DON'T JUST RELATE— ADVOCATE!

DON'T JUST RELATE— ADVOCATE!
A Blueprint for Profit in the Era of Customer Power

Glen Urban

Ideas. Action. Impact.
**Wharton School
Publishing**

Library of Congress Number: 2005921382

Vice President, Editor-in-Chief: Tim Moore
Acquisitions Editor: Paula Sinnott
Editorial Assistant: Kate E. Stephenson
Development Editor: Russ Hall
Marketing Manager: Martin Litkowski
International Marketing Manager: Tim Galligan
Cover Designer: Chuti Prasertsith
Managing Editor: Gina Kanouse
Project Editor: Michael Thurston
Copy Editor: Ben Lawson
Indexer: Lisa Stumpf
Interior Designer: Gail Cocker-Bogusz
Compositor: The Scan Group, Inc.
Manufacturing Buyer: Dan Uhrig

Ideas. Action. Impact.
**Wharton School
Publishing**

© 2005 by Pearson Education, Inc.
Publishing as Wharton School Publishing
Upper Saddle River, New Jersey 07458

Wharton School Publishing offers excellent discounts on this book when ordered in quantity for bulk purchases or special sales. For more information, please contact U.S. Corporate and Government Sales, 1-800-382-3419, corpsales@pearsontechgroup.com. For sales outside the U.S., please contact International Sales at international@pearsoned.com.

Printed in the United States of America
Second Printing: July 2005

ISBN 0-13-191361-1

Pearson Education LTD.
Pearson Education Australia PTY, Limited.
Pearson Education Singapore, Pte. Ltd.
Pearson Education North Asia, Ltd.
Pearson Education Canada, Ltd.
Pearson Educatión de Mexico, S.A. de C.V.
Pearson Education—Japan
Pearson Education Malaysia, Pte. Ltd.

Ideas. Action. Impact.
Wharton School Publishing

Bernard Baumohl
THE SECRETS OF ECONOMIC INDICATORS
Hidden Clues to Future Economic Trends and Investment Opportunities

Sayan Chatterjee
FAILSAFE STRATEGIES
Profit and Grow from Risks That Others Avoid

Sunil Gupta, Donald R. Lehmann
MANAGING CUSTOMERS AS INVESTMENTS
The Strategic Value of Customers in the Long Run

Stuart L. Hart
CAPITALISM AT THE CROSSROADS
The Unlimited Business Opportunities in Solving the World's Most Difficult Problems

Lawrence G. Hrebiniak
MAKING STRATEGY WORK
Leading Effective Execution and Change

Robert Mittelstaedt
WILL YOUR NEXT MISTAKE BE FATAL?
Avoiding the Chain of Mistakes That Can Destroy Your Organization

Mukul Pandya, Robbie Shell, Susan Warner, Sandeep Junnarkar, Jeffrey Brown
NIGHTLY BUSINESS REPORT PRESENTS LASTING LEADERSHIP
What You Can Learn from the Top 25 Business People of Our Times

C. K. Prahalad
THE FORTUNE AT THE BOTTOM OF THE PYRAMID
Eradicating Poverty Through Profits

Arthur Rubinfeld
BUILT FOR GROWTH
Expanding Your Business Around the Corner or Across the Globe

Scott A. Shane
FINDING FERTILE GROUND
Identifying Extraordinary Opportunities for New Ventures

Oded Shenkar
THE CHINESE CENTURY
The Rising Chinese Economy and Its Impact on the Global Economy, the Balance of Power, and Your Job

David Sirota, Louis A. Mischkind, and Michael Irwin Meltzer
THE ENTHUSIASTIC EMPLOYEE
How Companies Profit by Giving Workers What They Want

Thomas T. Stallkamp
SCORE!
A Better Way to Do Busine$$: Moving from Conflict to Collaboration

Yoram (Jerry)Wind, Colin Crook, with Robert Gunther
THE POWER OF IMPOSSIBLE THINKING
Transform the Business of Your Life and the Life of Your Business

CONTENTS

ACKNOWLEDGMENTS   XI

ABOUT THE AUTHOR   XV

CHAPTER 1   NOW IS THE TIME TO ADVOCATE FOR YOUR
             CUSTOMERS   1

    WATCH OUT FOR GROWING CUSTOMER POWER!   2

    HOW SHOULD YOUR COMPANY RESPOND?   7

    BUILDING ADVOCACY   11

    WHAT IS NEW HERE?   17

    THE NEW TOOLS WORK WELL   20

    THE PARADIGM IS SHIFTING—PIONEERS WILL
        GAIN ADVANTAGES   22

    WHAT YOU WILL LEARN IN THIS BOOK   23

CHAPTER 2   THE INTERNET CREATES CUSTOMER
             POWER   25

    THE INTERNET IS PERVASIVE   26

    THE TRAVEL REVOLUTION   28

    SOURCES OF CUSTOMER POWER   31

    AUTO BUYING—IT IS NOT YOUR FATHER'S
        BUYING PROCESS   32

CUSTOMER POWER IS HEALTHY   36

POWER HAS BEEN GRANTED   39

CHAPTER 3   THE BALANCE OF PUSH AND TRUST IS SHIFTING   41

THE BALANCE BETWEEN PUSH/PULL AND TRUST/ADVOCACY   42

THE BALANCE IS SHIFTING IN THE TRAVEL INDUSTRY   44

IN AUTOMOBILES THE SHIFT IS TO TRUST   49

HEALTH—THE NEED FOR TRUST IS INCREASING   56

POWER, BALANCE, AND IMPACT   58

CHAPTER 4   CUSTOMER POWER IS ALL AROUND YOU   59

INDUSTRIES ARE CHANGING DRAMATICALLY   60

CONVERGING FORCES ARE AMPLIFYING THE IMPACT OF
THE CUSTOMER POWER SHIFT   72

THE PARADIGM IS SHIFTING   76

CHAPTER 5   THEORY A—THE NEW PARADIGM   79

RULES OF TRADITIONAL PUSH/PULL MARKETING   80

THE MCGREGOR REVOLUTION IN ORGANIZATION THEORY
AND ITS ANALOGY IN MARKETING   85

RULES OF MARKETING BASED ON THEORY A   88

ANTECEDENTS OF THEORY A   91

ADVOCACY IN MARKETING LEADS TO ADVOCACY-BASED
MANAGEMENT   92

CHAPTER 6   WHERE ARE YOU POSITIONED ON THE TRUST
DIMENSIONS?   95

WHERE ARE YOU POSITIONED ON THE OVERALL TRUST DIMENSION?   96

WHERE ARE YOU POSITIONED ON THE TRUST COMPONENTS?   98

CHAPTER 7   IS ADVOCACY FOR YOU?   121

DOES ADVOCACY FIT YOU?   122

BUILDING AN ADVOCACY-BASED STRATEGY   128

EVOLUTIONARY STRATEGIES   136

CHAPTER 8   TOOLS FOR ADVOCACY   139

BUILDING THE FOUNDATION OF THE ADVOCACY PYRAMID   140

THE DREAM VERSUS REALITY IN CRM   141

CONTINUOUS LEARNING TO BUILD TRUST AND
    CROSS-CHANNEL COHERENCE   146

BUILDING TRUST WITH A VIRTUAL TRUSTED ADVISOR   148

"LISTEN IN" TO LEARN CUSTOMER NEEDS   154

BUILDING A VIRTUAL ADVOCATE   158

NEW TOOLS ARE EMERGING   160

CHAPTER 9   QUESTIONS AND ANSWERS ABOUT CUSTOMER
ADVOCACY   161

WILL CUSTOMER ADVOCACY REALLY WORK?   162

CAN YOU TRUST YOUR CUSTOMERS?   164

WHAT IS THE ROLE OF ADVERTISING IN A WORLD OF
    CUSTOMER POWER?   167

HOW WIDELY CAN YOU APPLY CUSTOMER ADVOCACY?   169

IS CUSTOMER ADVOCACY REALLY A PARADIGM SHIFT?   174

CHAPTER 10   MOVING TO ADVOCACY   179

EMPATHIZE WITH YOUR CUSTOMERS   180

CHANGE THE CULTURE OF YOUR COMPANY   182

PEOPLE, MEASURES, INCENTIVES, AND ORGANIZATION   188

CONSISTENCY AND COORDINATION   192

TRUST FOR ALL STAKEHOLDERS   196

VISION, COURAGE, AND PASSION   197

BUILDING THE TOTAL PYRAMID   198

CHAPTER 11   THE ADVOCACY IMPERATIVE   199

WHAT IS MOST IMPORTANT TO REMEMBER?   200

THE FUTURE OF TRUST AND ADVOCACY   203

THE ADVOCACY IMPERATIVE—IF YOU DO NOT DO IT, YOUR
COMPETITORS WILL!   207

THE ADVOCACY CHECKLIST   211

THE CHALLENGE OF CUSTOMER ADVOCACY   216

AFTERWORD: AUTHOR'S NOTE   219

INDEX   223

Acknowledgments

Many people have contributed to the content and ideas underlying this book. I have tried to footnote the key inputs, but I am sure I have missed some people that have influenced my thinking. The biggest source of ideas and findings has been from my MIT research teams, sponsoring companies, and professional friends. Thanks to all of you!

Here is a list of credits by research projects and groups. I hope I have not omitted anyone who should be on this list—if I have I apologize and thank you. So let's roll the credits!

TRUCKTOWN/LISTENING IN

Design and testing of a trusted advisor and finding opportunities for new products by listening to the dialogue between a virtual advisor and a real customer.

MIT—John Hauser, Bill Qualls, and Fareena Sultan (faculty). Iakov Bart, Ahmed Benabadji, Rupa Bhagwat, Brian Bower, Brian Chen, Hann-Ching Chao, Mitul Chatterjee, Shy-Ren Chen, Thomas Cheng, Stanley Cheung, Frank Days, Ben Fu, Salman Khan, Christopher Mann, Rami Musa, Joe Kim, Ken Lynch, James Ryan, Bilal Shirazi, Jonathon Shoemaker, Polly Slade, Andy Tian, Xingheng Wang, and Bruce Weinberg (research assistants).

GM—Vince Barabba, Gary Cowger, Lance Elson, Andy Norton, and Nick Pudar.

CROSS-SECTIONAL TRUST STUDY

Statistical analysis of 25 Internet sites based on responses from more than 6,000 respondents to identify determinants of trust.

MIT—Venkatesh Shankar and Fareena Sultan (faculty). Iakov Bart, Roy Henric, and Kim Wegbreit (research assistants).

McCann Erickson/NFO—Ronny Bindra, Joe Plummer, Laura Schaible, and Hank Schuyler.

ADAPTIVE SITE DESIGN

Three year study of site design to build trust based on five market experiments at Intel on their download site.

MIT—John Hauser, Tom Stoker, and Fareena Sultan (faculty). Iakov Bart, Matt Bilotti, Stanley Cheung, Roy Hendrichs, Mahesh Kumar, Lauren McCann, Rami Musa, Dmitriy Rogozhnikov, Max Rosenblat, Daria Silinskaia, Kendell Timmers, Yufei Wang, and Gabe Weinberg (research assistants).

Intel—Amy Auler, Tom Gardos, Ginny Gray, Dennis Harris, Jon McDermott, Cris McKean, Tom McLaren, Mary Murphy-Hoye, Brian Rhoads, Pam Romano, Kathy Rosen, and Debra Townsend.

DREAM CRM—MY AUTO ADVOCATE

Two year study of effects of trust and advocacy programs on trust, consideration, preference, dealer visit, and purchase of new autos.

MIT—John Hauser and Eric Bradlow (faculty). Sanjay Grover, Stephen Kao, Mahesh Kumar, Sha Ma, Darrin Parker, Dmitriy Rogozhnikov, David Verrill, and Yufei Wang (research assistants).

GM—Roger Adams, Vince Barabba, Jack Bowen, Gary Cowger, Melissa Dietrich, Dave Duganne, Karen Ebben, Henry Ferry, C. J. Fraleigh, Madeleine Freind, Patricia Hawkins, Brian Hoglund, Janis McFaul, Kerri Miller, Nick Pudar, Maria Rapp, Daniel Roesch, Pam Rosenthal, Joyce Salisbury, Keith Schoonover, Leeann Starr, Kevin Thompson, and Steve Tihany.

MY WIRELESS ADVOCATE

Study of unbiased advisor to help customers select the best wireless plan for them.

MIT—Stephen Kao, Sha Ma, and Birgi Martin.

Qwest/British Telecom—Steve Stokols and Al-Noor Ramji.

FINANCIAL SITE DESIGN

Benchmarking of worldwide financial sites and design of prototype advocacy site.

MIT—Harry Reddy (research assistant).

Suruga Bank—Tetsuya Yuge and Mitsuyoshi Okano.

INSITE MARKETING TECHNOLOGY INC. AND EXPERION SYSTEMS INC.

I was a co-founder of both these companies. They commercially implemented trusted advisors and thereby contributed much to my thinking and supplied examples for this text. InSite was acquired by Silknet in 1999 and Experion is still independent.

Experion and Insite Marketing Technology—Ross Blair, Jeff Cernak, Kev Coleman, Tony Deigh, John D. C. Little, Stefania Nappi, and Jeff Staymen.

Credit Unions—Neville Billimoria, Tony Budet, Jeff Farber, Doug Ferraro, John Parsons, Tom Sargent, and Ron Shevlin.

CUSTOMER POWER RESEARCH

I had a team of students research the prevalence and impact of customers and the Internet for our MIT Sloan School of Management 50th Anniversary conference (2002). They investigated autos, financial services, and health. Thanks to: David Gagnon, Susan Lee, Fernando Ramirez, Siva Ravakumar, Jessica Santiago, and Telmo Valido.

EDITORIAL SUPPORT

Wharton School Publishing was great, from original encouragement by Tim Moore to final execution from Paula Sinnott. Editorial guidance was provided by Jerry Wind. Thanks to Russ Hall, Tili Kalisky, Ben Lawson, Andrea and Dana Meyer, Michael Thurston, and Dianne Wilson. Special thanks to my assistant Sandra Crawford-Jenkins who proofed every word of this book, drew rough figures, and fought for permissions.

FAMILY SUPPORT

You cannot complete a book without family support, and I had it. My wife Andrea was a constant source of encouragement and often stated, "Of course that is right—that is just common sense." My daughter Danielle Pedreira was a great critical reader and sounding board for an MBA's reaction (she is an MIT Sloan MBA) and her husband Henry was a source of reinforcement. And special thanks to my new granddaughter Carmen, who makes it all worthwhile.

About the Author

Glen Urban is a leading educator, prize-winning researcher specializing in marketing and new product development, entrepreneur, and author. He has been a member of the MIT Sloan School of Management faculty since 1966, was Deputy Dean at the school from 1987 to 1992, and Dean from 1993 to 1998.

Urban's research focus is on management science models that improve the productivity of new product development and marketing. For example, in a methodology he devised called Information Acceleration, he uses multi-media computer technology to simulate future sales of products such as cars, computer systems, telecommunications, and drugs.

Information Acceleration emerged from Urban's earlier groundbreaking work in premarket forecasting for frequently-purchased consumer (nondurable) goods called Assessor. Since the Assessor concept publication, it has been used to forecast the success and profitability of more than 3,000 new consumer products around the world. Dr. Urban's recent research is to develop a trust-based marketing system on the Internet. An extension of the Information Acceleration research, the system uses pickup trucks for a prototype Web site that integrates attribute screening, expert advice, collaborative filtering, and community interaction. This is being extended to understanding how the click stream from such an advisor/customer dialogue can be used to discover unmet needs. Finally research is underway to find the determinants of trust on the Internet and design a real-time adaptive experimentation system to increase the levels of trust on a Web site.

Trained initially in engineering and business—earning a BS in mechanical engineering in 1963 and an MBA in 1964, both from the University of Wisconsin—Urban went on to earn a Ph.D. in marketing at Northwestern University in 1966. He is co-author of six books, including *Digital Marketing Strategy* (2004), *Design and Marketing of New Products* (second edition, 1993), *Advanced Marketing Strategy* (1991), and *Essentials of New Product Management* (1986). He has also published more than 30 articles on premarket forecasting of new products, test marketing, product line planning, leading-edge users in new product development, and consumer budgeting. His papers have won several prestigious awards, including two O'Dells—in 1983 and 1986—for the best papers published in marketing research. In 1996 he received the American Marketing Association Paul D. Converse Award for outstanding contributions to the development of the science of marketing, and the Journal of Marketing award for best paper in that year. In 1999 he was winner of the American Marketing Association and The Wharton School of the University of Pennsylvania Charles Coolidge Parlin Award for recognition of a body of work in marketing research. In 2000 he presented the Wroe Alderson Lecture at the Wharton School.

With two other researchers, Urban founded Management Decision Systems, Inc., a marketing consulting firm that merged with Information Resources, Inc. in 1985. He also co-founded Management Science for Health and its spin-off John Snow, Inc., both consulting firms specializing in international healthcare and family planning that have grown to several hundred employees worldwide. He co-founded Marketing Technology Interface, Inc., a company that uses multimedia computing to support strategic new product design, which merged in 1993 with Mercer Management, a consulting firm. In 1998 he co-founded InSite Marketing Technology, a software firm for trust-based marketing on the Internet (sold to Silknet in October 1999). His newest firm is called Experion Systems and was founded in December 1999.

1

Now Is the Time to Advocate for Your Customers

What would you do if your customers knew everything about your company and your competitors' products and services—even your disadvantages? The rise of the Internet enables your customers to find third-party information about your products, ratings of your products, people who was ever dissatisfied with your products or services, and the same full information on your competitors' offerings. On the Internet, your company, your biggest competitor, and the smallest unknown upstart competitor are the same distance from the customer. Each is only an online search away. The Internet has enabled an unprecedented increase in consumer power!

Customer power is growing, and you must decide what to do about it! I propose that you advocate for your customers and earn their trust. In this book, I will show you why you should do this, how you can do this, and what other leading edge companies are doing in this arena. In taking my own advice and advocating for my readers, I will also explain how you can tell if trust and advocacy are not right for your company.

Already some forward-looking companies are pursuing customer advocacy. They are providing customers with open, honest, and complete information—and then finding the best products for them, even if those offerings are from competitors. In short, they are truly representing their customers' best interests, essentially becoming advocates for them. The strategy is this: If a company advocates for its customers, customers will reciprocate with their trust, loyalty, and purchases—they will advocate for you now and in the future. Your firm can then command higher prices for its products and services because many customers will be willing to pay for the extra trusted value and the superior products you will offer. With trust, customers will increase the number and range of products they buy from you. Finally, when people trust your company, they will often tell others about it, helping to reduce your costs for acquiring new customers. The marketing paradigm is shifting, and you should too. Advocate for your customers to find business success in an era of customer power!

WATCH OUT FOR GROWING CUSTOMER POWER!

New technologies such as the Internet provide easy access to tremendous amounts of information, and people have been taking advantage of that to become smarter shoppers. They are using digital technologies to gather information, to find competing products, and to talk to other customers. Increasingly, they are using the Internet to avoid pushy marketers and to help them make their own purchasing decisions. The Internet is a great enabler of customer power. What many hoped would happen with the Internet is actually occurring, and it will change how you do business.

The five proven sources of increased customer power are

1. **Increasing access to information:** Customers now have access to information about a company and its products from a multitude of sources. From ConsumerReports.org for third-party information to Amazon.com for customer reviews and eBay for seller ratings, consumers now enjoy much greater access to independent information about a company's products and services. For example, more than 64% of car buyers now use the Internet to research car

models, features, and prices.[1] Sixty-eight percent of new car buyers rate third-party sites as very or extremely important sources of information, and they visit an average of seven different sites, such as Kelly Blue Book, Autobytel, and Edmunds.[2] Many prospective buyers start their online research months before setting foot on a dealer's lot. And 6% go on to save an average of $450 per vehicle by using an Internet buying service.[3] The implication: old-style marketing is less effective when customers have independent means to research a company's claims and obtain cost information.

2. **Access to more alternatives:** Customers can find competing products more easily. Search engines, comparison sites, and online reviews all enable customers to find the best products at the lowest price. For example, travelers now enjoy a range of web sites (e.g., Expedia, Orbitz, and Travelocity) that help them find the lowest fares on flights. Over 63% of leisure travelers and 69% of business travelers utilize the Internet for research.[4] Internet sales grew 37% in 2002 to $28 billion, even as total travel services fell 5%—indeed, 35 million people bought tickets online in 2003.[5] Leisure and business travelers increasingly refuse to pay high fares, causing much financial misery for airlines.

The Internet has also impacted the real estate market by making wider-spanning and richer information available to homebuyers. Online real estate buying services (such as

[1] J.D. Power, "2002 New Autoshopper.Com Study" (J.D. Power, West Lake Village, CA), October 2002, reports 64% and Jupiter Research, 2003, reports 77%, Cospirit Research found 83% of UK car shoppers found the Internet an aid to them.

[2] J.D. Power, "2002 New Autoshopper.Com Study" (J.D. Power, West Lake Village, CA), October 2002.

[3] Morton, Fiona S., Florian Zettelmeyer, and Jorge Silva Risso, "Internet Car Retailing." *The Journal of Industrial Economics*, December 2001:501-19.

[4] Yesawich Partners, "Consumer Travel Plans Include Visit to Net," May 6, 2004.

[5] Sileo, Lorraine and Joshua Friedman. "PhoCus Wright's Online Travel Overview: Market Size and Forecasts 2002-2005," February 2003.

eReality and ZipReality) rebate up to 1% of the purchase price, thereby lowering commissions and saving customers thousands of dollars on the purchase of a house.

3. **More simplified direct transactions:** Customers can buy from anywhere, regardless of physical location. The Internet simplifies transactions for both consumers and industrial customers. Customers can connect directly with providers to buy goods and services. For example, online ordering and direct shipment make buying books and electronics possible at any time without leaving home. Electronic airline tickets eliminate the need to obtain paper tickets, thereby reducing people's dependency on local travel agents. Simplified transactions also enable switching—the Internet gives customers the power to find and buy from a wider array of potential providers.

4. **Increasing communication between customers:** Prospective customers can find out if a company has mistreated former customers by consulting and collaborating with them through the Internet. In 2002, 110 million Americans looked on the Internet for healthcare information. An additional 48 million consumers in Japan went online for healthcare information, 31 million went online in Germany, and 14 million went online in France for health data.[6] Active online communities exist for virtually every disease. Patients exchange information about the effectiveness of products and provide advice to each other about how to take control of their medical treatments. When a customer requests a specific prescription, 84% of the time that request is honored by the doctor.[7] Sites such as epinions.com or planetfeedback.com make it easy for customers to submit their opinion of a company or product and for other potential customers to find these ratings.

Increasing communication between customers amplifies and accelerates word-of-mouth marketing. In the past, bad

[6] "Four Nation Survey Shows Widespread but Different Levels of Internet Use for Health Purposes." *Health Care News*, v.2, No. 11 (May, 2002) Harris Interactive, 2002.

[7] "Cybercitzen Health—The Integration of Information Technology and Consumer Healthcare." Manhattan Research, 2002.

companies lost customers one at a time. At worst, the occasional exasperated ex-customer might convince a few friends to stop buying from the company. But now, the Internet provides global reach for the disgruntled. Web sites such as thecomplaintstation.com, rating services, and discussion forums accelerate the process of weeding out bad products, bad service, and bad companies. On eBay, customers give positive and negative comments on sellers, and even a few negative comments can immobilize the seller's auction by reducing the number of bidders. Very visible star ratings summarize the seller's reputation in terms of the quality and quantity of comments.

5. **Increasing control over contacts:** Customers can avoid a company's marketing efforts. Consumers have more control over the flow of marketing messages into their homes and lives. Consumers' distaste for junk mail, telemarketing calls, spam, and pop-up ads means that these pushy messages are more likely to earn ire than profits. Technology empowers consumers by letting them mute or zap TV commercials, screen telephone calls, block pop-up ads, stop telemarketing, or send spam straight to the trashcan. For example, 94% of people "distrust" pop-up ads,[8] over 20 million have installed pop-up blockers,[9] and over 50 million people signed up for "no call" protection.

Customers are taking advantage of these five trends to become more powerful consumers. They are tired of corporate hype and corporate scandal. More than two-thirds (69%) of Americans agree with the statement, "I don't know whom to trust anymore," according to a February 2002 Golin/Harris Poll.[10] Companies tarnished their images through accounting scandals and product recalls. CEOs lost credibility with fat salaries, while workaday staffers lost 401k retirement savings in a market downturn.

[8] Intelliseek, December 2003, "distrust" means "distrust completely" and "distrust somewhat."

[9] Neff, Jack. "Spam Research Reveals Disgust with Pop-up Ads." *Advertising Age*, vol. 74, issue 44, August 2003.

[10] "American Business Faces a Crisis of Trust." *Trust*, February 2002.

According to a 2004 Gallup International and World Economic Forum study, there is a dramatic lack of trust in global and large national companies, and trust is even lower when it comes to NGOs, trade unions, and media organizations across the world. Global companies and large domestic companies are not trusted to operate in the best interest of society—48% of the 36,000 respondents across 47 nations had little or no trust in global companies, and 52% had little or no trust in large national companies.[11] The highest level of distrust of any institution was 52%. In 2003, two-thirds of Americans believed that "if the opportunity arises, most businesses will take advantage of the public if they feel they are not likely to be found out."[12] Furthermore, customers are resentful of current marketing tactics. Sixty-four percent of consumers are "furious" about pop-up ads on their screens (96% were "angry" or "furious")—the same percentage as those who are furious over spam.[13] Ninety percent of customers say "they think less of brands featured in pop-ups."[14] These resentments make consumers fight back and exercise the increasing power granted to them by these five dimensions of customer power.

In an era of customer power, untrustworthy companies can be out of business. In a few short months, the venerable Arthur Andersen went out of business because a few employees broke the trust (shredded Enron evidence); over 100 years of tradition were gone, and 20,000 employees lost their jobs. In 2005, Merck is facing a major crisis because it is now evident that Vioxx increases the risk of heart attacks and stroke. Although legal damage suits will continue for years, the court of public opinion has already dealt a severe penalty to Merck stock value. The firm's health itself is in question because of its failure to be completely candid with customers.

[11] Voice of People Survey, "Trust in Global Companies," World Economic Forum, 31 March 2004.

[12] Craig Wood, "Crisis of Confidence: Rebuilding the Bonds of Trust" (Chicago, IL, Yankelovich, 2003), p. 8.

[13] Neff, Jack. "Spam Research Reveals Disgust with Pop-up Ads." *Advertising Age*, vol. 74, issue 44, August 2003.

[14] Blackshaw, Petel. "Pull the Plug on Pop-up?" *Adverstising Age*, vol. 74, issue 44, November 2003.

Untrustworthy companies may not all go out of business, but at least they will suffer a competitive disadvantage. Customers' abilities to verify marketers' messages make traditional hype a very risky strategy. This new transparent reality will weed out those companies that do not honestly deliver information and real value to customers. In the face of this Darwinian trend, companies have no recourse but to change their relationship with customers and build trust.

The point is that the Internet and other computer-augmented technologies enable consumer power, and companies' pushy tactics and lack of trust encourage customers to use that power. Today's consumers are more educated and more informed than ever before. With more tools for verifying a company's claims, customers can seek out superior product and service options. There are no secrets any more! Companies must decide what to do in the face of this growing force.

HOW SHOULD YOUR COMPANY RESPOND?

In the face of increasing customer power, your company can choose among three possible strategies. These strategies range from amplifying the traditional push/pull model of marketing, to strengthening relationships with customers, to embracing true customer advocacy. I'll introduce these strategies in this section and then discuss their relative merits in depth in Chapter 6, "Where Are You Positioned on the Trust Dimensions?"

Push/Pull Harder: You may be tempted to respond to your customers' new power with good old-fashioned marketing push and pull. Increased pull by media advertising, aggressive push by price promotions (perhaps with higher initial prices or hidden fees to maintain profits), and potentially misleading one-sided communications might get the job done. After all, those time-tested tactics have been the core of marketing for the last 50 years. But modern-day consumers are wiser and more elusive than their more gullible predecessors. Even as consumers have embraced a greater influx of information, the media channels by which a company might push information to consumers have become less effective. Media fragmentation, consumer skepticism, and the time pressures of a modern lifestyle mean that pushing information and products on unsuspecting customers is an uphill battle.

In the halcyon days of mass media, everyone read his or her local newspaper and watched one of the three national broadcast TV channels. In the past, a company could reach a large mass of consumers through any of these mass-media outlets. But now, daily newspaper readers are in the minority, national broadcasts have lost market share to a dizzying array of cable channels, and the Internet has diverted peoples' attention to a fragmented web of online sites. The national broadcast networks have seen their market share of prime-time audiences decline 50% since 1970. When today's figures are compared to the 1960s, the decline is even worse. The hundreds of channels available on cable or via satellite fragment the TV's power, making it harder for marketers to push their messages to the millions of viewers that they need. Surprisingly, advertising costs have not fallen—in fact, they are way up! Network prime time TV cost per thousand exposures rose 18% from 2000 to 2003.[15]

Even if a prospective customer is exposed to your TV ad, only one-third actually watch the ad—the vast majority mute it, switch channels, or leave the room.[16] In a 2004 study, Yankelovich found that 79% of viewers flip channels during commercials compared to 51% in 1986, and 53% turn down the volume versus 25% in 1986.[17] Ads lose out in the competition with the refrigerator, the bathroom, family members, other TV channels, electronic games, and the Internet. Average use of the Internet is almost the same as TV viewing time, at 15 hours per week, and 36% of people say they are watching less TV.[18] Some people under 21 never watch TV and

[15] Media Dynamics, Inc. *TV Dimensions 2003.* p. 74.

[16] Tandemar Corporation, "Quality of TV Viewing Experience." (Tandemar Corporation, Canada) 2000.

[17] Smith, J. Walker, Ann Clurman, and Craig Wood, *Coming to Concurrence* (Racom Communication, Evanston, IL, 2005), p. 125.

[18] Jupiter Research, "Marketing and Branding Forecast: Online Advertising and E-mail Marketing Through 2007," *Marketing and Branding*, v.2 (Jupiter Research, New York, NY) 2002.

prefer to use the Internet and mobile devices. Even on the Internet, with its deftly targeted pop-up and banner ads, click-through rates have fallen dramatically since the early Internet days of 1998 to 2005. Internet service providers and software vendors now tout their capability to block pop-ups and spam. Junk mail gets tossed, and telephone calls are screened by Caller-ID, answering machines, and no-call registries. The effectiveness per dollar of push/pull marketing has dropped dramatically!

Admittedly, a company may continue to thrive using a push strategy in this brave new world of fragmented media and attention-deficient addled customers. Clever, funny, or engaging ads can draw customers in. Shrewd selection of highly specific media with refined targeting can help a company reach its intended niche audience. But aggressive push can be a false victory—winning the sale but losing the customer if excessive hype or questionable (but not illegal) pricing tactics leave the buyer embittered and resentful if they find out the facts. And in today's world, they *will* find out the facts!

Strengthen Relationships: In trying to appeal to a more powerful customer base, your company might pursue a strategy of relationship marketing. In recent years, many leading companies have refocused on their customers by emphasizing customer satisfaction metrics, creating consistency in customer interfaces, building better products through Total Quality Management, and emphasizing more personalized service. *Customer Relationship Management (CRM)* software often backs these efforts by giving a company the data and functionality it needs for one-to-one marketing and creating a consistent one-face-to-the-customer interface. CRM helps a company to understand each customer and then deliver a consistent message or service to that customer. By putting the "custom" back in customers, these companies can target their customers better and can deliver persuasive information and promotions more efficiently.

Customers may enjoy this new emphasis on one-to-one connections, but only if your company is very careful about how it uses the data. The dream of CRM is for a close positive relationship with customers, but the reality is often more invasive marketing. Too many CRM programs are based on building a huge data warehouse, mining the data, and then hitting the identified segments with aggressive email, phone, or Internet promotions, with or without customer permission. For some companies, CRM is merely a more efficient means of push/pull marketing, targeting customers in the sense of drawing accurate cross-hairs on their chests. Impertinence and aggressive cross-selling can make your customers treat your company as if it were a cheeky acquaintance—making the customer cross the street to avoid contact with you. No wonder 55% of CRMs have not succeeded.[19] If your CRM is a push system, it is not going to work well in this world of customer power. You need to fulfill the dream of CRM by building a long-run trust, but even this may not be enough. Advocacy is an effective new strategy and you should consider it.

Customer Advocacy: Your company might choose to embrace advocacy by becoming a faithful representative of your customers' interests. Under this approach, you provide customers and prospects with open, honest, and complete information. You give them advice so that they can find the best products, even if those products are not your company's products. Far from being foolish, the honesty of advocacy reflects the reality that customers will learn the truth anyway. If your company is distorting the truth, your customers will detect those falsehoods and will act accordingly.

Of course, if you embrace honesty, you will need to have very good, if not the best, products. With transparency, this is the only way you can earn the customer's purchase. You will invest more in product design and quality and less in pushy promotion and advertising.

Advocacy is not a way for your company to speak *at* customers. Rather, it is a mutual dialogue that assumes that if you advocate for your customers, those customers will reciprocate with their trust, purchases, and an enduring loyalty (see Figure 1-1). It is a partnership between you and your customers for everyone's mutual benefit. You advocate for their interest, and they advocate for you by buying your products and helping you design better products. Most importantly, they tell other customers about your firm and products. Advocacy has duality—the partnership created by

---

[19] John Freeland, *The Ultimate CRM Handbook* (McGraw Hill, New York, 2003) p. 3.

advocacy is mutual and reciprocal. If customers tell others about the positive partnership, then customer acquisition costs will decline, and customer preference for your product will grow. Companies that advocate for customers will enjoy more opportunities to sell a wider range of products to more people. This can lead to growth in sales as customers and their friends choose your company's products. It also leads to greater profit margins as customers come to realize that you offer an extra value that is reflected in an honest, reasonable price. General Motors, Intel, Leading Credit Unions, and John Deere are a few of the companies that are testing and implementing advocacy programs, and we will discuss these cases in depth later in this book.

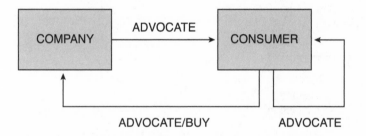

Figure 1-1 Company Advocates for Consumer and Consumer Advocates for the Firm

BUILDING ADVOCACY

Advocacy is a major step forward in the evolving interaction between a firm and its customers. Push/pull marketing is driven by the economics of mass production—efficient processes that created mounds of low-cost goods. Relationship marketing is impelled by the saturation of push marketing and intense rivalries, particularly around quality and price. Advocacy will be the next imperative because of the accelerating growth of customer power.

The Advocacy Pyramid: Figure 1-2 shows the pyramid of advocacy that defines the underpinnings of this strategy. Total Quality Management (TQM) and customer satisfaction are at the base of the pyramid. They are necessary conditions for trust and advocacy. If your company wants to honestly recommend its own products, then it must have products that are good enough to recommend. Advocacy is supported in the middle by relationship marketing because CRM provides the tools needed to personalize your company's advocacy relationship with each customer. The pinnacle is advocacy.

Figure 1-2   The Advocacy Pyramid

As you reach the top of the pyramid, you won't use CRM as you did in the past. Instead of targeting promotions and company communications at your customers, you will design CRM to build trusted and partnering relationships with your customers. You will use CRM and related systems to provide balanced, transparent, and relevant information plus unbiased advice on how to make the best decision. CRM, seen in this light, would be better called a "Dream CRM" strategy since it makes the dream of CRM real. Likewise, one-to-one and permission marketing shifts in the company's intentions toward customers. But instead of creating more micro granularity in spewing out promotions and hyping tangentially relevant company product information, these methods should become a mutual dialogue between individual customers and your firm to maximize customer interest over the available products in the market.

EBAY BECOMES THE KILLER APPLICATION THROUGH TRUST

Who would have thought that a site started by a French-Iranian immigrant (Pierre Omidayar) to help a girlfriend to trade her Pez candy dispenser collection would become the killer application of the Internet? Who would have thought that millions of people who have never met would buy and sell billions of dollars of goods over the Internet, including thousands of used cars? Yet this is exactly what eBay did—in 2003, over 20 billion dollars of goods exchanged hands at the online auction site.[20] eBay is a microcosm for the economy as a whole—it illustrates both customer power and the profits created by trust.

The keys to eBay's success are the mechanisms that help buyers and sellers trust each other. This trust has enabled eBay to create a new marketplace for buying and selling. One trust mechanism tracks the reputations of participants through the feedback between buyers and sellers. Buyers may enter feedback (positive, neutral, or negative rating and description) about a seller, and vice versa. The percent of positive comments is displayed for each seller. Sellers garner star ratings based on the number of net positive votes (yellow at 10 to 49, and on to green at 5,000 to 9,999, and shooting stars for higher numbers), and the stars appear next to their items. Every auction contains simple, clear information on the reputation of the seller. Because of this rating system, buyers and sellers trust each other enough to exchange large amounts of money without even seeing an item in person. Sellers are upgraded to "Power Sellers" if they embrace the core values of the eBay community and maintain 98% positive feedback. This results in a "Power Seller" label next to the item they offer for sale.

The behavior of bidders on eBay illustrates the profitability of creating trust through reputation. Trustworthy eBay sellers—those who build a good reputation with buyers through multiple transactions—enjoy

[20] Maney, Kevin. "The economy according to eBay" USAToday.com, http://www. usatoday.com/money/industries/retail/2003-12-29-ebay-cover_x.htm, December 2003.

higher prices for their goods at auction. A controlled experiment found that buyers bid 7.6% more for otherwise identical goods that are listed by repeat sellers with high reputations.[21] Ebay's feedback systems create the transparency needed for buyers to assign higher monetary values to good reputations.

eBay also has an aggressive fraud protection program, ensuring that less than .01% of transactions are affected by fraud.[22] PayPal is available for making payments on eBay, and along with credit card companies, it protects against fraud losses. Participants who have changed IDs in the last 30 days are flagged with a pair of sunglasses to indicate that there may be a reason why the person changed his or her ID. You are encouraged to "get to know your seller" by asking email questions, and you can easily report suspicious activity. For more valuable items, eBay offers an escrow service, Escrow.com, that ensures that both the money and the goods reach their respective parties. Another partner company, Squaretrade.com, provides a range of reputation-enhancing services, including ID verification, dispute resolution, and a seal that eBay sellers can display to protect buyers from fraud; in addition, purchases can be protected up to $250 after a $25 deductible.

These trust builders have enabled eBay to grow and support commerce between millions of seemingly anonymous buyers and sellers. eBay has even become a major force in used car sales ($2.5 billion in 2002).[23] Some buyers trust eBay's used car selling system so much that they will travel hundreds of miles to pick up a used car that they've only seen on the web site. Most cars are sold by used car

[21] Resnick, Paul, Richard Zeckhauser, John Swanson, and Kate Lockwood, "The Value of Reputation on eBay: A Controlled Experiment." Working Paper RWP03-007 (John F. Kennedy School of Government), July 6, 2002.

[22] Mainelli, Tom. "eBay Identity Theft Hits Close to Home." Quote from Kevin Pursglove, eBay spokesman, CNN.com, http://www.cnn.com/2002/TECH/ internet/02/18/ebay.identity.theft.idg, February, 2002.

[23] Wingfield, Nick and Karen Lundegaard. "Clicking the Tires: Ebay Is Emberging As Unlikely Giant in Used-Car Sales." Wall Street Journal, Feb. 7, 2003, p.A1.

dealers. These people are the most abusive marketers in the offline world, but eBay's seller ratings have forced honesty and trustworthiness upon them. Reputation is so important on eBay that these used car sellers are especially diligent about documenting the features as well as the flaws of the cars they offer. eBay illustrates the increasing role of transparency and reputation for the creation of trust that underpins all commercial transactions.

Benefits of Advocacy: Advocacy builds trust. Trust is more than just a self-congratulatory adjective to be appended to a company's press releases. Trust means advocating for the customer's long-term interests. Trust is hard to earn—and easy to lose—but if your company earns trust, it will enjoy sustained benefits. Trust increases customer loyalty because satisfied customers buy repeatedly, purchase a wider variety of products, and recruit their friends to become customers. This can mean profitable growth. Advocacy creates business benefits in four areas:

- **Reduced Customer Acquisitions Costs:** Advocacy can reduce your customer acquisition costs in two ways. First, it lowers the cost of acquiring each new customer. Instead of wasting money on ads that play to empty couches, a trustworthy company enjoys a beneficial word-of-mouth reputation. Second, trust lowers the number of new customers that a company needs to acquire to maintain top-line growth. Acquisition costs are much lower than retention costs for most industries. With advocacy, a company is not constantly forced to acquire new customers to replace the departing dissatisfied customers. The advocacy-based company retains loyal customers.

- **Higher Profit Margins:** Trust can increase the prices that your company is able to charge. Customers are willing to pay more for a quality product from a trustworthy supplier. Although some customers are deal-prone, many are willing to pay more to get more. In a busy world, consumers will pay to buy a brand they can trust to avoid the aggravation of problems.

- **Growth:** Advocacy can also help your company diversify and expand its share of wallet (percent of total expenditure by customer) with satisfied customers. When a company becomes a trusted provider, customers will look to that company for more products and services in more categories. Although push-based companies can engage in up-selling and cross-selling, trust-based companies will be more successful because customers are more likely to believe the company's recommendations. Advocacy-based companies are also more likely to understand and respect each customer and therefore make meaningful suggestions that lead to higher conversion rates.
- **Long-Term Competitive Advantage:** Advocacy lays the foundation for long-term competitive advantage. A better, more consultative relationship with valued customers helps the company to innovate in market-leading directions. Instead of guessing what customers might want, a trust-based company has a good understanding of its customers and their buying patterns. Customers will help advocacy firms to create successful new products. Trust also builds the brand by fostering a better reputation for the company. When times are turbulent, customers will stick with firms they trust.

These benefits are even more applicable when the customer is a business rather than an individual consumer. In industrial marketing, the 20% of salespeople who sell 80% of the total sales volume for the firm owe much of their success to building trust-based relationships with clients. Moreover, customer power is also rising among industrial customers. Companies ranging from Wal-Mart to Sony to GM all have supplier performance programs. Such systems entail a range of tactics, such as supplier scorecards, supplier pre-certification, requirements for adhering to ISO 9000 quality management standards, and software systems to track supplier performance.

Many companies use software, such as ERP (Enterprise Resource Management), SCM (Supply Chain Management), or other specialized SPM (Supplier Performance Management) software packages to track and evaluate suppliers. In some cases, the customer company might even have better quality and performance data about the supplier than the supplier itself does.

The sales of commodity items may be done on a cost-based push approach, but sales of the strategic raw materials and component parts that go directly into manufactured goods are a different matter. In fact, trust is far more important in the supply chain, where companies establish long-term relationships with strategic suppliers. Collaborative development of products—co-creating the supplier's products to mesh perfectly with the customer's products—is a good example of a trusted-based strategic relationship in the supply chain. As companies move to lean production methods, just-in-time manufacturing, or outsourcing, they become even more dependent on suppliers. Thus, good suppliers must be trustworthy.

WHAT IS NEW HERE?

Many authors have stressed the importance of focusing on customers and developing an intimacy with them.[24] CRM has been offered as a methodology for building loyalty.[25] These concepts should be viewed as squarely in the middle of the advocacy pyramid, but this is not enough. What is new is the top level of the pyramid. Customer advocacy draws on the past work in strategic management, but it represents a revolutionary set of principles, tools, and tactics. It is like the shift from subsonic to supersonic flight. The development of supersonic flight involved an extreme overhauling of previous assumptions about and methods of flight. Subsonic flight principles are based on laminar flow over a curved wing profile, whereas supersonic flight principles are based on turbulent airflow and impact of the mass of air on the flat wing surface. Customer advocacy requires a new set of assumptions about customers and a new theory of marketing success. So many things are new.

[24] For some examples, review: Tracey, Michael and Fred Wiersema. *The Discipline of Market Leaders* (Perseus Publishing, New York, 1995); Day, George. *Market Driven Strategy* (Free Press, New York, 1999); Slywotzky, Adrian and Richard Wise. *How to Grow When Markets Don't* (Warner Books, New York, 2003); and Peppers, Don, et al. *One to One Field Book* (Doubleday, New York, 1999).

[25] For example, see: Freeland, John. *The Ultimate CRM Handbook* (McGraw Hill, 2003).

A NEW PHILOSOPHY

Relationship building is based on understanding customers and meeting their needs, but advocacy is based on maximizing the customers' interests and partnering with customers. This goes beyond customer focus to actively representing the customers' interests like a good friend. This philosophy is based on the realization that customers are in control, so the path to success is to help them make the best decisions possible in the complex world of buying. The philosophy is based on mutuality of interest. If the firm helps the customer, it will learn what products and services customers really want and then can provide the products that honest advice would recommend. The customer advocates for the manufacturer by telling others about the firm and developing a long-term trust and loyalty for the firm.

NEW EVIDENCE

Although early Internet visionaries predicted that customers would gain decision alternatives and better information from its development, when the Internet bubble broke in 2000, many people rejected these notions.[26] In this book, I review the new evidence that establishes that customers actually have acquired new power. It is all around you and the effects are being felt in industries like travel, autos, and health services. I spend three chapters showing how power has grown and is changing the balance from push/pull marketing to trust-based marketing.

THE NEED FOR TRANSPARENCY

One tenant of the new philosophy of customer advocacy is transparency. You need to be completely honest and present full and complete information. In this book I show how you can use

---

[26] For examples of predictions, see: Bakos, Yannis, "Reducing Buyer Search Costs: Implications for Electronic Marketplaces," *Management Science,* December, 1997, Brynjolfsson, Erik and Michael Smith, "Frictionless Commerce? A Comparison of Internet and Conventional Retailers," *Management Science*, April, 2000, and Wind, Yoram, et al. Convergence Marketing (Prentice Hall, Upper Saddle River, NJ, 2002).

transparency to build trust with your customers and earn loyalty that assures profits even in turbulent times.

ADVICE IS REQUIRED

The complexity and number of options in your product offerings are probably high. For example, if you are a bank, you may offer 25 different mortgages; if you are a computer manufacturer, you may sell eight models and 100 configurations of computers; or if you are an auto producer, you may sell four brands and 25 models for each brand. Customers need honest help and complete information in order to pick the best product for themselves—not the product that maximizes the manufacturer's profit. The product should be the one a trusted friend would recommend. For the customer to have confidence, belief, and willingness to accept your advice, you must establish trust with a carefully instructed advisor virtually on the web or in person. A transparent and intelligent advisor who is genuinely in the corner of the customer represents advocacy for the customer across your firm's product offerings. This need is amplified by the fact that customers want to make good decisions efficiently. They want to trust an advisor to save time and make a better decision.

COMPARE YOURSELF TO COMPETITION

It is useful to give advice across your product offerings, but true advocacy demands that you provide information and advice across all offerings in the market. You should compare yourself to competitors, even if you are not the best, because customers are doing it anyway. You need to go beyond transparency and be proactive in representing your customers' best interests. If you do not come out on top in the honest comparison and advice you give, redesign your products so that they are the best. This may sound counterintuitive, but it is like stopping the production line if even one quality defect occurs. It is a severe reaction, but it should seldom be necessary, and quality will improve when everyone knows that you are serious about having the best products. In this book, I will tell you how you can "listen in" to this advice session, how to learn what is needed to make your product number one, and how to uncover hidden opportunities for new products.

SPEND LESS ON ADVERTISING AND PROMOTION

Advertising reach and effectiveness is going down, and prices are going up (in terms of cost per thousand viewers), so the cost/benefit ratio is decreasing and you should probably spend less in any case because of this declining productivity. But even more important in this context is that for customer advocacy, you should be concentrating on two-sided and unbiased information and advice. More money should go to Internet advisors, providing comparative product trials, and building peer communities composed of customers and your company. Promotion is a heavy-handed attempt to buy sales. With advocacy, you want to have superior products and represent them based on their value. You will not need as much price off promotion. You should allocate old advertising budgets to product improvement, communicating new products, and building new trustful communication channels.

NEW TOOLS ARE AVAILABLE

The good news is that a range of new tools is available to provide transparency, advice, and input to improve products. In this book, I explain how virtual advisors can be implemented on the web. These virtual personas function like a friend to provide help and honest guidance to help the buyer make the best decision for him or her. These complementary tools allow firms to build improved products based on the information customers provide about their needs and desires while talking to the persona. I also suggest methods to convert a CRM system that may be push-oriented into a CRM that fulfills the dream of a positive relationship by becoming a tool for advocacy.

THE NEW TOOLS WORK WELL

Not only are new tools available to build trust, but also they actually work. In this book, I will give numerous examples of tools for advocacy and evidence that they work. Here are a few brief examples that I will expand upon later in this book.

Credit Unions like First Tech in Portland, Mission Federal in San Diego, Bellco in Denver, and University Federal in San Antonio are finding that a trusted advisor for mortgages and loans builds trust with customers, substantially increases loan volume, reduces costs by requiring fewer loan officers and shorter customer sales sessions, and earns recommendations from users (95% would recommend the advisor to a friend).

General Motors created and experimentally tested a Dream CRM that converted their push/pull CRM into an advocacy tool by giving fair advice across all cars, providing comparative test drives across GM and competitive vehicles in a non-selling situation, building communities, and providing individualized product information customized to consumers' preferences. The results of market experiments were statistically significant and implied the potential for large increases in market share for those exposed to all the Dream CRM components. A complementary analysis of the dialog between the advisor and customers yielded opportunities for new models with an estimated hundreds of millions of dollars of sales. Most recent experiments are based on extending the Dream CRM into a full auto advocacy system.

Intel refined its customer support download site by conducting five sequential market experiments and found that adding improved navigation, a logic wizard, and persona resulted in a one-third improvement in download success and millions of dollars of lower costs in meeting the customers' download requirements with the Internet instead of with personnel from the call center or channel members.

Other companies such as John Deere, travel sites like Travelocity.com, Expedia.com, and Orbitz.com, and retailers such as Epinions.com, Amazon.com, Shopping.com, and Cnet.com have had positive experience with full information and honest comparisons. The pioneers have proved that the new methods work, and now many firms are considering adopting these techniques as they shift the balance of their marketing efforts from push/pull to trust and advocacy.

IS ADVOCACY FOR YOU?

Many things are new in customer advocacy, from philosophy to strategies of communication and product development. But you need to decide if they will work for you and your firm. If I am to follow my own advice, I must alert you, the reader (my customer), to the alternatives to trust-based marketing and note that an advocacy strategy is not suitable for everyone. Indeed, many companies face competitive situations, operating conditions, or customer characteristics that preclude the use of advocacy. Yet, with each reason to not build trust, there are exceptions to the exception— reasons why conditions that preclude trust might change or where trust might provide competitive advantage by moving from push to relationship or full advocacy.

An advocacy strategy is not suitable for every organization. For instance, a company's products could be undifferentiated, highly standardized commodities requiring little involvement from customers. Or buyers could be deal-prone individuals who evaluate offerings only on price. Or a company could enjoy a monopoly position. In addition, an organization's goals can be a major impediment to implementing an advocacy strategy. If short-term results are crucial, then advocacy might not be the best approach because it requires a long-term outlook and patience for return on investment in relationships with customers. We will discuss where trust may not work (and the counter-arguments for why it might still work) in a range of business scenarios in Chapter 7, "Is Advocacy for You?". All that being said, I believe customer advocacy will be relevant to most organizations and will be the strategy of choice for the industry leaders and most successful firms. In this book, I will teach you how to tell if advocacy is for you.

THE PARADIGM IS SHIFTING—PIONEERS WILL GAIN ADVANTAGES

Evidence is building that the paradigm of marketing is changing from the push strategies suited to the last 50 years of mass media to relationship marketing and now to advocacy-based strategies. The new age of customer power drives this shift. Managers need to decide where their firm should be in the spectrum from push/pull to advocacy. Intermediate points that build trust can be an end-point in the trust level or can be evolutionary steps on the way to an advocacy strategy. But relationships are not likely to be enough to achieve success in a world of customer power.

There are advantages to being a first mover in this strategy space because when customers develop trust based on advocacy with a particular firm, they are not likely to quickly switch to a competitor. Trust creates a barrier to entry by increasing customer loyalty and by forcing would-be competitors to spend more time and resources to develop a trusted reputation. For second-movers, trust is a chicken-and-egg problem—they cannot create trust without a track record of sales, and they cannot gain sales without trust. Even if later entrants try to compete on the trust dimension, the pioneers will have a superior position if they continue to innovate in the design of advocacy programs. Therefore, not embracing advocacy creates a risk to firms' growth and profits if competitors gain the trust of customers first. The movement to a trust-based strategy does present short-run challenges, but it also offers major long-run opportunities.

Although trust is not the best response in all situations, innovative firms are moving beyond CRM to implement advocacy-based strategies, and early adopters are formulating action plans to advocate and partner with customers. I predict advocacy will increasingly become the norm of behavior in the next ten years as the new paradigm becomes established and firms meet the threat (and opportunity) of growing customer power. Pioneers will gain advantages, but all firms will have to learn to compete in a world of trust.

WHAT YOU WILL LEARN IN THIS BOOK

In this book, you will learn that the growth of customer power is pervasive and that it requires us to develop a new theory for market strategy—Theory A (for Advocacy). Based on this theory, you will learn how to determine whether an advocacy-based strategy is right for your firm and how to build the trust necessary for this strategy. I provide you with new tools for advocacy building that you can apply to your business, and I identify the leadership skills and cross-functional requirements that you will need to make a successful response in this rapidly changing era of consumer power. You will learn what you need to do to change your firm's culture, create incentives, develop measure of success, and redefine your organization. Finally, I discuss the future of advocacy and argue that advocacy will become an imperative and not a choice. Those who lead in advocacy will gain profits, and customers will be reluctant to switch from these pioneers. Those who do not lead will have to respond to be competitive and will suffer a disadvantage because of their late adoption of customer advocacy. Relationship will not be enough and customer advocacy will become the key to profits in this age of customer power.

2

The Internet Creates Customer Power

It is perhaps not too surprising that the Internet has become such an important factor in our lives. The unexpected aspect of the Internet is not that people will use the Internet for purchasing, but that it has fundamentally changed the relationship between customers and companies. The Internet has generated a phenomenal growth in customer power. The Internet is to business in the 2000s what TV was to business in the 1950s. TV produced branding and promotion—the critical ingredients for traditional marketing and advocacy. The Internet is producing Customer Power—the critical driver of trust-based marketing. This chapter builds on the ideas summarized in the first chapter of this book. After reviewing the current extent of Internet usage, I describe the basic theory of customer power using examples from the travel, automobile, and health industries.

THE INTERNET IS PERVASIVE

The Internet has a profound and growing effect on business. Access to information, choices, and other customers combines to create a strong base for customer power. To understand this source of power, let's look at how Internet usage has grown and changed in recent times.

Some people think the Internet came and went with the dot-com bubble. Even as Internet stock prices declined, Internet usage continued its booming growth trajectory. In 1998, only 33 million or 33% of U.S. households went online, but in 2003 nearly 70% of households used the Internet—over two times larger in five years.[1] And this only measures penetration of the Internet in the home. Adding in Internet access in the workplace and libraries boosts the overall access rate to about 75% in 2004.[2] This is one of the fastest diffusion rates in the history of business. In the same five years, online buying went from 22% to 51% of consumers, and consumers increased the average number of categories purchased by four-fold (from about two to over eight categories). Average online spending was $95 per buyer in 2003.[3] In addition, 25.4% of online buyers said they often shop online and then buy in stores.[4]

Table 2-1 documents the five years of growth from 1998 to 2003 in terms of homes connected, buying proportion, and hours online. Most of the potential of the Internet that was over-promised during the Internet bubble is coming true, but at a bit slower rate than the unrealistic level originally expected. The

---

[1] Schadler, Ted. "Benchmark 2004 Data Overview," Forrester (Cambridge, MA), July 25, 2003, p. 3.

[2] The USC Annenberg School. Center for the Digital Future, "The Digital Future Report: Surveying the Digital Future, Year Four," September 2004, p. 27.

[3] The USC Annenberg School. Center for the Digital Future, "The Digital Future Report: Surveying the Digital Future, Year Four," September 2004, p. 57.

[4] The USC Annenberg School. Center for the Digital Future, "The Digital Future Report: Surveying the Digital Future, Year Four," September 2004, p. 60.

Internet investment bubble broke, but the underlying use and impact has grown steadily. If this growth continues, the Internet will be the most important force affecting business strategy in the future. The users of the Internet have shifted from young, predominantly male geeks to mainstream America. Table 2-2 documents these demographic shifts. For example, now only 41% of Internet users have college degrees, and the demographic split of male/female is almost equal. Attitudes toward technology (based on those who agree with the statement that "technology is important to me") have decreased from the geek-dominated level of 47% to a more typical 30%. Table 2-3 shows Internet use by age group. In the under-18 age group, 97.5% use the Internet. In the 18-35 age group, 88.5% use the Internet, and 38% of people over the age of 65 use the Internet. As the younger groups age, virtually everyone will use the Internet.

A final striking figure is the growth of broadband at home. Broadband has grown from 1% in 1998 to 23% in 2003, and it is accelerating. The significance of this growth comes from broadband's "always-on" features and the fact that it does not disrupt telephone use. More consumers are willing to pay more money for a constant, high-speed connection to the Internet. This suggests an increasing integration of the Internet at home. In turn, the high speed and low latency of broadband encourages consumers to gather even more information.

Now let's examine three industries in depth to understand the nature of the transformation in the relationship between customers and manufacturers.

Table 2-1 • Internet Growth Is Astounding

	1998	1999	2000	2001	2002	2003
Connected households	25%	33%	43%	57%	61%	64%
Buy online	22%	27%	50%	49%	51%	51%
Hours online/week for personal reasons	N/A	7.2	9.9	9.5	9.0	8.5

Source: Forrester (Cambridge, MA), "Consumer Technologies 1998-2003 Benchmark Studies," July 25, 2003.

Table 2-2   Internet Is Every Person's Tool

	1998	1999	2000	2001	2002	2003
Average age	40.5	41.0	41.5	44.9	45.0	46.6
Male	57%	56%	53%	49%	50%	49%
College degree	49%	46%	44%	42%	42%	41%
Agree with statement: "Technology is important to me"	47%	43%	41%	33%	31%	30%
Have broadband at home	1%	2%	6%	10%	17%	23%

Source: Forrester (Cambridge, MA), "Consumer Technologies 1998-2003 Benchmark Studies," July 25, 2003.

Table 2-3   Internet Use by Age and Year

Age	2000	2001	2002	2003
12-15	83%	91%	97%	98%
16-18	91%	96%	97%	97%
19-24	82%	81%	87%	92%
25-35	81%	82%	81%	85%
36-45	72%	81%	73%	87%
46-55	73%	76%	72%	78%
56-65	55%	59%	64%	67%
over 65	29%	31%	34%	38%

Source: The USC Annenberg School. Center for the Digital Future, "The Digital Future Report: Surveying the Digital Future, Year Four," September 2004, p. 31.

THE TRAVEL REVOLUTION

Consider travel from the perspective of the customer—planning a trip involves decisions about a myriad of potential flight combinations (airlines, routes, fares, and travel times), rental car options, and possible accommodations. In the past, gathering all the information needed was the domain of the travel agent with specialized computer terminals connected to massive central reservation systems like Sabre and Galileo. Five years ago, 75%–80% of all travel was booked through travel agencies.

The Internet changed that dynamic by enabling the traveler to gather information about distant destinations and to access computerized reservation systems directly. Today, billions of dollars worth of flights are booked online, and the structure of the industry has changed enormously. As discussed in Chapter 1, "Now Is the Time to Advocate for Your Customers," over 63% of leisure travelers utilize the Internet for research. Fully 20% of all travel bookings were purchased online in 2003.[5] Online buying accounted for almost 24% of leisure and unmanaged business travel and 10% of managed business travel.[6]

The Internet has created a vast repository of information as well as extensive marketing and service opportunities. This has led to the birth of large companies like Orbitz.com, Travelocity.com, and Expedia.com, which are growing and profitable. These companies are based on Internet technology. Jeff Katz, CEO of Orbitz.com, believes that travel is one of the industries that has truly succeeded in taking advantage of the Internet's resources. In this particular case, "the Internet has increased consumers' power by 100%," Katz says. Figure 2-1 shows the Orbitz search-and-compare engine, which gives not only rates on a requested flight, but also advice on how much you can save by leaving or returning one day earlier or later. In this case, the price drops by $41 if I leave one day earlier and return one day later.

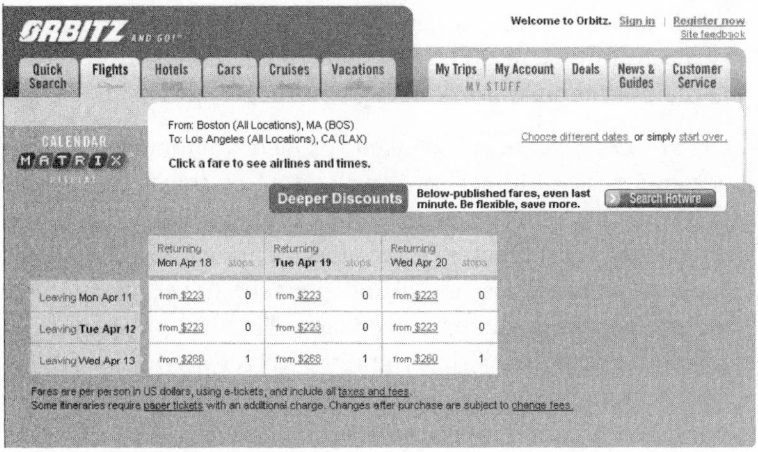

Figure 2-1   Orbitz Lower Fare Options

[5] Jupiter Research, "Internet Travel" June 2003.

[6] Jupiter Research, "Internet Travel" June 2003.

The Internet is a purchase tool that reduces the need for travel agents. Fewer leisure travelers now use travel agents when planning their vacations: 22% used a travel agent in 2003, down from 33% in 1999. In 2004, that figure fell even further to 16%, and during the same period, usage of the Internet grew by 53% in 2004 versus 36% in 2001.[7] In 2001, 36% of leisure travelers used the Internet to gather travel information, up from 24% in 1999. Among heavy leisure air travelers (those taking three or more trips a year), 80% report using the Internet for research in 2004. Among online air travelers—defined as air travelers who have an email address—the switch is even more dramatic. By 2001, over 93% of online leisure travelers used the Internet as an information source, up from 57% in 1999. The portion of online business air travelers who consulted with travel agents in 2001 dropped 17% since 1999, when 59% of business travelers relied on agents as an information source.[8]

Perhaps the more important issue is how the Internet has changed travelers' booking practices. According to the TNS Plog survey, agents continue to see an erosion of market share. In 2004, only 12% of business travelers surveyed typically booked through agents, down from 23% in 2001. Nearly one out of three business travelers typically booked through the Internet in 2004, up from 7% in 2000. On the other hand, 43% of leisure travelers say they purchased tickets online in 2004, up from 22% in 2003. The percentage of leisure travelers booking their vacations through an agent dropped to 14% in 2004.

Although 87% of travel is still booked through traditional direct-to-supplier venues (i.e., airlines' own web sites) or travel agents, the Internet has enabled a new way of travel planning and has increased the leverage that consumers hold over the traditional travel industry players. As a result, thousands of independent travel agents have gone out of business in the past five years. This has pulled out the shield of protection that airlines granted travel agents by paying them 5%–7% commissions. Today, virtually no airline pays a travel agent commissions, and the agents must add fees to cover their costs (often over $40 per ticket and often $40 more for rebooking). Customers can now avoid those added costs by going to the Internet.

[7] 2004 TNS Plog American Traveler Survey.

[8] 2004 TNS Plog American Traveler Survey.

SOURCES OF CUSTOMER POWER

The travel industry example illustrates how the Internet provides a new channel for buying products and services by giving customers more options when buying a given product or service. Consumers have more power when they can more easily find, select, and buy competing product or service offerings. Figure 2-2 shows a general conceptual model that indicates that customer power in the Internet era is largely dictated by three factors: *more options*, *more information*, and *simpler transactions*.

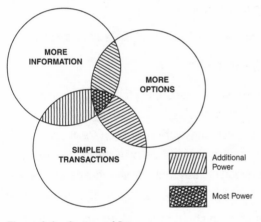

Figure 2-2 Sources of Power

- **More Options:** The Internet creates new purchase and distribution channels in addition to being a resource for additional information. The Internet lessens the distances between competitors in the sense that customers can easily access competing sites with a simple click of the mouse. Industries that have adopted online sales channels typically provide consumers with a greater degree of power.

- **More Information:** With the Internet, consumers enjoy access to timely and valuable information regarding the price, availability, and specifications of available products. Online tools further enhance the value of this information when the tool provides direct comparisons between the relevant choices. The increased availability of well-organized information available on the Internet helps customers make better choices and find or negotiate better prices.

- **Simpler Transactions:** Simpler transactions translate into greater consumer power. The Internet empowers customers by facilitating transactions that are easier to evaluate and more convenient to execute.

AUTO BUYING—IT IS NOT YOUR FATHER'S BUYING PROCESS

Now let's apply the theory of customer power to the automobile industry. We start with a story (see sidebar) about how buying has changed and then examine Internet usage for automobile buying and how customer power is generated.

A STORY OF AUTO BUYING TODAY

In the last 25 years, if a woman was shopping for a car, she was likely to be viewed as an easy mark for a commission-hungry salesman. Most women did not know cars well and were no match for the wily floor salesman. Often women paid higher prices or were treated to comments like "When you are ready to buy, bring in your husband." Yet the following story illustrates how customer power is shifting this paradigm.

A female former student of mine shared with me her most recent car-buying experience. After a prosperous year in consulting, she earned a large bonus and wanted to buy her dream car—a brand new red foreign sports car convertible. She visited a local dealer showroom and asked about her dream car. The salesman warned, "These are really impossible to get, but I will work hard to try to find you one." She said she wanted to spend about $36,000 ($1,000 above invoice), but the salesman only shook his head. He made it clear that such a hot model could not be discounted and that she would have to pay $40,000 or more. Frustrated with this experience, she went to the Internet. There she found her car for her $36,000 price, with all the features she wanted. New car keys in hand, she visited the original salesman to tell him of her find. He said, "That is impossible! Where did you buy the car?" To which she replied, "At your dealership." She had worked with the Internet sales representative of the very same dealer to get the deal!

All stories are not as dramatic as our sidebar, but customer power has changed the world of auto marketing for most buyers. The Internet is having a tremendous impact on consumer behavior in the U.S. automotive industry, which sold 16.7 million vehicles in 2003.[9] New sources of unbiased information and online buying channels combine to restrain the trickery of the stereotypical pushy car salesperson. Most dealers now have a special sales representative to deal with Internet-savvy customers, and many customers arrive at the dealer sales floor with a printout of prices and features.

Although Internet sales account for only about one out of every ten (10.6%) new vehicle purchases, 64% of all new vehicle buyers research their vehicle online before making a purchase.[10] These buyers are empowered by information on features and prices for all models through sites like Kelly Blue Book (KBB) or Edmonds. Figure 2-3 shows KBB's price comparison information. Notice that this comparison includes the invoice price as well as retail pricing. In the early days of the Internet (1997), after I showed this kind of Internet information to an audience of auto executives, one of them said, "We have to stop this!" Little did he realize that the power of the customer in bargaining for a car had increased and would never go back to the "old days" of incomplete information! As mentioned in Chapter 1, those who use the Internet for auto shopping visit seven web sites on average and focus on two types of auto web sites: automotive manufacturer sites (original equipment manufacturers like Ford, GM, etc.) and third-party sites. Seventy-eight percent of Internet auto shoppers say they visit at least one OEM site.[11] Table 2-4 shows the increase in Internet use in the vehicle purchase process.

[9] *Automotive News*, May 24, 2004, p. 25.

[10] According to J.D. Power and Associates, November 8, 2004.

[11] J.D. Power, "2002 New Autoshopper.Com Study" (J.D. Power, West Lake Village, CA), October 2002.

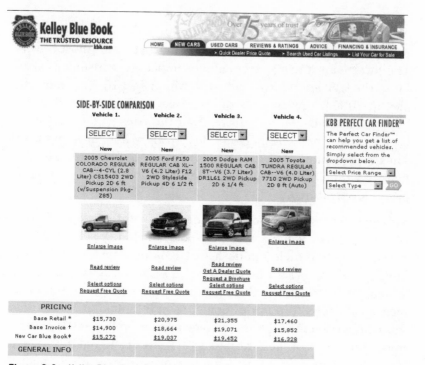

Figure 2-3 Kelley Blue Book Comparisons

Table 2-4 Internet Use in Auto Purchasing

	2000	2001	2002	2003	2004
Percentage of customers who use the Internet for research purposes in the new vehicle shopping process	54%	60%	60%	64%	64%

Source: JD Power and Associates[12]

The majority of Internet shoppers visit a third-party site to compare vehicle specifications and to narrow their set of alternatives to a few models. They then review detailed information for each model at the manufacturer or dealer site. Although some of the most popular sites are Internet extensions of traditional auto information companies—such as KBB.com of Kelly's Blue Book or edmunds.com of Edmunds—many of the popular third-party information sites

---

[12] JD Power survey data used in Table 2-4 refers to the fact that data acquired in 2000 and 2001 cannot be compared to 2004 due to differences in data acquisition methods.

provide services only on the Internet, such as Carpoint.com, AOL Auto, and AutoVantage.com. These companies strive mainly to provide information and impartial recommendations.

Another type of auto Internet site is the Internet Buying Service (IBS), such as Autobytel.com, CarsDirect.com, and AutoNation's Retail Network. These firms forge marketing relationships with dealers and serve as intermediaries to help consumers reach purchase agreements with dealers in exchange for a commission. Autobytel, for example, can solicit bids from their network of dealers and help complete the buying process. CarsDirect.com gives you the final price you should expect to pay. KBB and Edmunds have now added the IBS feature to their sites.

The generation and sale of customer leads via the Internet has rapidly developed into a complex, multi-level distribution system. There are agents who sometimes serve as wholesale middlemen, aggregating this demand information and selling it to dealerships so they can respond to the Internet requests for a price quote. The high customer acquisition costs that dealers incur through the traditional marketing process (generally on the order of several hundred dollars per customer) allow great room for improvement through Internet lead generation. The consumer also benefits because many of these services offer a combination of no-haggle pricing and convenience, and they produce more competition between sellers.

Not to be left out of the Internet action, manufacturers and dealerships have made varied levels of effort in creating their online presence. Most manufacturers have introduced web sites that are aimed at providing and collecting information, much like an interactive brochure. FordDirect.com and GMBuyPower.com connect consumers to their dealer networks with access to inventory, vehicle configuration tools, and current incentives.

Surprisingly, used cars are also sold on the Internet. eBay sold over $7 billion worth of used cars in 2003.[13] This is a major increase from the 2002 value reported in Chapter 1. This is

[13] Maney, Kevin. "The economy according to eBay," USAToday.com, http://www. usatoday.com/money/industries/retail/2003-12-29-ebay-cover_x.htm December 2003.

astounding because used car salesmen on the real used car lot are notorious for ripping off customers and duping them. How did eBay overcome this reputation and successfully sell used cars? First, eBay is trusted, as noted in the sidebar in Chapter 1. Disreputable sellers get negative comments and are not patronized or, worse yet, are removed by eBay. Complete information is provided through multiple pictures and guarantees that if the car is not as it was represented, eBay will help the buyer reverse the transaction. The transaction is easy—the price is specified, and delivery or pickup is also specified (some buyers drive 100 miles or more to get exactly the car they want). The risk is further reduced by the escrow service. In short, all the ingredients for customer power are present: more information, new options (eBaymotors and others like Cars.com, Autobytel.com, and Craigslist.org), and simplified transactions. eBay has taught used car salespeople how to behave if they want to sell in an environment where customers have the power.

CUSTOMER POWER IS HEALTHY

The complexity of medicine, the nature of medical terminology, and the risks of self-diagnosis or treatment force people to rely on highly skilled professionals such as doctors when dealing with health issues, and the high cost of medical care makes people rely on insurance companies to pay the bills. Government regulations all but guarantee a powerful role for doctors by limiting most treatments to those prescribed by a doctor. With such powerful, entrenched players, one might think that customer power is low in healthcare.

But in 2003, 110 million American adults sought health information on the Internet. This is 66% of all adults who have Internet access.[14] And this is a global phenomenon. Although less prevalent in Europe (35% of adults with online access search for health

[14] "Four Nation Survey Shows Widespread but Different Levels of Internet Use for Health Purposes." *Health Care News*, v.2, No. 11 (May 2002) Harris Interactive, 2002.

information in France, 44% in Germany, and 42% in Japan), it is growing rapidly.[15]

Consumers can now access a wide range of information from pharmaceutical companies, government agencies, insurance companies, hospitals, health product retailers, HMOs, and community groups. Merck's Internet site gives customers free access to the Merck Manual, a highly renowned source on health information. Figure 2-4 shows the Mayo Clinic site, which encourages patients to take control of their bodies by offering tips for healthy living, guides for disease identification, and information about treatments. Consumer-oriented healthcare information is growing globally. For example, Japanese pharmaceutical companies like Takeda, Sankyo, Eisai, and Yamanouchi provide direct customer information on the Internet in Japan despite a local medical system that is highly dominated by doctors.

More than just accessing information, consumers are using the information in a powerful and self-directed fashion. Thirty-eight percent of consumers look for information on their own, without consulting their doctor. These consumers are taking control of their healthcare. Patients often see ads for drugs; over $2.5 billion was spent on direct-to-customer advertising in 2002. Fifty-five percent of consumers have researched a drug they recall seeing in an ad.[16] Customers use web pharmacy sites—sometimes in foreign countries—to get the lowest prices for their prescriptions. In almost every company employees have a choice of health benefit plans, and they get information on them from their company and insurer sites. Rating information on the quality of hospitals is available from HMOs (and even Blue Cross/Blue Shield is considering making this information available), and customers exert their preferences by their choice of hospitals for treatment.

[15] "Four Nation Survey Shows Widespread but Different Levels of Internet Use for Health Purposes." *Health Care News*, v.2, No. 11 (May 2002) Harris Interactive, 2002.

[16] "Four Nation Survey Shows Widespread but Different Levels of Internet Use for Health Purposes." *Health Care News*, v.2, No. 11 (May 2002) Harris Interactive, 2002.

Doing this kind of research changes how patients behave when they go to the doctor. Forty-six percent bring their printouts to their doctors, showing that patients are more educated when they arrive for a visit. Emboldened by their own knowledge, patients have newfound control of the doctor-patient relationship. Rather than dictating treatments to patients, doctors are being forced to answer questions based on the patient's new information.[17] These powerful consumers even ask for specific treatments. Of those who have online access, 13% have requested a specific brand of a prescription drug. Perhaps most interesting, as I said in Chapter 1, 84% of the time the doctor honors that specific request. These patients are taking an active role in their healthcare, and physicians are feeling the pressure: 47% of physicians in the U.S. said they feel "a little or somewhat pressured" to prescribe advertised drugs that their patients request.[18]

Figure 2-4   Mayo Clinic Decision Guides
© Mayo Foundation for Medical Education. All rights reserved. Used with Permission.

[17] Manhattan Research, *Cybercitizen Health*, vol 2, 2002.

[18] FDA study of 250 general practitioners and 250 specialists (reported in *Ad Age*, January 20, 2003, p. 6).

In the health field, customers have vastly increased access to information, new options are being exercised, and transactions are becoming simpler.

POWER HAS BEEN GRANTED

The three industries analyzed in this chapter demonstrate how customers have gained power through information access, new options, and more simplified buying. Now let's look at how this power has shifted the balance from push/pull to trust-based strategies in these industries.

3

The Balance of Push and Trust Is Shifting

 As described in the last chapter, customer power springs from three sources: more purchase options, more valuable and timely information, and a greater degree of transaction simplicity. The new power of the customer is causing manufacturers and dealers to move from push/pull marketing strategies to trust-based strategies. This suggests that each industry has a balance of forces that determines whether push/pull- or trust/advocacy-oriented marketing strategies will work in that industry.

THE BALANCE BETWEEN PUSH/PULL AND TRUST/ADVOCACY

Figure 3-1 presents a weights-and-balance scale analogy of the balance between push/pull and trust/advocacy marketing strategies. The scale analogy displays the trade-off between the two extreme ends of the strategy spectrum. At one extreme is the pure push/pull business model, which involves virtually no trust. In a push-based business model, a company tries to manipulate customers into buying products and services. The goal is to get as many sales as possible, especially sales of high-margin items. Alluring, flashy ads create hype that drives sales; advertising and marketing emphasize form over substance. Fulfillment and after-sale support are minimal and very cost-oriented. Under the push business model, the goal is to get the next sale, rather than the sale after that.

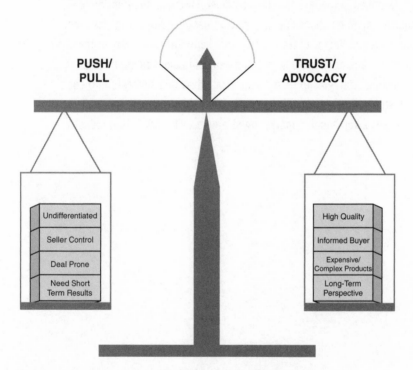

PUSH/PULL

TRUST/ADVOCACY

| Undifferentiated |
| Seller Control |
| Deal Prone |
| Need Short Term Results |

| High Quality |
| Informed Buyer |
| Expensive/Complex Products |
| Long-Term Perspective |

Figure 3-1   Balance Beam for Push/Pull and Trust Strategies

At the other extreme is an advocacy strategy that seeks to earn customers' trust by acting on their behalf at all times. Sales, marketing, fulfillment, and support all work together to under-promise and over-deliver. In seeking to unconditionally serve and satisfy customers, an advocacy-based business will occasionally act against its own short-term interests (e.g., recommending a competitor's product or covering the cost of some extreme level of service). Because an advocacy-based company tries to build customers for life, these companies strive to create reputations for impeccable honesty. Although a fully trust-based business can lose customers (whose needs or circumstances change), the quality of the experience means that even ex-customers become delegates of that company's marketing department.

In between the two extremes is a strategy based on building relationships with customers. This is often an evolutionary stop on the way to an advocacy strategy that builds complete trust. A relationship strategy is one that tries to connect to customers and create loyalty. The sales processes of such a company try to honestly match customers to the products offered by that company. Such a company offers extensive and largely unbiased information about its own products, although it will not necessarily provide any useful comparisons to competing products. A company that is building relationships has a value-based pricing strategy so that customers know that they are getting what they pay for. Because trust is one element of this intermediate business model, companies in this category will have adequate fulfillment and support services that deliver the promised value to the customer (e.g., high-quality products, adequate returns processes, and service guarantees).

If an industry has undifferentiated products, and the sellers have market power, then push is likely to be the observed strategy. This would also be true if customers are deal-prone and have very high price sensitivities. Another factor that impels the push effort is the necessity to get short-term results. Aggressive promotion is often an effective lever to get short-term sales movement.

On the other hand, if an industry has high-quality, differentiated products, and buyers are highly informed, then advocacy strategies are likely to be effectively utilized. Customers will get the information on their own, so giving fair comparisons makes sense because customers are likely to make them anyway. If products are high-quality and the design feedback from customers to manufacturers is good, then an advocacy strategy can work because firms are likely to have very responsive products.

Another factor impelling trust is the complexity and cost of products in the industry. If the risk associated with buying the products is high, or the uncertainty of information is great, then trust strategies can be very effective in winning customer loyalty. Finally, if the firm is committed to building long-term value and is not under short-term earning pressures, it can afford to develop a trust program and underwrite the higher initial costs because of the longer-term ROI.

Figure 3-1 shows these factors as blocks. Subtract one and see how the balance shifts. If your product is differentiated, remove the "undifferentiated" block. If your customers control the market instead of you as a seller, remove the "seller control" block. If you are striving for long-term success, remove the "short term" block. Removing these blocks causes the scale to tip strongly toward trust and advocacy.

Now let's apply the balancing-scale analogy to the travel, auto, and health industries in order to understand the balancing factors at a more granular level. Figure 3-1 gives the general factors, but as you will see in the following sections, the specific influences vary across industries. You may have different blocks, but the balance of forces will be indicated as your market changes.

THE BALANCE IS SHIFTING IN THE TRAVEL INDUSTRY

In the 1960s and 1970s, airline services were of high quality and were often differentiated. Travelers were largely businessmen, and they were very informed. Airlines had a long-term perspective and invested in customer satisfaction and loyalty. These factors pushed the balance toward the trust side of the scale. But in the 1980s and 1990s, the markets shifted. Price-sensitive leisure travelers entered the market, and capacity grew faster than demand. In order to fill those seats, airlines resorted to "load management" pricing and discriminated heavily between business travelers and vacationers, as well as between last-minute travelers and those who planned ahead. Rates became complex, and price became the dominant factor. Cyclical fluctuations, combined with high fixed investment, increased the pressure to cover short-term costs and make the quarterly numbers the stock market expected. Prices declined, and costs were cut, resulting in lower service quality and higher customer dissatisfaction. These trends intensified in the 1990s as discount airlines (like Southwest Air and Virgin Airlines) entered the market and capacity increased more while prices eroded even more. By the 2000s, price wars were common. With the drop in travel due to the events of September 11, 2001, airlines faced a tougher environment. Dissatisfied customers were deal-prone and had little loyalty. Big airlines like Pan Am and TWA disappeared, and giant United Airlines and USAIR have been operating under direction from the bankruptcy court. Thus, the airline industry slipped from trust and quality differentiation to price competition and push strategies over a period of 20 years.

On the other hand, the reservation and ticketing industry developed high levels of trust as third-party services (Orbitz, Expedia, and Travelocity) help customers find the best flights and prices for the customer by using full, honest information and acting to maximize the customer's interest, not the airlines. Buyers became informed and found reliable, high-quality ticketing and reservations for airlines and then for hotels. New services reduced the risk of having a poor flight or paying too much. These new companies became profitable, and some now have market capitalizations greater than many airlines. The Internet and electronic tickets enabled trust to be built as customers increased market influence and could exercise more decision options (e.g., using alternate third-party sites, going to the airlines directly, or using the traditional travel agent).

CUSTOMER POWER MEANS LOWER RATES

For most consumers, a key benefit of the shift in balance toward trust and the newfound power in ticketing is the ability to save money as well as the ability to easily make reservations and get tickets. Online price quotes allow consumers to price-shop when it comes to travel planning. Travel sites let consumers go beyond the price quotes from a travel agent and instead explore thousands of possible flights almost instantly. What's more, the cost of obtaining information is virtually zero for consumers with Internet access, and only a small charge is added for the ticketing services ($6–$11 typically, but as high as $15 for some international airlines). Finally, the abundance of online information provides consumers with reviews of airlines, hotels, and other travel amenities that they may not have had access to in the past. This enables informed tradeoffs between price and quality. In addition to saving money, customer power raises the importance of service quality. Tourist information sites provide consumers with destination information on restaurants, sightseeing tours, and tickets to local events. With the development of online travel sites, consumers now have the ability to plan their travel any time, day or night. More travel sites are offering one-stop shopping. With a few clicks, a consumer can do everything, from purchasing airline tickets to shopping for concert tickets, renting a car, and planning a complete vacation with overnights at small bed and breakfasts.

Growth in power is not restricted to final consumers; it also affects business customers. Before the Internet, small businesses relied on travel agents for their business travel needs, paying a combination of management and transaction fees. Unless they spent millions a year on travel, suppliers would not offer them discounted fares. Furthermore, small-sized businesses typically did not have dedicated travel managers to keep track of travel expenses.

With the advent of B2B online travel agents that target small and mid-size companies, such as GetThere.com, Yatra.net, Delta's MYOBTravel.com, and Continental's RewardOne program, these smaller businesses can now have more control than ever over one of their biggest expenses. The B2B online agencies not only provide standard travel management tools, such as customer profiles and real-time tracking reports, but they also aggregate purchasing power of multiple customers to negotiate deals with suppliers. As competition heats up in this historically underserved B2B travel market, suppliers are providing additional incentives for these small businesses to book directly through them. For example, MYOBTravel.com customers receive a discount on the first, fifth, and tenth bookings through the site, representing 10%, 20%, and 30%, respectively, off the published fares. The percentage of business air travel transactions conducted online increased from 9.5% in 2001 to 34% in 2003.[1]

THE TRAVEL INDUSTRY IS RESPONDING

In response to emerging customer power and the slip toward the push/pull end of the scale, some players in the travel industry have decided to further empower consumers with a straightforward business model to build trust and loyalty; others have chosen to use the Internet as a tool to target different market segments. Southwest Airlines's Internet strategy is apparent throughout its web site— direct and simple. No matter what the route is, the web site offers nine standard fares (e.g., Refundable, Child, Senior Citizen, Roundtrip Fare in the time period Mon-Fri 6:00 AM–6:59 PM, Discount, etc.). Southwest also lets customers cancel reservations online or apply funds from a previously unused trip to a new purchase. According to Nielsen/NetRatings and Harris Interactive, Southwest Airlines is a top-ranked online travel site for customer satisfaction. The rankings for customer satisfaction include factors such as site ease-of-use, information availability, flight options, pricing, duration of shopping experience, and customer service. At Southwest Airlines, you are told exactly what you will get, and the business delivers on its promise. The quality/price tradeoff is understood, and trust builds as those expectations are consistently fulfilled.

Customer salience is increasing within established airlines like Delta. According to Delta Airlines's former CEO Leo Mullin, the Internet enables his company to generate incremental revenue by providing different value propositions to different segments of travelers.[2] By partnering with these other discount web sites, Delta can better manage available inventory by selling off unsold seats. Furthermore, with the consumer data harvested through these

---

[1] Reed, Keith. "Flight Control: Companies turn to online booking to cut travel costs." *Boston Globe.* 14 August 2003. pp. E1 and E4.

[2] Leo Mullin retired from his position of CEO at Delta Airlines in May 2004.

sites, Delta migrates selected price-conscious travelers to become loyal customers by offering targeted promotions.

Likewise, Orbitz, Expedia, and Travelocity have aimed to further empower customers. Travelocity's business model is to provide travelers with choices and control at the best value. "We provide our customers savings in terms of time, as well as money, by offering great choices, deals, 24/7 customer service and convenience, such as FareWatch emails," says Mike Stacey, Director of Loyalty at Travelocity. As the leading online travel agency, Travelocity is much more than a web site that sells plane tickets. In the wake of airlines' zero-commission policy, Travelocity is diversifying its revenue mix to rely less on transactional air-ticket sales and more on high-margin products like cruises and vacation packages. Although airline tickets remain the biggest segment of Travelocity's business, much of Travelocity's growth has come from other travel needs. Having realized that consumers look for more personal interactions when it comes to purchasing complex products like cruise packages, Travelocity recently added call centers in Pennsylvania and Virginia that focus strictly on cruise and vacation sales. Shoppers can now call Travelocity's trained agents seven days a week for information, or even to book via the phone. To further reduce reliance on airline commissions, Travelocity recently agreed to buy Site59.com Inc., a last-minute travel company, for $43 million. Site59.com, named for the 59th minute in an hour, sells bundled vacation packages through partnerships with hotels, rental car companies, and airlines. Acquiring Site59 will enable Travelocity to expand its high-margin merchant business, in which it buys hotel rooms and airline seats on consignment at a discount and then sells them for profit.

Although 4,500 travel agencies have gone out of business, travel agencies, both big and small, are here to stay.[3] But the boundary between online and traditional sales channels will disappear. Because of the intense competition for travel dollars, consumers can now choose from a variety of ways to buy travel: through a traditional agent, through an aggregator site, or by booking directly

[3] Heartland Information Research. "E-Commerce's Impact on the Travel Agency Industry," October 2001, p. 2.

with the supplier. Instead of fighting this rising consumer power, travel industry players are embracing it by offering open and honest information, more options, better advice, and simplified procedures. Travel agents are differentiating in order to service travelers who want personal service and who are willing to pay for it.

Customer power is creating a travel revolution as new intermediaries are forming and old market structures are adapting.

IN AUTOMOBILES THE SHIFT IS TO TRUST

In the 1950 to 1995 period, push strategies dominated the auto industry. Dealers had the power, and customers had limited information about a risky and complex decision. The unflattering stereotype of the pushy car salesperson is familiar to anyone who has purchased a vehicle from a dealership. Unfortunately for consumers, it existed for good reasons. Before the Internet, dealer sales representatives could be pushy because it paid to do so. Consumers generally had little knowledge of invoice pricing and quality ratings of automobiles and were unfamiliar with what inventory they could expect the dealer to have. Furthermore, finding out what inventory other dealers had typically meant visiting those dealerships—an inconvenient, time-consuming process. In the past, many a slick salesperson convinced many an uninformed customer to pay too much for too little. Consumers found themselves relying on the dealership for almost all of the vehicle information, a scenario that rewarded pushy sales tactics.

With the Internet (see Figure 3-2), consumers have as much information as they want, including pricing and even dealer inventory in some cases. As a result, informed consumers can walk into a dealership and tell the sales representative exactly what vehicle they want, how much they are willing to pay for it, and where they will go for the next best alternative in the event that negotiations at the first dealership fail. The major factor that keeps the scales from tipping further in the direction of trust-based marketing is that 35% of consumers still do not conduct research on the Internet (they often mistakenly think that they can outsmart the dealer), and so the dealerships that are quick to identify these consumers are still able to rely on some level of push marketing.

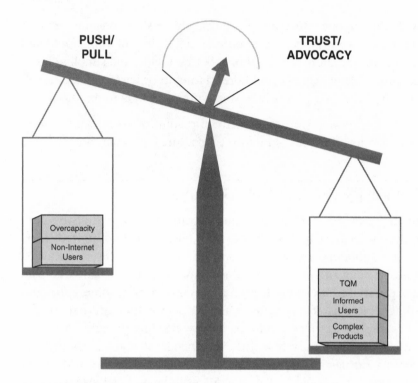

Figure 3-2 Balance Beam for Auto Industry

THE VULNERABLE BUYER SAVES THE MOST MONEY

This new power has resulted in lower prices for automobiles. As cited in Chapter 1, "Now Is the Time to Advocate for Your Customers," customers save an average of $450 by using an Internet buying service when purchasing a vehicle.[4] Seventy-five percent of this savings stems from the provision of information. Online buyers enjoy better prices than the 65% of offline customers. According to research, there are two sources of savings: of the total savings of $450, $378 is due to better information and referral to a dealer, and $72 is due to buying from low-cost dealers affiliated with the IBS.

[4] Fiona Scott Morton, Florian Zettelmeyer, and Jorge Silva-Risso, "Internet Car Retailing," *Journal of Industrial Economics.* vol XLIX, no. 4 (December 2001), pp. 501-19.

The savings from using the Internet are greatest for the most vulnerable segments in the market—women and minorities. Research shows that African American and Hispanic customers pay approximately 2% more ($400 on a $20,000 car) than other customers if they buy offline.[5] This is largely due to income, education, and neighborhood differences. Women pay 2% more than men. For minorities who use the Internet, the difference is zero, so they save the premium they would have paid ($400) and gain the Internet saving of $450. The Internet is the equalizer by giving disadvantaged buyers better information and providing them with education about autos.

The empowering effect is very evident when one compares the impact of the Internet on auto buyers who like to bargain versus those who do not like to bargain and are therefore more vulnerable to push auto selling methods. Table 3-1 presents the results from a study that examined the impact of using the Internet for information only versus using the Internet both for information and to gain a referral.[6] The first column in the table shows those who do not use the Internet and the price premium they pay relative to the base of the people who like bargaining and do not use the Internet—zero premium. As you would expect for non-Internet purchasers, those who dislike bargaining do pay a price premium— a higher price by about 2.1%. The second column shows the price premium for those who use the Internet but do not take the referral to a dealer from the buying service. These people pay no premium if they like bargaining and .4% price premium if they dislike bargaining. For those who do not like to bargain and use the Internet, this is a lower price by 1.7% relative to those who dislike bargaining and do not use the Internet (2.1%–.4%). In other words, by using information on the Internet, people who dislike bargaining

[5] Fiona Scott Morton, Florian Zettelmeyer, and Jorge Silva-Risso, "Consumer Information and Discrimination: Does the Internet Affect the Pricing of New Cars to Women and Minorities?" *Quantitative Marketing and Economics*. vol 1 (2003), pp. 65-92.

[6] Fiona Scott Morton, Florian Zettelmeyer, and Jorge Silva-Risso, "The Effect of Information and Institutions on Price Negotiations: Evidence from Matched Survey and Auto Transaction Data," Working Paper (Hass School of Business, University of California Berkely) December 2002.

save 1.7%. Using the Internet provides no lower price for those who like bargaining (0% versus 0% in Table 3-1). The third column shows the effect of Internet use with a dealer referral. The lowest prices are paid by those who use the buying service referral: –.8% for those who like to bargain and –.04% premium for those who dislike bargaining. For the vulnerable buyers who do not like to bargain, they can save 1.7% if they use the Internet (but not the dealer referral) and 2.14% if they buy the car through the Internet Buying Service (2.1% + .04%). Using the Internet Referral reduces the premium difference for those who dislike bargaining to almost zero relative to those who relish bargaining (–.04% versus –.08% or only .04% more). The vulnerable buyers who do not like to haggle gain the most from the Internet power they accrue.

Table 3.1   Price Premiums for Autos for Those Who Use the Internet Versus Preference for Bargaining

	Do Not Use Internet	Use Internet no referral	Requested referral
Like Bargaining	0%	0%	–.08%
Dislike Bargaining	2.1%	.4%	–.04%

Source: Fiona Scott Morton, Florian Zettelmeyer, and Jorge Silva-Risso, "The Effect of Information and Institutions on Price Negotiations: Evidence from Matched Survey and Auto Transaction Data," Working Paper (Hass School of Business, University of California Berkeley) December 2002.

These price benefits are complemented by a reduction of the time it takes to shop for a car.[7] The net impact of lower prices and less effort to buy are explicit measures of increases of customer power benefits.

INDUSTRY MARKETING IS SHIFTING

The benefits of a $450 savings may seem small when compared to the $20,000 price for a car, but the savings are real for customers. For the dealer, this $450 represents as much as 33% of their contribution margin. This has caused the beginning of a revolution in automobile marketing strategies.

[7] M. S. Lee, B. T. Ratchford, and D. Talukdar, "Impact of Internet on Information Search for Automobiles," Working Paper (University of Maryland, Bethesda, MD) 2002.

Vehicle manufacturers have taken advantage of the Internet to cultivate a better relationship with consumers. The Internet has proven to be a powerful point of contact that enables two-way communication with the consumer. One recent initiative, which aims to expand the role of the manufacturer, is Auto Choice Advisor, created by General Motors (GM). This service provides impartial recommendations from a database of over 300 vehicles, most of which are non-GM products, and is available on impartial sites such as Kelly Blue Book and Car Talk. The consumer enters a variety of preferences for major attributes desired, and the service applies an algorithm to rank the "best" vehicles based on those individual preferences. GM hopes that this tool will provide meaningful insight into which vehicle attributes customers value the most. The success of this advisory web site depends largely on how much trust the consumer is willing to place in GM as a source of advice, which GM is attempting to bolster by partnering with trusted sources such as J.D. Power and AIC (see Chapter 7, "Is Advocacy for You?" for more details).

Once heavily threatened by the potential of the Internet as an alternative purchase channel, the dealer network has responded with its own Internet tools. The response, however, has been slow due to the federal franchise laws that require all new vehicle sales to be made through an authorized dealership, thus reducing the perceived threat from the Internet entrants who cannot sell directly to consumers. The Internet has presented dealers with an opportunity to redefine their relationship with the consumer. The task is not easy, though, because the industry suffers from a long history of strong distrust between consumers and dealership sales representatives. The most progressive dealers have responded by establishing a customized sales process to cater to Internet-savvy consumers. Because many consumers now walk into a dealership with full knowledge of invoice pricing and vehicle availability, there is higher potential for a trust-based sales process, with more emphasis on matching customers with their desired vehicles, and less effort expended on trying to manipulate the customer's opinion. Currently in my experience, about a third of dealers are innovatively forging a new customer sales strategy, and almost all of these have special sales representatives to deal with Internet customers.

As more customers rely on the Internet for research in the shopping process, the scale clearly tips toward the trust side. The customer, armed with Internet-provided information, is able to quickly verify dealer claims about invoice pricing, options content, rebates, and even regional availability. Thus, the Internet presents a breakthrough opportunity for dealers to change the mindset of many customers in how they perceive the trustworthiness of the dealership. As the role of the Internet continues to expand in the automotive sales industry, the effectiveness of trust-based strategies is expected to increase. Although many dealers are caught in the middle between push and trust today, the industry appears to be steadily progressing toward the full-trust model in the long term.

Outside of the United States, the impact of the Internet on automotive shopping has been most prominent in Europe, a market largely similar to the U.S. European markets have also seen the emergence of rapidly growing automotive web sites that provide research tools for pricing, specifications, options, and availability.[8] This market is experiencing a lag compared to the U.S. in terms of percentage of new car shoppers that utilize the Internet in their search process. This effect is due primarily to the overall lag of Internet adoption in Europe compared to the U.S.

One major impact of the Internet in the European market has been on unofficial imports across the European Union's now-open national borders. Due in large part to highly variable tax structures in different countries, the prices of automobiles can vary by 30% to 50% from one country to another. Britain has seen a surge in vehicles that are imported into the country by individuals purchasing in lower-cost countries such as the Netherlands. More than 5% of new car registrations in Britain are now from unofficial import purchases.[9] Such import sales are also on the rise in Germany, Austria, and France.

[8] Britt, Bill. "Internet Proves a Powerful Sales Tool for Automakers." *Automotive News Europe*. 8 (15): 7 July 28, 2003.

[9] Mitchener, Brandon. "Tax Arbitrage: For a Good Deal on a British Car, You'll Need a Boat." *The Wall Street Journal*. 19 July, 1999.

The Internet is a major enabler of this import process, giving broad access to pricing and availability in other countries. This instant access to more options is a key source of customer power. In fact, importing intermediaries, which operate primarily through a web site, are providing shoppers with nearly all the vehicle information as well as the transaction logistic details needed to make a purchase. In contrast, dealers in low-price countries are taking a cautious approach to selling cars for export. Many have avoided overt promotions of this business, citing contractual arrangements with the manufacturers. However, by law, any EU citizen can freely purchase a car in any other EU country. Empowered by pricing and logistical information, British customers are finding it easier to import cars and can even schedule a "Car Cruise" journey for the round-trip journey to select their vehicle.[10]

The extent to which one considers the Internet to be a paradigm shift in the automotive industry depends on one's initial vision of the Internet. For those who saw the Internet as a new way to purchase cars that would make the existing dealer network obsolete, the Internet has been a disappointment. Consumers still prefer to "kick the tires" prior to making a purchase, and dealer franchising laws protect the traditional process for completing a sales transaction.

From the standpoint of reaching customers in the research process, the Internet has indeed created a paradigm shift. Increased access to information (unbiased information on pricing and features), purchase options (more dealerships and alternative referral channel models), and simplified transactions (no-haggle sales or import support intermediaries) all contribute to increasing customer power and decreasing profit margins for dealers. The business of marketing to consumers in the automotive industry is undergoing a radical shift in reaction to the increase in consumer power. The ability of customers to aggregate information, compare brands, and shop across dealers of the same brand is increasing in scale and scope. The auto industry shows how customer power shifts the balance between push and trust.

[10] Mitchener, Brandon. "Tax Arbitrage: For a Good Deal on a British Car, You'll Need a Boat." *The Wall Street Journal.* 19 July, 1999.

HEALTH—THE NEED FOR TRUST IS INCREASING

As we saw in the last chapter, customers have access to more health information. Web sites, such as CDC.gov, and the availability of information in direct-to-customer ads (e.g., the special supplements in the Sunday edition of *The New York Times*), along with increased government regulations requiring disclosure, have dramatically increased information availability, thereby moderating the traditional control of the doctor. This is a force toward trust-building in the industry, but just as significant is the increase in the number of decisions patients must make. Employees now must choose between different health plans offered by their employer and, increasingly, they may choose the brand of prescription they want. In the U.S., customers are offered options when they go to a pharmacy. Typically, they are offered the health plan's generic brand for a $10 co-payment, a branded product on the formulary of the plan for a $20 co-payment, or a branded product outside the formulary for a $30 co-payment. This decision puts the customer in a more powerful position and provides an opportunity to make a choice. Many plans let members choose their doctor and their hospital. Due to liability exposure, doctors are more often explaining the options for treatment and asking the client to choose than making the final choice for the customer. For example, in cancer treatment, the doctor may explain the advantages and disadvantages of chemotherapy, radiation, or surgery, but often the patient must make the final choice with (or sometimes without) the doctor's recommendation. These new decision requirements have shifted the balance toward patient power over medical decisions and the need for trust building by medical system members.

Another structural change that is shifting the balance in the health industry is online community groups, which provide an important source of information when patients must make treatment decisions. Virtually every major disease has a community group where people share stories and exchange information. (For example, heart disease has communities at Heartcenteronline.com, arthritis has RAacademy.com by Aventis, cancer has Wellnesscommunity.org, and Herpes has a site called The Herpes Outreach Center by Novartis). Figure 3-3 shows Wellnesscommunity.org, sponsored by a consortium of drug companies (Roche, Amgen, and Lilly, among others). People join these communities to find support, information, and like-minded souls. Whereas doctors may have little time to spare for each patient, these online forums offer a venue in which people can take their time and explain their problems, ask for advice, and find information. People share information about the progress of their disease, coping strategies for everyday living (e.g., kitchen tools that can be used by sufferers of rheumatoid arthritis to open jars and cans), links to other informative web sites, stories of adverse reactions to drugs, experimental treatments, tips for working with insurance companies, and so on. In turn, these groups create customer power when the newly knowledgeable participants go to their doctors and demand particular treatments.

Figure 3-3 Communities in Health Empower Consumers

The widespread acceptance of HMOs, the growth of generic drugs, and the advent of communities also build the level of trust patients possess and grant patients more influence. The scale is tipping because of easy access to information, growing knowledge of customers, and patient communities.

FUTURE RELATIONSHIPS WILL BE COMPLEX

Although it is clear that the paradigm is shifting in the travel and automobile industries, the situation in the health industry is more complex because of the intricate relationships between industry participants. Pharmaceutical firms, hospitals, doctors, regulators, insurers, retailers, and HMOs all participate in responding to increasing customer power. All these participants in the health system are perceiving the importance of patients, and many are developing Total Quality Management programs.

To date, however, it is not clear which group might become the consumer's advocate and gain the trust of consumers. Doctors and hospitals were the source of trust in the past, but the impact of HMO patient scheduling, liability, and spiraling costs has eroded trust in doctors. HMOs could be the trust leaders, but cost pressures and incentives sometimes work against patient trust. Pharmaceutical companies could be leaders, but they are often concentrated only in specific disease classes. Insurers could be a viable leadership group because by encouraging preventive care and good practice, they can reduce their costs. The government often provides unbiased information (scoring high on that trust dimension) and regulation to protect customers, but it plays too small a role in delivery to be the major trusted provider of health services. Perhaps the future will see a consortium of system participants who will respond to customer needs and demands for more information, choices, and simplicity.

Although it is not clear who will take the lead in responding to customer power, all members of this industry are moving to accommodate more educated and demanding customers. Industry participants will need to earn the trust of patients to be successful. Patients are moving to control their healthcare, and they are increasingly making choices about whom to favor with their patronage.

POWER, BALANCE, AND IMPACT

We have seen that consumer power is increasing in the travel, health, and automobile industries. The balance is shifting from push/pull to trust/advocacy strategies, and the impact on the industry structure and consumer savings is real. In the next chapter, we will see that these trends are not restricted to these three industries but in fact are evident in many industries.

4

Customer Power Is All Around You

In the past two chapters, we've seen that the Internet drives customer power, and that it results from more information, new options, and simplified transactions. This power, along with industry trends, has tipped the balance toward trust-based marketing in the travel, auto, and health industries (see Table 4-1 for a summary). But almost every industry is feeling these effects to some degree. Customer power and its reactions are all around us. In this chapter, we will see how this power is reflected in finance, real estate, insurance, job placement, retailing, industrial marketing, and other industries. We can expect these trends to continue as a convergence of forces makes the old push tactics less effective and advocacy more desirable.

Table 4-1 Summary of Three Industries

Industry	Evidence of Customer Usage	Change in Industry Structure and Leadership	Evidence of Consumer Power	Corporate Response
Travel	63% of leisure travelers use the Net for research. Over 20% of all airline tickets are sold via the Internet.	Consumers can research and purchase their travel without an agent, diminishing the role of travel agents.	Airlines discontinued commissions to agents. About 4,500 brick and mortar travel agents have disappeared.	Third-party companies are a big success. Travel agents are trying to reposition themselves as personalized service providers.
Auto	64% of new car buyers use the Net for research; 10.6% use Internet buying services.	Prominent emergence of third-party information and selling services. Dealer network still intact, but changed.	Online purchase transactions using a buying service save an average of $450 per vehicle over the traditional buying processes.	Many dealers offer sophisticated Internet buying tools and special Internet representatives.
Health Care	Over 66% of adults online conduct health-related research via the Internet.	Comprehensive research sites on the Net empower consumers to research their health needs.	Customers select HMOs, research illnesses online, ask doctors for specific products, and use community groups.	Community sites proliferate. Pharmaceutical manufacturers market directly to consumers, encouraging them to ask their physicians about specific products.

INDUSTRIES ARE CHANGING DRAMATICALLY

STOCK BUYING GETS BETTER AND CHEAPER

A revolution in consumer investing began in 1996 when companies like eTrade widely marketed Internet trading. The price of trading a block of stock was dramatically lower. This caused a number of other firms to lower prices. Ameritrade, Schwab, and others entered the market, and customers enjoyed lower costs and gained more alternatives. The price of trades dropped by more than 50% compared to offline commissions in the 1990s.

As traditional brokerage firms and more new entrants joined the online market, customers gained more information and advice. Many brokers didn't simply compete on low cost. Rather, they offered access to exclusive information sources (e.g., free access to Standard and Poor's) and extensive online financial management tools. Companies like TD Waterhouse acknowledged customer power with "You're in Control" marketing messages, and Ameritrade added a "5-second" guarantee on execution—it will make the trade in less than 5 seconds. Customers clearly benefited from this empowerment, gaining lower prices, better information, more alternatives for service, and faster transactions.

An example of a trust-building financial company is Charles Schwab. Unlike many brokerage houses, Schwab does not pay its brokers on a commission basis. They receive a salary, rather than a cut of the fees and trading revenue created by the customer. Their mission is to "provide the most useful and ethical financial services in the world." Schwab developed ads that describe how the company treats customers as partners and how it advocates for its customers. For example, one ad showed a doctor next to a Schwab financial advisor and stressed that the Schwab broker was a trusted advisor who works for you like your doctor does. The headline was, "Both are pillars of trust. Only one can assess the health of your portfolio." Schwab's web site supports this customer advocacy strategy. The web site provides advice and valuable information sources to its customers, including major sections on "Education Resources to Invest with Confidence" and "Advice Planning: Bringing Your Future into Focus."

The rate reductions provoked traditional suppliers like Merrill Lynch to respond. Merrill Lynch did so in a very creative way, differentiating its personal brokerage network to provide a bundle of services and personal assistance to segments of the market. It did not match the discount prices, but created more value for customers with premium services at lower prices. These responses led to better information and lower costs based on comprehensive personal advice. This, in turn, led eTrade to position itself as a bank with a wide range of services. Schwab likewise responded by segmenting its markets based on three groups: Independent Investing, Active Trading, and Advised Investing. These alternative service plans were designed to build trust in each segment and add value on the dimension most important to each group of people. As a result, independent investors get research and online tools, active traders can trade on their own or team up with trade specialists, and advised investors can determine the level of personal attention they want and access premium services, including an Independent Financial Advisor.

Individual securities trading has undergone a transformation with more power to customers, and industry trends have tipped the balance toward more trust and consultative selling practices.

DAILY FINANCIAL RATES ACROSS BANKS EMPOWER BORROWERS

Recent developments in the financial services industry further empower consumers. Internet sites such as Bankrate.com and money-rates.com provide daily information on interest rates for loans, mortgages, CDs, and other financial services. Because people are taking advantage of this information, financial providers feel pressured to both supply comparisons and justify performance. If the customer has access to the information anyway, it is better for a provider to offer this comparison and then justify the difference in costs of its products instead of allowing competitors to be first in presenting this information to customers. Comparison information empowers buyers and leads them to reward honest vendors. Mortgage rates are updated daily, and consumers can get instant mortgage services from sites like LendingTree.com, credit unions, and major banks like CitiBank. Customers can apply online and in some cases can be approved without a personal visit. More information and simplified procedures have generated benefits for customers and have given them a whole new range of purchasing options.

SEE MANY MORE HOMES AND SAVE MONEY

The real estate industry has responded to customer needs in the booming housing market. According to the California Association of Realtors (CAR), 56% of homebuyers go online, or over one-half of home buyers can be classified as "Internet buyers."[1] Consumers go online and see a wide-ranging set of homes—some even in full-motion video—through services like eReality.com and zipReality.com. These sites work with realtors, pooling realtors' lists of available options and providing in-depth information to prospective buyers. Typically 10,000 or more homes are available in a metro area. The sites also simplify the buying process by automating the paperwork. They pass these savings on to customers as 1% rebates on purchases. As you can see, 1% of $500,000 is $5,000—a substantial saving. eReality estimates that it saved clients more than $8.3 million last year. More options, lower costs, and easier buying processes are important to customers. More information, direct discounts, and simplified procedures are big gains for customers.

Some of the new intermediaries actually bypass the traditional realtor altogether by listing houses and letting the seller close the deal (e.g., ISoldMyHouse.com), but most systems leverage existing realtors. Existing realtors have responded with their own sites and competitive rates. The National Association of Realtors now shows listings for all member agents on Realtor.com. They offer over two million homes and have a search capability that allows consumers to specify the location, house features, and price range to find their ideal house. Consumers can then view details on the house, see a picture of the agent, and take a video tour. All this means more alternatives, better information, and trusted advice.

Other realty companies are using third-party surveys to determine the level of customer satisfaction and are displaying those results on their realty signs. For example, GMAC Real Estate's Premier Service program establishes expectations for service and then commits to those service standards in writing. When the transaction is complete, a third-party surveyor, Quality Service Certification, assesses how GMAC performed. GMAC knew that in-house surveys could be viewed with skepticism, so they chose an independent party to conduct them.

[1] Iankelevich, David. "Internet Home Buyers Changing the House Rules." *eMarketer*, July 2004.

COMPARISON SHOPPING DRIVES COMPETITION IN AUTO INSURANCE

It is now easy to compare auto insurance prices. Previously, consumers had to call each company individually, fill out a different application form at each company, and wait to receive a quote. Now firms like Progressive and AllQuotesInsurance.com let consumers fill out one application and compare policies and prices directly. The firms offer consumers a rate and compare it to the consumer's existing policy and quotes from other insurers in the state where they operate. Typically, customers will save money over their existing rates. If the company's proposed rate is more expensive, they will explain why it is more expensive. Progressive goes beyond offering just a price quote—it offers a ranking on quality and service of other providers (see Figure 4-1). Progressive even provides customers with the URLs of competitors. These actions earn customer trust and reflect the reality of more competition and open comparison.

Traditional insurance companies have responded to increased customer power, and many now offer instant quotes online. The industry is much more competitive, and companies are fighting for customer trust and loyalty. Many financial institutions now offer auto insurance as well as their traditional products. For example, eTrade, Lendingtree, and CitiBank offer insurance services. These companies want to build on the trust they have earned with customers to sell a full line of services.

There is one caveat in this increased customer power, though. Progressive prices its policies individually depending on the customer's driving record and demographics. They may compare a consumer's individual rate (which may be low because of the consumer's good driving record or credit rating) to averages of other firms (obtained from state records). In most cases, Progressive will solicit and accept good drivers and let bad drivers pass on to other suppliers unless they are willing to pay the higher premium. Progressive is not yet at the full advocacy end of the trust scale, but these types of comparisons have increased customer power in the auto insurance business, and Progressive does supply the contact information of competitors so that consumers can get an individually priced quote from other companies.

Close Window

California Company Comparison Chart

Here's how other big-name companies compare in 20 areas. We may not be able to provide rates for every company, but we'll give you the information you need to make shopping fast and easy.

Note: Information in this chart is current as of 07/01/2004 and was obtained from company Web sites, financial rating companies and publicly filed information from the state government.

	Hide	Hide	Hide	Hide	Hide	Hide
Stability and Size of Company (back to top)	Progressive Direct	State Farm	Allstate	Farmers	GEICO	Liberty Mutual
A.M. Best rating	A+ *	A++	A+	A	A++	A
State market share for auto (2003)	3.0% *	14.5%	8.7%	10.4%	2.9%	0.8%
National market share for auto (2003)	6.9% *	19.2%	11.1%	5.2%	5.1%	2.4%

* Ratings and market share percentages represent two specific brands, Progressive Direct and Drive Insurance from Progressive. By itself, Progressive Direct represents the tenth largest auto insurance group of companies in the country.

Ease of Purchase (back to top)	Progressive Direct	State Farm	Allstate	Farmers	GEICO	Liberty Mutual
Are online quotes available?	Yes	Yes	Yes	Yes	Yes	Yes
Does the Web site provide rates for other big-name insurance companies?	Yes	No	No	No	No	No
Can policies be purchased online?	Yes	Yes	No	No	Yes	No
Can policies be purchased through a toll-free number 24 hours a day, 7 days a week?	Yes	No	No	No	Yes	No
Can payments be made in installments?	Yes	Yes	Yes	Yes	Yes	Yes
Can policies be purchased using a credit card?	Yes	Yes	Yes	No	Yes	No

Ease of Customer Service (back to top)	Progressive Direct	State Farm	Allstate	Farmers	GEICO	Liberty Mutual
Is there a customer service toll-free number available 24 hours a day, 7 days a week?	Yes	Must call local agent	Yes	Yes	Yes	No
Can you make an instant policy change online?	Yes	No	No	No	Yes	Yes
Can payments be made online?	Yes	Yes	Yes	Yes	Yes	Yes

Ease of Claims (back to top)	Progressive Direct	State Farm	Allstate	Farmers	GEICO	Liberty Mutual
Can claims be reported 24 hours a day, 7 days a week via a toll-free number?	Yes	Must call local agent	Yes	Yes	Yes	Yes
Can claims be reported online?	No (why?)	Yes	Yes	Yes	Yes	Yes
Can claim status be tracked online?	Yes	No	Yes	Yes	Yes	Yes
Do authorized repair facilities guarantee repairs for as long as I own my car?	Yes	Yes	Yes	Yes	Yes	Yes

Access (back to top)	Progressive Direct	State Farm	Allstate	Farmers	GEICO	Liberty Mutual
Web site address	progressive .com	statefarm .com	allstate .com	farmers .com	geico .com	libertymutual .com
Toll-free number	1-800-PROGRESSIVE	Must call local agent	1-800-255-7828	1-888-490-2801	1-800-861-8380	Click for info

Product Lines (back to top)	Progressive Direct	State Farm	Allstate	Farmers	GEICO	Liberty Mutual
What other personal products are available?	Motorcycle ATV Boat/PWC Motor Home Travel Trailer RV Segway HT	Motorcycle ATV Boat/PWC Motor Home Travel Trailer RV Mobile Home Life Home Health	Motorcycle ATV Boat/PWC Motor Home Travel Trailer RV Mobile Home Life Home	Motorcycle ATV Boat/PWC Motor Home Travel Trailer RV Mobile Home Life Home Health	Motorcycle Boat/PWC Motor Home Travel Trailer RV Mobile Home Home	Motorcycle ATV Motor Home Travel Trailer RV Mobile Home Life Home
Are financial services offered?	No	Yes	Yes	Yes	No	No

Figure 4-1   Progressive's Non-Price Comparisons in California

COMMUNITIES BUILD BRAND EQUITY FOR PACKAGED GOODS

As we have seen, the health industry has many online communities. But even consumer packaged goods companies now use online communities to build trust. Proctor & Gamble's Pampers site, the Pampers Parenting Institute, helps young and expectant mothers with information and an online community. The site does not explicitly sell P&G products, but the company hopes that providing the site will foster a more favorable brand image when consumers do buy. This community is not just a "chat room"—it is a monitored set of discussion topics and information resources.

Proctor & Gamble and Lever Brothers offer these kinds of community sites in almost every country over a range of products. For example, in Saudi Arabia, Unilever's teen health and beauty site is the second most visited site in the country, and it helps the company maintain its market share lead in consumer goods.

MORE JOB ALTERNATIVES MEANS MORE OPPORTUNITY

With the resumes of over 20% of all working-age adults posted online, people have real power to find a better job and higher salary. Sites like Monster.com provide a wide forum for exchange and are the first step in the job-matching process. Monster has added career advice and a special "Network Now" capability that gives you personal links to individuals in your profession and geographic area. Competition in the resume-matching process has grown with new sites like Jobs.com and Careerfish.com.

Prospective employees benefit from having more options and simplified methods of contacting employers, all with lower costs for everyone. This shift to online job matching has not put traditional recruitment companies out of business, though. Sometimes job sites provide too many options, and employers need a person to screen the many applicants. Thus, these service providers need to change in order to reflect both job seekers' and employers' newfound power to directly connect. Creating a better relationship with their customers (usually employers) and becoming a trusted source for qualified job seekers could help these companies add value in the matching process. Clearly, the market is more efficient, and everyone can gain from better matching.

INTERNET DATING: FIND LOVE ONLINE

Searching for a potential significant other has been made easy by the Internet—in fact, tens of thousands of sites are currently available for all sorts of population segments and interests: religion, race, ethnicity, geographic location, and sexual preferences. Interest sites range from broad-based interests, such as gender and location-based sites, to more specific interest groups, such as sites catering to vegetarians, avid runners, single parents, or people over 50. Internet dating has become a welcome alternative to the bar scene for many. In fact, more than 17 million people viewed online personals in 2002, and 2.5 million people have paid for online personals, according to Jupiter Research.[2]

With all the possibilities out there, you would not post your profile if you did not trust the site. Most sites, such as Match.com and AmericanSingles.com, offer a secure environment where you can check out hundreds of profiles and photos and exchange emails anonymously. Trust is created through privacy policies and acceptable conduct policies on many sites. The majority of sites will not resell your email address, and most prohibit sexually explicit photos and language and forbid you to contact other members for the sole purpose of promoting a business, product, or service. For example, eHarmony.com and Match.com, both licensees of eTrust, have dedicated entire web sections explaining site user privacy and how users can protect personal information.

In order to provide users with even greater discriminating power, a number of sites provide comparison information and evaluations of Internet dating sites available. ConsumersReview.org and DatingSitesReviews.com provide information, forums, and chat rooms, as well as news blurbs about featured sites.

A number of sites generate member loyalty by offering advice on everything from how to write a personal profile to posting a photo and setting up that first face-to-face meeting. They also provide safety tips, such as scheduling the first few dates in public venues. In fact, the most popular sites appear to be those that provide users with the greatest decision-making power (such as the ability to take a tour of the site, free trials, and excellent privacy options explained in great detail) and empowerment in use of the service (such as tips on using the site itself and dating).

[2] "Yahoo adds Video, Voice to Online Dating Service." 12 January 2003, http://www.siliconvalley.com/mld/siliconvalley/4933379.htm.

These web sites achieve consumer advocacy in online dating by promoting trust through service transparency and consumer privacy. By partnering with site users through empowerment tips, online dating services are also able to generate increased loyalty.

CONSUMER DURABLES—A BUYER'S MARKET

The advent of information-providing intermediaries like Amazon.com, Dealtime.com, CNet.com, Bizrate.com, and ePinions.com has increased buyer power. Consumers may compare products across a range of product attributes and may compare prices across brands and retailers. Intermediary sites often include peer group ratings or retailer ratings (see the sidebar). These new intermediaries are innovating. For example, Amazon.com provides customized individual recommendations based on what other people have bought when they made a purchase like yours. This helps customers find the right products in multi-purchase categories, like music, books, and DVDs, where the vast range of offerings can be daunting.

BUYING A TREADMILL

I wanted to buy a treadmill for my mother who needs exercise to build her ankle strength. First, I searched on Google and found over 100 models by various manufacturers. Reading the manufacturers specifications, retail offerings, and fitness information across five or six sites, I soon learned I needed something special. I didn't want a runner's treadmill with a long track and high speed, but rather a walking treadmill with a short track and slow speed. I also needed arm braces for easy on and off and safety in case my mother fell. The model I wanted was a Pro-Form "Trail Runner." Then I went to ePinions.com. Its product ratings confirmed my judgment (although there were only five reviews), and it gave eight retail alternatives with customer ratings on delivery and service (hundreds of reviews on the retailers). The best-ranked retailer was Fogdog.com, but its price was $100 higher after shipping. I was about to make a price/quality tradeoff when I noticed a box called "check for the lowest prices." Doing this resulted in a price that matched the lowest price on the retailer table. So I had it shipped (for free, incidentally) to my mother in Wisconsin, and I began assembling it the next time I visited her. There was a problem because one part was missing. I called Fogdog.com, and a courteous representative sent a local repairman out who put in the part, finished the assembly, and tested the machine. Now that was the good service I expected! I can see why it was ranked well.

In the end, I had many buying options, published health and customer ratings, a very good price, and outstanding service. I probably could have found this machine near my home (in Boston), but delivering it would have meant a lot of driving and, in the end, a special order. Best of all, my mother is walking more strongly because she can get physical exercise even during an icy Wisconsin winter.

In response, established retailers created online features of their own. Wal-Mart has a very expansive online site, which includes a link called "What's New at Your Wal-Mart." This multi-channel use of the Internet is the trend. Customers may use the Internet for information first and then visit the physical store later for "hands-on" examination and purchase pick-up. For example, Circuit City lets customers buy online and then pick up the merchandise at a local store, thereby saving shipment costs and providing a convenient point of presence for servicing products as well. Another trend in multi-channel retailing is the "opt-in" system, by which a buyer can sign up to receive the latest discounts and new product information by email. For example, J.C. Penney has over 9,000,000 people signed up for its service, and major retailers like Wal-Mart and Sears work hard to get customers onto their lists. These lists give the retailer easy access to interested buyers, while customers, in turn, get added information on products and prices. Although the new Internet channel has changed retailing dramatically, existing physical outlets will not disappear. In the future, traditional retailers will provide better information, decision support, quality, and service by integrating the Internet with the store—and customers will benefit.

INDUSTRIAL BUYERS SAVE WITH REVERSE AUCTIONS

Although B2B Internet exchanges have largely faded out of existence, most companies now have integrated supply chains that include electronic bidding. These reverse auctions (the company auctions off a contract to the lowest-bidding supplier) reduce costs by encouraging new bidders and enhancing the rivalry from existing suppliers. They also reduce costs by simplifying the procurement process. Industrial buyers have gained power through the same mechanisms as consumers—more options (bidders), more information, and simplified transactions.

The phenomenon of increasing buyer power is not limited to retail consumer products. There is one important difference, however. In the case of industrial products, the bidders (suppliers) often can lose trust in the buyer as they are being subjected to increased price-bidding pressures. The level of partnership may decrease, so buyers must balance this long-term effect against the short-term gains of the lower price.

REDUCING THE COST OF BUILDING TRUST WITH SMALL BUSINESS CUSTOMERS

Small business customers of industrial firms are often neglected because of the high costs of selling to them. But new Internet initiatives have provided better service and lowered costs while building trust with small business.

For example, OSRAM Sylvania has created a site called mySylvania.com that provides comprehensive information on products as well as a channel for efficient ordering and tracking. The site also provides product availability information and generates automated price quotes in real time. The information provided includes a tutorial and a customers' guide to the thousands of light bulbs offered by this company, giving customers the information they need (specs, availability, delivery, and cost) quickly. Customers can then compare this information to other sources and gain the advantage of selecting the best price with a minimum of effort.

GE Plastics has been an innovator since the beginning of the Internet. GE Plastics's web site goes far beyond supplying data sheets by providing "engineering calculators" as well as materials selection guides. For example, wizards are available for technical tasks such as calculating stiffness, fatigue, and costs of plastics. These calculators do not substitute for the firm's engineering staff, but they leverage it dramatically. This partnering to provide design support builds goodwill with all customers, but it is especially valuable to small customers who do not have large devoted engineering staffs. The customer and GE both benefit.

THE CUSTOMER POWER PHENOMENON IS SPREADING WORLDWIDE

Although the U.S. leads the revolution with the Internet and trust, the rest of the world is catching up fast. One mechanism is the globalization of U.S. sites like eBay and GE. For example, in travel, Orbitz, Travelocity, and Expedia are expanding worldwide. Dedicated travel sites have also developed overseas, such as sites like lastminute.com or easyJet.com in Europe. A first mover in South America, Despegar.com has formed an alliance with Yahoo! to provide travel services to users of Yahoo!'s Latin American sites. Despegar now has presence in Argentina, Brazil, Chile, Colombia, Mexico, Uruguay, Venezuela, Spain, and the U.S. and has also moved into the corporate travel market.[3] In banking, CitiBank and eTrade are global, but EGG and Barclays Bank are pushing the trust frontier in banking in the European Union. Vauxhall and BMW have innovative trust-building sites in Europe for automobiles. Pharmaceutical companies in Japan, like Takeda, are innovating by providing extensive consumer information in a healthcare system traditionally dominated by doctors. In England, Netdoctor.com is a collaboration site between doctors and information providers to

[3] Iankelevich, David. "Online Travel Market in Latin America Getting Ready for Takeoff." *eMarketer,* March 2001.

empower patients with education and service. Health on the Net Foundation (HON.ch) in Switzerland aims to "guide lay persons and medical practitioners to useful and reliable online medical and health information." Clearly, worldwide innovation is taking place.

CONVERGING FORCES ARE AMPLIFYING THE IMPACT OF THE CUSTOMER POWER SHIFT

As is clear from the consideration of the many industries listed in this chapter, customer power is growing, and the scale is tipping away from push marketing and toward trust. But the changes are even more pronounced because this growth trend is amplified by several important converging forces that make the old strategies of the 1950–2000 period less effective.

INCREASING SKEPTICISM

Corporate scandals soured many people on the merits of capitalism. The early 2000s witnessed a string of accounting scandals (Enron, MCI-Worldcom, Tyco, Parmalat), declining 401k account balances, layoffs, insider trading accusations, obstruction of justice charges (Martha Stewart), and anti-globalization protests. Meanwhile, the unending flow of "Buy" recommendations on plummeting stocks reinforced consumer cynicism. The combined assaults of these events have created widespread distrust of business. Indeed, bad press does real damage. As I stated in Chapter 1, "Now Is the Time to Advocate for Your Customers," people do not know whom to trust anymore, but they certainly do not trust business. Recall that the World Economic Forum found that 52% of customers across the world do not trust large corporations, and Golin/Harris found that two-thirds of U.S. customers feel that companies will take advantage of the public if they can without getting caught. According to a 2001 Booth-Harris Trust Monitor survey, the majority of consumers have stopped using some products due to negative media coverage.[4]

---

[4] Booth-Harris, "Trust the Emotional Glue Behind Customer Loyalty." *Trust Monitor.* (M. Booth and Associates, New York, NY) 2001.

And according to the Cone Corporate Citizenship Study, a national study conducted on more than 1,000 adults, 91% of those surveyed would consider switching to another company's products or services if they found out about a company's negative corporate citizenship practices, and 83% would refuse to invest in that company's stock.[5]

REGULATION AND ENFORCEMENT

The government is responding to voter outrage by aggressive enforcement and consideration of new laws. Executives who are not honest and do not provide complete information to stockholders are being treated as criminals. Breaking trust is not just a poor practice—it can put you in jail or subject you to large civil liabilities. Martha Stewart is a good example of strict enforcement and desire by the government to make salient the need for honesty. Enron and Tyco provide similar lessons—it does not pay to behave in an untrustworthy manner.

Regulation by the FDA has required much more complete product information. All drug advertising contains warnings about side effects and drug interactions (although in very small print). Tobacco packages and ads contain explicit warnings, and tobacco companies run anti-smoking campaigns for youth. Their sites explicitly state health risks, product ingredients, and the dangers of second-hand smoke (for an example, see RJ Reynolds—rjrt.com). These are all good trust cues and reflect transparency and responsibility. However, we should realize these are largely mandated by the Master Settlement agreement (November 23, 1998) with 46 states. In this settlement, companies agreed to stop many push marketing practices (e.g., free sampling, payments for use of cigarettes in movies and TV, and cartoon characters), begin new preventative programs, and pay over $200 billion penalty to the states over the next 25 years. Whatever the source, the consumer is benefiting from open, honest information and prohibition of many push marketing practices in this industry. If companies do not move toward trust, they may find the government passing regulations to force them to do so.

---

[5] 2002 Cone Corporate Citizenship Study at www.coneinc.com.

The government is sometimes proactive in supplying information to empower citizens. For example, in advance of the new U.S. Medicare drug program, Medicare (Medicare.gov) provided comparisons of prices for specific drugs across the dozens of new drug discount cards and retail stores. This allows citizens to better compare prices, select the best value, and exercise their purchasing power.

DECREASING MEDIA POWER

Modern-day consumers are far harder to reach and sway than their more gullible forefathers. Even as consumers have increased their consumption of information, the media channels by which companies push information to consumers have become less effective. Media fragmentation, consumer skepticism, and the time pressures of a modern lifestyle make it harder for companies to push their products onto an unsuspecting public. As a result, push/pull marketing's reach and effectiveness have dropped dramatically.

OVERCAPACITY, COMMODITIZATION, AND SATURATION OF MARKETS

The economic downturn of 2000-2003 reduced consumer demand, but even before the recession, capacity was increasing relative to demand. It is estimated that automobile production capacity is 33% above demand. The United States Census Bureau reports that sales are 72% of capacity across all industrial sectors on average for years 1997 through 2001.[6] Whether it is autos, consumer electronics, financial services, travel, or telecommunications, capacity substantially exceeds demand. This excess capacity causes companies to widen their product lines. Over 300 major automobile models exist, and even Coke has over 30 variants (flavors and package types). This overcapacity increases rivalry, and it is further intensified by commoditization as firms quickly copy each other's products and technology.

[6] U.S. Census Bureau, "Manufacturers' Utilization of Plant Capacity: 1997-2001" (U.S. Department of Commerce, Washington D.C.), October 2002, www.census.gov/prod/2000pubs.

With more choice, customers gain the privilege of selecting the exact product they want, often at promotional prices. Manufacturers faced with excess inventory and shortfall in sales growth have resorted to price reductions. The resulting price wars have been destructive to profits and stock prices. United Airlines and USAirways testify that bankruptcy is increasingly common as the slippery slope of price cuts leads to matching cuts from competitors, lower service quality, reduced demand, more price cuts, and the failure to gain sales and/or profits. At the same time, customers are trained to think only of price and are rewarded for disloyalty. Telecom companies are training people to be disloyal with their aggressive deals that promote switching between providers.

The net effect of these converging forces is a revolution in the environment in which firms must search for success. Although customer skepticism, media fragmentation, and product commoditization will present challenges to management, the dominant new consideration will be the growth of customer power. Taken together, these forces will create a turbulent environment for managers.

RESPONSE TO BETRAYAL IS PUNISHMENT

In addition to the forces described previously, one more force is emerging—customers are reacting negatively to push marketing. As I commented in Chapter 1, over 90% of customers said they were "angry" or "furious" about pop-ups on their screens.[7] It is striking that this is the same level of annoyance that customers have for spam email. Most large firms do not use spam, but their pop-up ads generate as much resentment. People react more negatively to heavy-handed push methods on the Internet than on TV. For comparison, regular TV ads rated only 15% on the "very annoyed" scale. The expectations for behavior on the Internet are much higher than on TV, and when those expectations are betrayed, customers are annoyed. The annoyance is not likely to increase sales. A 2004 Yankelovich study found that 54% of consumers said that they avoid

[7] Neff, Jack. "Spam Research Reveals Disgust with Pop-up Ads." *Advertising Age.* vol. 74, issue 44, August 2003.

buying products that overwhelm them with marketing and advertising.[8] Millions of people have used their browser tools or have installed software to screen out pop-up ads.[9] A free piece of software called FireFox can be downloaded and 10 million people have done so to block pop-ups and spyware. Customers do not like to be pushed around.

If that push turns to lack of trust, the penalty is greater. Recent surveys have also shown that when customers feel that a company has not behaved in a trustworthy way, they will refuse to buy from that company. A Harris Booth study found that 96% of customers take action (switch suppliers or stop buying) if they do not trust a company, and 84% refuse to purchase from such a company.[10] Expectations are critical. If customers expect trust, high quality, and good service, then betrayal of that trust will result in punishment. In a recent study by Stanford, researchers found that firms that generate a trust personality may be punished more for bad product service than a company that has not raised expectations.[11] This is an important caveat in dealing with powerful customers. Do not build expectations unless you can meet them. *Trust is difficult to earn and easy to lose.*

THE PARADIGM IS SHIFTING

Customer power has changed the marketing environment. The 50 years between 1950 and 2000 represent an era of push marketing, engendered by the availability of new technology (TV) and the growth of customer demand. Firms were in power and pushed products down on customers. The year 2000 heralded

---

[8] Smith, J. Walker, Ann Clurman, and Craig Wood. *Coming to Concurrence* (RaCom Communications, Evanston, IL), 2005, p. 128.

[9] Neff, Jack. "Spam Research Reveals Disgust with Pop-up Ads." *Advertising Age*. vol. 74, issue 44, August 2003.

[10] Booth-Harris, "Trust the Emotional Glue Behind Customer Loyalty." *Trust Monitor*. (M. Booth and Associates, New York, NY) 2001.

[11] Aaker, Jennifer et al. "When Good Brands Do Bad." *Journal of Consumer Research*. 31 (2004) p. 1.

the new paradigm in which the technology of the Internet, the saturation of markets, decreases in media effectiveness, and increased competition put the customer in charge. Customers are now in control, and firms will be increasingly unsuccessful in pushing products onto these potential buyers.

The trends toward increasing customer power across most industries are clear. If they continue, the balance will tip toward trust, and a paradigm of customer advocacy will be established. This results in a new theory of management—Theory Advocacy or Theory A. In the next chapter, you will learn about this theory, and in the following chapters, you will learn how to use this theory to decide if the advocacy strategy is right for your company.

5

Theory A— The New Paradigm

In the last three chapters, we learned that the growth of customer power is pervasive and cannot be ignored. Fueled by a set of converging forces, a tsunami is heading toward companies. Companies must now ask, "What are we going to do about Customer Power? We could push harder with promotion or pull more with advertising—our traditional marketing techniques," but the emerging alternative is advocacy. In this chapter, I examine a new trust methodology based on "Theory A" (A is for Advocacy) as an answer to increasing customer power, and I contrast it to "Theory P" (P is for Push/Pull marketing).

RULES OF TRADITIONAL PUSH/PULL MARKETING

Traditional marketing has been successful over the past 50 years. It is based on the notions that the customer is King/Queen and that a firm should identify consumer needs and build products to meet those needs. The traditional view is that the customer is the recipient of the firm's efforts and that large resources need to be spent to establish premier positioning in the market and convince customers to buy the company's product. Under this model, promotion is aggressively used to impel purchase. I call this push/pull marketing. The practice of traditional marketing has led to the development of seven rules for successful push/pull marketing.

1. CAVEAT EMPTOR

"Buyer Beware" is the watchword in marketing. Because of the way that companies ply their wares, customers should have a healthy cynicism about these claims and should realize that the motivation of the firm is to make money. Within legal constraints, marketing uses its considerable skills of persuasion to convince customers to buy its products. The emphasis is not upon supplying information fairly but rather supplying it effectively to get the sale.

A prime example of this is ads for wireless phone service. Recent ads trumpet thousands of free outgoing minutes, free long distance, and unlimited weekend calling at low bargain prices like $59.99. This seems like a good deal, right? Wrong! Almost impossible to read without a magnifying glass is the fine print. The fine print may take up an inch or more on the bottom of the ad. This fine print often reveals that there is an installation fee (typically $35 to $50) and monthly taxes and fees (about $5/month in taxes and often $5 to $10 for costs called "taxes" but not paid to the government), which are not included in the advertised price. In addition, there is often a high cancellation fee (typically around $200) if the customer wants to leave the plan in less than two years. This means the customer could be paying more than the market price if prices drop (a likely event) in the future. Furthermore, the unlimited service is only available on the supplier's network. If you roam off the network, you may pay a high per-minute fee (typical-ly $.59/min to $.79/min). And it is not easy to know if you are roaming off the network. Is that incoming call from off the net-work? If so, you are likely to pay the high per-minute rate for the incoming call as well. Of course, incoming calls refer to domestic calls only, and you may be liable for international fees in some plans if the call is coming from outside the country. Outgoing calls are often rounded up to the next full minute. And if the customer uses more than the allotted free minutes, the fee is high in many plans (in some cases $.79/minute). Maybe this is not such a good deal. Almost everyone is surprised by their first wireless monthly bill. The ads do not lie, and consumers who carefully review all the fine print get the facts. The onus, however, falls on the customer— it is "buyer beware" because the buyer has to figure it all out. In the world of "caveat emptor," it is ok to present one-sided and slanted information to achieve sales.

Other examples include banks, which offer low-fee checking accounts but have high fees for checks returned due to insufficient funds and fees for using ATMs not owned by the bank. Likewise, credit cards may be free, but consumers could pay $29.95 for late payment if they do not get a check in the mail in as little as 14 days (most payment periods are for 21 to 28 days, but the bill is dated when issued and often is not received until a week later). Credit card issuers can unilaterally raise the interest rate on your balances (often from that low promotion rate) if they think your financial status has changed (like late payment on any bill or cred-it card). All the information is in the credit contract, but have you studied its many pages? I have not. In fact, the *New York Times* recently reported about the lack of transparency for which credit card companies are becoming notorious. According to the article, late payments may be slapped with an interest rate of as much as 28%. And 80,000 people lodged complaints with the Office Comptroller of Currency in 2003, with the single biggest source of ire being credit cards.[1] As another example of "caveat emptor," an auto dealer may broadcast a special price of $13,999, but buyers

[1] McGeehan, Patrick. "The Plastic Trap: Soaring Interest Compounds Credit Card Pain for Millions." *New York Times*, 21 Nov. 2004, online edition.

must figure out that this applies only to one specific car in the inventory, which may not be available when they go to the dealer. But the dealer did get the consumer into the dealership and can now try to sell him or her a more expensive car. Being somewhat misleading is ok as long as the marketer stays inside the law. It is the customer's job to figure things out and make the right decision.

2. SPEND HEAVILY ON ADVERTISING AND SELLING

Convincing customers to buy is an expensive proposition. In 2004, $264.5 billion was spent on advertising in the U.S. alone (probably twice that worldwide), and that figure is growing.[2] For some frequently purchased consumer products, advertising and promotion accounts for up to 33% of the product price. In personal selling of pharmaceutical products, 87,000 salespeople or "detailers" call on doctors—or about one detailer per 4.7 doctors who have offices. The sales call typically lasts less than ten minutes with the doctor. The detailer explains a few products and leaves some free samples with the doctor. It costs over $150,000 per year to keep that salesperson in the field, including expenses and overhead, which translates to $13.2 billion for selling expenses in the health industry alone.[3]

3. MAXIMIZE YOUR MARKET POSITION

The primary purpose of large advertising expenditures is to cut through the clutter of messages and establish a point of difference in the mind of customers. The idea is to establish a brand image. For example, a company may advertise that its toothpaste makes teeth whiter or that its brokerage services are based on better information. The goal is to build the brand as a psychological

[2] Emarketer: Comparative Estimates: Total Advertising Spending in the United States, 2000-2007.

[3] Darves, Bonnie. "Too Close for Comfort? How Some Physicians Are Re-examining Their Dealings with Drug Detailers." American College of Physicians (ACP) Observer, 2003.

differentiator in a segment of the market. Often, this positioning concentrates on customers' psychological desires. Chrysler's new Crossfire is positioned as a fun, sporty car for women in their 30s and above. Although the physical car is mostly built from Mercedes Benz components, the effort is to create a psychological association of fun, freedom, and excitement with the Chrysler brand name.

4. COMPETE AGGRESSIVELY ON PRICE AND OFFER DIFFERENT PRICES TO DIFFERENT CUSTOMERS

Firms use price and promotion as a competitive weapon. Sunday newspapers often contain over 50 pages of Free Standing Inserts (FSI) that describe special deals and supply coupons. "Price off" is a dominant tool of retailers. If most products are sold "on sale," the manufacturers' suggested price has little meaning. In fact, higher retail prices leave more room for a bigger customer discount. In many markets, the risk of a price war is high, and the competitive structure often is unstable. Airlines are a good example of an industry in which services are relatively homogeneous. When one firm cuts prices, others must match the price cut or cut even further. The answer for the airlines is price discrimination. Price discrimination means charging different customers different prices for the same service. This often breeds ill will and may result in a similar price war, but one that is confined to demographic segments, particularly when arbitrary and complex restrictions are used to define discrimination policies.

5. BUILD QUALITY PRODUCTS AND PROVIDE GOOD SERVICE

In the last 20 years, firms have made great progress toward increasing the quality level of their products. The Total Quality Movement has made a substantial impact. At the beginning of a product life cycle, the design of quality products is aimed at customer wants. Through extensive market research, companies identify what consumers want and then produce those products at high quality levels.

Marketing concentrates on effectively launching the new product with a large advertising and promotion budget and selling the products down the channel. Firms look at needs but presume they must force buying through large advertising budgets and price incentives to distributors and retailers as well as customers.

Service is important in total quality, and it determines the likelihood of repeat purchasing. But often service is not the highest priority. Great service costs money and can lead to higher costs and prices. With the intense competition cited previously, it is often difficult or impossible to allow service level costs to get too high. Retailers often cannot do the job and, increasingly, manufacturers have mail-in service capabilities. For example, with copiers and computers, consumers must send in the product and wait for its return, paying the cost of repair if the product is out of warranty or if the flaw is not covered in the guarantee. If you drop your cellular phone and it breaks, you will be billed a high fee for repairs (typically a $250 flat fee). Your cellular phone itself may have been free when you signed the contract, but you will have a high fee if it is dropped or gets wet, which is fairly likely over a two-year contract.

6. GET SALES RESULTS

When it come to getting sales, companies do whatever is necessary to get the sale. Marketing is about getting orders. Sales force incentives and quotas are structured to get short-term sales results. "Close the sale" is the first law of personal selling. This culture and incentive structure often results in heavy sales pressure and mustering of all resources to overcome customer objections and concerns. Sometimes this leads to an adversarial relationship between the seller and buyer.

7. MEASURE SALES AND MARKET SHARE

Marketing is often controlled by comparing actual sales to the sales plan and achieving the sales forecast. Market share can also be used as a measure of success. These measures tend to be assessed quarterly or even more frequently. Some packaged goods firms look at daily market share by region or retail chain. The measures and typical bonus incentives lead to maximizing short-term results and often forgoing long-term strategies that may lead to sustained success.

THE MCGREGOR REVOLUTION IN ORGANIZATION THEORY AND ITS ANALOGY IN MARKETING

The rules outlined previously for traditional pull/push marketing are strong and have worked very well in the past. It is no surprise that when these rules are observed, little trust is engendered in customers. Now we face an age of customer power where those rules are likely to be insufficient for success in the future.

The old view is that customers need to be convinced or maybe even coerced to buy. Old-style marketing assumes that customers do not have much information, are not very good decision makers, and can be easily influenced. One fairly recent statement of push/pull marketing is "Torment Your Customers (They'll Love It)" by Stephen Brown, which was published in the prestigious *Harvard Business Review*.[4] The subheading says, "Customers are sick of being pandered to. They yearn to be teased, tantalized, and tortured by marketers and their wares." The author goes on to say "Customers don't know what they want. They never have. They never will." These are strong underlying assumptions about customers. Some marketers may consider these statements to be extreme and even embarrassing, but nonetheless, it's striking how many of these statements underlie traditional marketing strategies.

Advocacy marketing (Theory A) contrasts with traditional push/pull marketing (Theory P) in the rules that govern its operation and in the assumptions that it makes about customers. The old paradigm of push/pull marketing assumed that customers do not know what is good for them, while Theory A assumes that customers are responsible and active decision-makers.

[4] Brown, Stephen. "Torment Your Customers (They'll Love It)." *Harvard Business Review*, vol.79, No.9, Oct. 2001, pp. 82-88.

In 1960, McGregor introduced Theory X and Theory Y on the management of employees.[5] Theory X represented an old style of management in which employees were mindless robots that had to be pushed into working through monetary incentives and tight control by management. Theory Y represented a new style of management in which employees were intelligent, responsible individuals who could be trusted to do a good job (see Table 5-1).

Table 5-1   Theory X Versus Y in Organization Theory and Theory P Versus A in Marketing

	Assumptions About Employees	Assumptions About Customers
Old Assumptions	**Theory X**	**Theory P—PUSH/PULL**
	Employees dislike work	Customers avoid decision-making responsibility
	Employees must be coerced before they will work	Customers are passive and must be coerced
	Employees prefer to be directed	Customers have difficulty learning and prefer to be influenced
	Employees avoid responsibility	Customers have little imagination
New Assumptions	**Theory Y**	**Theory A—ADVOCACY**
	Employees will exercise self-direction	Customer decision-making is natural
	Employees will become committed based on ego satisfaction	Customers are active and want to control the buying process
	Employees seek and accept responsibility	Customers prefer to learn and make an informed decision
	Employees have imagination, ingenuity, and creativity	Customers have imagination, ingenuity, and creativity

More specifically, the traditional view, Theory X, held that employees dislike work, avoid responsibility, and prefer to be told what to do. This led to authority and control as the key factors in organizations. In contrast, McGregor proposed in Theory Y that employees are creative, willing to exercise self-direction, and willing to accept responsibility. This led to participatory management, management by objectives, and teamwork as critical success factors in organizations. Quality circles would never have been possible under Theory X, but they flourish under Theory Y.

[5] McGregor, Douglas. *The Human Side of Enterprise*. New York, McGraw Hill, 1960.

It may be difficult to think of business without management by objectives and teams, but in 1960, good management was based on power and span of control. McGregor was viewed as radical by many traditional managers in 1960.

The contrast between push/pull marketing and advocacy marketing parallels McGregor's Theory X and Theory Y. The key is in changing the assumptions that companies hold about their customers. Just as Theory Y provides a new view of empowered employees, Theory A provides a new view of customers. Theory P marketing led to push promotions and pull with one-sided advertising. Theory A, on the other hand, provides a view of empowered customers. The implications for Theory A marketing are trust-based marketing and companies advocating for their consumers. Theory P thinking leads to a push/pull view of marketing—that companies must "make" reluctant, apathetic customers buy products. In contrast, Theory A points to and creates a mutually beneficial relationship with an empowered, responsible, loyal customer following. For example, under Theory A, a company has the opportunity to partner with its customers and use the Internet as an enabler to provide information and offer customized advice. Charles Schwab ran an interesting ad that quotes a customer as saying, "I'm smarter than my old broker thought I was." She switched her money to Schwab, where the company's recognition of her ability matched her own assumptions. This is a customer who fits Theory A assumptions.

The question is, "What do you assume about your customers?" You must examine your markets and test your assumptions. The last three chapters have documented the growth in many markets of empowered customers who are active, responsible, and creative in their decision-making. If these descriptions characterize users in your markets, you should be operating under Theory A. This new view is a paradigm shift in marketing, as Theory Y was in organizational theory in the 1960s. It may take 5 to 10 years, but the world of marketing will never be the same. Those who practice Theory A now may be viewed as radical, but I believe that Theory A will become the dominant approach to marketing in the future.

RULES OF MARKETING BASED ON THEORY A

Just as the rules of Theory P or traditional push/pull marketing are driven by its assumptions, so is Theory A. If you take the assumptions of Theory A seriously, the rules of the game change dramatically. Here are seven rules for advocacy marketing.

1. ADVOCATE FOR YOUR CUSTOMERS

The paramount rule of Theory A is to advocate for your customers. Give them full, honest, unbiased information. Be transparent and genuine. Build your brand as a trust mark. It is good to give your brand a personality, but its primary function is to capture, in one or a few memorable words, the trustworthiness of your product and firm. A favorite TV ad of mine was run by Saint Paul Insurance. It showed a small girl walking out on the Serengeti Plane as a rhinoceros charged directly at her. She calmly held her ground and the rhino stopped just inches from her—the ad ends as she pats the side of the rhino's face. The voice over says, "Trust is not being afraid even if you're vulnerable." This is a good definition of trust. Vulnerability is a key aspect of trust and advocacy. If the customer is vulnerable, it is our job to protect them from that vulnerability, be it a product risk or the risk of making a poor decision.

2. INVEST HEAVILY IN PRODUCT SUPERIORITY

Advertising is important in Theory A as a means of launching new products and establishing your brand as a trust mark. But Theory A dictates that companies should spend much less on advertising, promotion, and selling than on developing product superiority. Advertising and selling can help make consumers aware of the quality features of the product, but with consumer power growing, consumers will have direct comparisons for products based on unbiased information. Slanted advertising has little function in the world of perfect information. The old rule of emphasizing the positives of the product and ignoring the negatives is not likely to work. One-sided advertising becomes two-sided comparisons in the world of transparency brought on by the Internet. Companies will no longer be able to hide the negatives about their products or services. Customers are looking for the best products and will be armed with information to use in making their assessments. In fact, if we obey Rule #1 of advocacy indicated previously, we will be helping customers do just that. You must strive to have not just high-quality products but the best products.

3. CREATE VALUE

Price is important, but if a company needs to promote heavily, it has probably not created products or services that are worth their price. High value—not low price—is the driving concept of Theory A. Customers want the most benefits per dollar and not necessarily just the lowest price. Added value features that customers want and need are the key to success. If you have built trust by advocacy, customers will believe your statement about added value and will have the confidence to act on your recommendations. The idea is to avoid price wars by competing on added value and innovation in the benefit space. Make sure your prices match your products' value. If you add little value, the price must be low. But if you can innovate and create new benefits, you may charge a higher price because customers will see that the price is a fair exchange for the value they receive.

4. WORK TOGETHER TO DESIGN PRODUCTS

Because value is our watchword, we must understand what customers value. We need to understand their needs and decision processes. This means we have to work closely with our customers. We can use the established market research tools to assess new product opportunities,[6] but an even better approach is to work jointly with your customers. The assumptions of Theory A are that customers are smart, understand their own needs, and are imaginative. In many cases, they will have solutions to their needs or will have developed ways of meeting their needs.[7]

[6] Urban, Glen L. and John H. Hauser. *Design and Marketing New Products* (Prentice Hall, Upper Saddle River, NJ), Second Edition, 1993.

[7] Von Hipple, Eric (2001). "Perspective: User Toolkits for Innovation." *Journal of Product Innovation.* v. 18, (2001): 247-257.

5. MAKE FULFILLMENT FLAWLESS

Trust is hard to earn. Customers slowly raise their levels of trust in your company as they gain confidence that you are actually working to maximize their interests. You must fulfill your promises. If you do not, trust is broken, and you may not be able to regain it. Do not follow an advocacy strategy if you cannot maintain trust through flawless execution. This means not only in your operation, but also throughout the channel. Slips in product or service execution are "trust busters"—you must avoid them. Trust is hard to earn but easy to lose. Fulfillment of promises is paramount.

6. BE LOYAL TO YOUR CUSTOMERS

Do not ask, "How can I make my customers loyal to me?" but rather "How do I make my firm loyal to our customers?" Build a positive long-term customer relationship. Create a mutuality of interest that promotes not only repeat purchases of your product but also the expansion of the relationship by purchase of services adjacent to the initial product. Have your firm deepen the relationship by creating bundles of services that meet wider needs. Concentrate on the share of needs met in your target market, not on the market share of a particular product segment. Think of the long run. Never jeopardize the long-term interest of customers to meet your short-term needs.

7. MEASURE THE LONG-RUN STRENGTH OF RELATIONSHIP WITH YOUR CUSTOMERS

Measure the trust customers have in you. This is the key correlation for long-term profits and return on investment. Look for long-run loyalty measured by repeat purchases and the share of wallet that the customer is allocating to your firm and its widening offerings. Track customers' confidence in your firm and keep it at the highest levels. Measure the level of positive recommendation you receive from your customers. Market share and profits are important, but consider average growth rates rather than short-term fluctuations as measures of advocacy success.

These Theory A rules differ from Theory P rules of push/pull marketing in significant ways. The philosophy of advocating for customers in Theory A is the opposite of "caveat emptor" in Theory P. The importance of marketing variables changes as you move from Theory P to Theory A. In Theory P, advertising and price are most important, while in Theory A, product superiority and value are paramount. Both Theory P and Theory A require quality, but in Theory P, quality is "nice to have," whereas in Theory A, quality is a "must-have." Similarly, the emphasis on service is much higher in Theory A than in Theory P. Both theories support innovation as an important activity, but in Theory A, innovation involves the customers more directly and becomes more critical to success than in Theory P. The types of measures used to track and control systems differ in Theory A and Theory P. Theory A uses a long-term set of measures of trust and loyalty leading to long-term profit maximization, while Theory P maximizes profits in the short run by paying careful attention to market share and sales.

ANTECEDENTS OF THEORY A

Theory A has antecedents in the history of marketing. Remember in the 1940s movie "Miracle on 34th Street" when the Macy's Santa told a mother to go to Gimbals rather than Macy's to find the right product? This was an early example of advocacy. Others exist. Trust departments of banks have always taken on the responsibility of protecting their trust fund benefactors. Private banks that cater to individuals with over $1,000,000 in assets have sometimes been in a deep trust relationship with their customers. Some clients even delegate investment authority to their team, with the confidence that the team has the clients' needs at heart and is not simply maximizing its commissions. Cooperatives such as credit unions, farmers' cooperatives, and some firms like REI have had an advocacy philosophy for a long time. Pharmacists at the corner drugstore are often viewed as advocates because they are knowledgeable about many products, they often offer advice to help the customer choose the best brand given certain medical plan co-payments, and they help patients understand the interaction effects of multiple drugs. The pharmacist often will recommend generic drugs at a lower price to help the customer. Similarly, relationship selling in industrial markets is based on helping customers solve their problems even if it does not produce an immediate sale. The salesperson may initiate a development effort at the firm to work with the customer to build a solution for their products. Efforts by firms in TQM and CRM are also evolutionary steps toward Theory A.

Now with the advent of customer power, we need to move from exceptions and special case antecedents to make advocacy standard practice. It is a giant step from push/pull methods to advocacy and a very big step from the Theory A precursors to full Theory A implementation.

ADVOCACY IN MARKETING LEADS TO ADVOCACY-BASED MANAGEMENT

Advocacy is a marketing concept, but it *should be* pervasive in the organization. All functions must adopt the philosophy. Figure 5-1 shows arrows emanating from marketing to other functions. Marketing information needs to get to other departments, and efforts must be coordinated across all functions. The proverbial functional chimneys must be broken down. A vision of advocating for the customer must unify the organization. Engineering must design products for buyer benefits; production must maintain costs and assure the highest quality; human resources must train and hire employees who embrace Theory A; finance must adopt a long-term profitability view and consider trust and loyalty measures as control parameters; distribution channels must be consistent with the manufacturers' advocacy programs; and customer service must assure the flawless delivery of promised benefits. In short, consumer advocacy should be pervasive throughout the organization. Corporate strategy and planning must reflect the new view of the company. Theory A is a corporate philosophy, not just a marketing viewpoint.

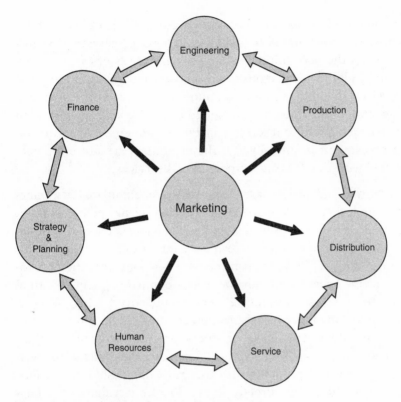

Figure 5-1 Advocacy as a Corporate Strategy

BENEFITS OF TRUST-BASED STRATEGIES

If you implement Theory A across the organization, benefits can accrue for everyone.

Trust-based businesses can extract themselves from margin-killing price competition by proving to customers and to the marketplace that they deliver true value. Businesses that are more trust-oriented have high customer retention and more stable revenue streams. Ultimately, trust-based businesses have higher sales volumes and lower marketing costs than push/pull businesses.

Push/pull businesses must acquire a continuous influx of new, uninformed customers to replace departing, dissatisfied customers. As the poor fulfillment and service levels of the company become widely known, a push-based business must spend increasingly large amounts of money on marketing to reach the next customer and to convince him or her to buy. Although money spent on advertising and marketing can buy customers, the return on that investment is short-lived if the customers are not ultimately satisfied with the delivered products and services.

By contrast, advocacy-based businesses accumulate customers with modest and decreasing marketing costs per customer. Satisfied customers, ratings agencies, and journalists all become very effective free marketing resources for trusted companies with high reputations. When a customer trusts a company, the cost-to-serve drops because the customer and company spend less time negotiating sales, inspecting goods, and overseeing service. Admittedly, advocacy-based businesses must spend more on creating and delivering good products and services because an advocacy-based business cannot honestly recommend its own products if those products are not truly the best. But because these expenditures go directly to providing real value to the customer, they have a high and long-lasting ROI.

QUESTIONS YOU NEED TO ASK

The first question is, "What should I do about customer power?" Your answer could be push/pull marketing or customer advocacy. Your decision will depend upon the way you view your customers, so you need to ask, "What assumptions am I making about my customers?" The assumptions-related questions to ask are: "Do I assume that my customers are active or passive decision makers?" "Do I assume they are proactive or that they need to be coerced into buying?" Next, think about strategy and ask, "Should I base my marketing on Theory P or Theory A?" Innovative firms are beginning to operate under Theory A. Should you? In the next chapter, we will discuss the answers to these questions and develop a structure to understand how much trust is appropriate for your firm as it moves toward advocacy.

6

Where Are You Positioned on the Trust Dimensions?

In the last chapter, I defined two extremes of push/pull (Theory P) versus advocacy (Theory A), but in reality, your firm is probably somewhere in between. You may have some elements of trust and relationship building, but not complete advocacy. In building a strategy to respond to the growth in consumer power, you must find out where you are on the overall and component trust dimensions, and then you must decide where you want to be and how to get there. Full advocacy may not be appropriate in your industry, but you need to determine how much trust to build. Often an evolutionary strategy is appropriate as you build trust. Relating positively to your customers may be the answer, but often it is not enough and advocacy is the best choice.

WHERE ARE YOU POSITIONED ON THE OVERALL TRUST DIMENSION?

The first step in formulating a strategy to cope with customer power is to evaluate your company's current position on the overall trust continuum (see Figure 6-1).

Distrust					High Trust
Skeptical Not Confident Disloyal	**P**		**R**		**A**	Belief Confident Loyal

P = Push
R = Relationship
A = Advocate

Figure 6-1   Overall Trust Rating for Three Markets

You and executives at your company can determine your company's overall trust position, but using executive judgment often can lead to biased results. Instead, it is better to conduct a market research survey with your customers (current and potential) to determine their attitude toward your firm. Customers often assign a different level of trust to the company than managers do. Most managers rate themselves higher on trust than customers. It is easy for managers to say, "We have the trust of our target market," but many managers would be surprised by what their market thinks of them.

You can measure overall trust by using a single scale, but it is good practice to have multiple measures on the components of the trust attitude represented by confidence (belief), competence (ability), and benevolence (helping others). These simple scales can be easily used in straightforward market research that confirms managerial judgment or provides some new information on customer opinion of your firm. These fixed scales can be elaborated by focus groups that search to find qualitative insight on trust beliefs. Look at the sidebar "Measuring Trust" for examples of trust rating scales.

MEASURING TRUST

A market research scale is not difficult to formulate or execute. For example, to determine overall trust, you could ask

Rate whether you agree or disagree with the following statement— 1 means strongly disagree, 2 disagree, 3 neither agree nor disagree, 4 agree, and 5 strongly agree:

Company X is very trustworthy __ __ __ __ __

                                      1   2   3   4   5

It is better to have multiple measures of attitudes, so three dimensions of trust—confidence, competence, and benevolence—should be used. I recommend that you measure overall trust and the following component measures:

Do you agree or disagree with the following statements:
    1   2   3   4   5

Promises made by Company X are likely to be reliable.

__ __ __ __ __

Company X understands the market they work in.

__ __ __ __ __

I expect that Company X puts customer interests before their own.

__ __ __ __ __

These are some examples of scales to measure first-order trust effects. A rigorous attitude measurement would include more component scales and a statistical analysis.[1]

---

[1] See David Gefen, "Reflections on the Dimensions of Trust and Trustworthiness Among Online Consumers" and Iakov Bart, V. Shankar, F. Sultan, G. Urban, "Determinants and Role of Trust on the Internet: A Large Scale Empirical Study: MIT Sloan Working Paper, 2004, for more details.

WHERE ARE YOU POSITIONED ON THE TRUST COMPONENTS?

In Figure 6-1, I evaluated the overall trust of three strategies: I rated push/pull strategies (P) low, advocacy strategies (A) high, and relationship programs (R) in the middle. It is necessary that you understand the underlying differentiating factors that determine the trust ratings. These underlying dimensions give a deeper view into trust. There are eight components that underlie trust:

1. Transparency
2. Products/Services Quality
3. Incentive
4. Partnering with Customers
5. Cooperating Design
6. Product Comparison and Advice
7. Supply Chain
8. Pervasive Advocacy

It should be noted that this chapter focuses only on these eight dimensions. This is not a complete list of advocacy dimensions, but these are the ones that I feel are most prominent in distinguishing between push and advocacy strategy. Chapter 11, "The Advocacy Imperative," presents a comprehensive checklist for customer advocacy.

Figure 6-2 summarizes eight dimensions as a respective set of distrust-to-trust scales. The left side represents practices that create distrust, which leads to skeptical customers, low confidence in the company, and disloyalty. The right side of each scale represents trust—customers who confidently believe in the company and thus are loyal. In the figure, I profile the position of each of the three marketing strategies (Push/pull, Relationship, and Advocacy) across these scales. Studying this example will make clearer what each scale means.

	P		R		A	
Transparency Distorted, HIdden Information	P		R		A	Full, Honest Information
Product/Service Quality Low product service quality fail to meet promises		P		R	A	Quality Best product and service to fulfill expectations
Incentive Incentives aligned for company, not customer gains	P			R	A	Incentives aligned so employees trust and meet customer need
Partnering with Customers Leave customers to work out their own problems	P			R	A	Help customers learn and help themselves
Cooperating Design Customers are sold company solutions	P		R		A	Customers help design products individually and through communities
Product Comparison and Advice No or biased comparisons and no advice	P			R	A	Compare to competitve products honestly and comprehensive communities
Supply Chain Customer trust conflict in channel	P		R		A	All supply chain partners aligned to build trust
Pervasive Advocacy Marketing pushes services and products	P	R			A	All functions work to build trust

Figure 6-2   Ratings of Three Strategies on Component Dimensions

1.   TRANSPARENCY[2]

How honest and open are you with your customers? Developing an advocacy-based relationship with customers means making the company more transparent to those customers. Companies such as Amazon.com offer very high levels of transparency, providing information about the book, reviews of the book (not just from publishers but also from other readers), and alternative suggestions to the book that customers may have recommended. Amazon also provides views into a few pages of the book and shows the book's overall sales ranking. Customers can click on the author's name to see if the author has written other books. Amazon even offers used copies of various books when they are available. Amazon tells customers whether the book is in stock and how quickly it will ship

---

[2] For more background information, see the following books: Pagano, Barbara et al. *The Transparency Edge: How Credibility Can Make or Break You in Business.* New York: McGraw Hill, October 2003, and Tapscott, Don et al. *The Naked Corporation: How the Age of Transparency Will Revolutionize Business.* Reed Business Information, 2003.

(from the next day to several weeks for out-of-print books). Customers may choose the shipping method, which ranges from expedited fast service down to slower free service if the customer spends over $25. If a customer places an order, Amazon sends an automatic confirmation with the full order information when the order is received and then sends another notification when the book is shipped. Thus, customers know about the product, alternatives to the product so that they can choose the best one, and even alternative pricing because Amazon offers them the option to buy the book used, if available, rather than new. Customers know when the book will ship, when it has shipped (and can track it if the shipping was expedited). In short, Amazon is sharing all that it knows about the product with the customer.

Evaluating your company on the transparency continuum might include examining your company's policies about pricing and publicizing product performance, as well as your company's candor about acknowledging faults or potential problems. Push/pull-oriented companies tend to hide bad information while hyping good information. They attempt to control all communications with an iron fist. In the last chapter, we described the lack of transparency in the wireless communication and credit card industries, and we cited them as two of the most opaque marketing industries. Transparent companies, those using an advocacy strategy, tend to publish both the good and the bad in a way that makes it easy for customers to use and understand the information.

At some level, transparency is unavoidable; increasing customer power ensures that customers will uncover the truth. The growth of customer power is a trend toward inevitable transparency in that customers and third parties will act to expose any company's deceitful practices, under-performing products, or poor service. Whether the company admits it or not, the data is out there from third parties or former customers. And if a consumer finds evidence of less-than-candid honesty, a "trust-buster" occurs that breaks the relationship. Some companies, such as software companies, may try to hide poor performance behind licensing terms that forbid customers from publishing or releasing benchmark performance data. But when customers find out that such data is hidden, their confidence wanes. Thus, transparency may not be optional in the future.

2. PRODUCT/SERVICE QUALITY[3]

Can you, in good conscience, recommend your products to your customers? Products and services must be of good quality, or they must be priced sufficiently low. Otherwise, companies can never honestly recommend their own products, making it difficult for them to gain customer trust. Quality is a prerequisite for advocacy.

As Figure 6-2 illustrates, advocacy requires a better level of quality than a relationship strategy and requires much higher quality than a push/pull strategy requires. Push/pull strategies can use hype or price to cover up marginal quality. Many airlines rate low on this quality scale because unilateral cost reductions, staff cuts, crowding of seats, and long check-in times have made travel distasteful.

Relationship strategies require higher product and service quality because a relationship strategy depends on customer loyalty, and customer loyalty is a function of quality. In the 1980s, U.S. auto companies were manufacturing vehicles that had more defects than their Japanese counterparts. As a result, American carmakers lost market share. But these firms worked hard to improve their quality, eventually achieving higher J.D. Powers' ratings. Now auto companies are in a situation where quality may be better than customer perceptions. Thus, auto companies need to rate the perceived quality in Figure 6-2 and then worry about how they can align perceptions with reality.

A company doesn't have to offer luxury goods to rate high on quality. Rather, the product must deliver on the company's promises and meet customers' expectations. One can sell low-performance goods at a low price. What matters is that the quality is as good as or better than expected and that the level of quality is competitive among similarly priced alternatives.

[3] For background information, see books such as the following: Gale, Bradley. *Managing Customer Value: Creating Quality and Service That Customers Can See*. Free Press, 1994, and Treacy, Michael et al. *The Discipline of Market Leaders: Choose Your Customers, Narrow Your Focus, Dominate Your Market*. New York: Perseus Books, 1997.

Your company can evaluate the quality of its goods and services using a variety of quality metrics such as defect rates, order accuracy, delay times, and so forth. But more important than absolute quality is quality with respect to both customer expectations and competitors' offerings. A review of your own marketing materials and sales pitches can help reveal the extent to which your company is creating an appropriate expectation of quality.

3. INCENTIVE

Do your employees have incentives to be true customer advocates? Advocacy means creating alignment between the interests of the company (and its employees) and those of the customers. Customers are sensitive to the seller's alignment of incentives. They give full trust only when they are convinced that the firm is serious about creating a mutually rewarding, long-term relationship.

A good example of a company that tries to maximize its alignment with customers is the discount broker Charles Schwab and Company. Unlike many other retail brokerage firms, Schwab's brokers receive a straight salary with no commissions for "churning" the client account. Schwab also eschews investment banking and is thus free to offer unbiased ratings of companies. The company provides a range of online tools that let customers research companies and make their own sound investment choices. Schwab would rate near the advocacy level on the incentives scale. In contrast, telemarketing companies who base all compensation on commissions would be rated low on this scale.

Evaluating your incentive structures will help you assess your company on this dimension. Performance metrics, employee evaluation criteria, and the structure of your business model will determine whether your business interests are aligned with those of your customers. In some cases, the competing interests of different customer groups or business partners may create misaligned incentives.

4. PARTNERING WITH CUSTOMERS

Does your company create collaborative, mutually beneficial partnerships with customers? Developing trust means showing customers that your company is "on their side." One good approach to this is to help customers help themselves. Thus, this dimension rates the helping relationship. A "helping relationship" is more like a pure consulting relationship than one tainted by selling. A good example is GE, which is sharing its knowledge of Six Sigma quality practices and business process improvement with its corporate customers. Although altruistic in appearance, helping customers in areas outside of the strict boundaries of the company's product line provides great value to the company. Look at the sidebar "GE—We Bring Good Management Ideas to Customers" to get more information about the GE programs.

Helping the customer actually helps a company in three ways. First, it creates a strong social bond that promotes customer loyalty. Second, it helps the company to more fully understand the needs and issues of its customers. By working on customers' problems, rather than push/pulling the company's solutions, the company gains insight into the pressing issues that its customers face. Third, in the business-to-business arena, improving a customer company's growth promotes sales growth back to the helping company. In mature industries, the growth rate of supplier companies is limited by the growth rate of the customer. Prosperity for customers means prosperity for the companies that supply them with needed goods and services.

Your company's rating on partnering will depend on how you interact with customers. Arms-length transactional relationships have lower ratings. A higher rating occurs when your people work with customers to provide individualized solutions or to solve unique problems. The highest ratings come when the company provides assistance on seemingly unrelated areas, such as GE's offer to help customers improve business processes.

GE—WE BRING GOOD MANAGEMENT IDEAS TO CUSTOMERS

GE's "At the Customer, For the Customer" program is an initiative to help customer companies learn from GE's management experience with Six Sigma, business process improvement, human resources, and IT. The program leverages GE's "Black Belts," who are trained leaders in process improvement. These leaders visit customer companies and help those companies improve specific processes. These small-scale consulting efforts are free of charge and are intended to help jump-start rather than actually perform the customer's entire process improvement effort. The program does not even have to relate to GE in any way—the goal is mainly to transfer best practices and help GE customers remain profitable.

The "At the Customer, For the Customer" program cuts across all of GE's divisions. For example, the GE Aircraft Engines division helped ailing airlines weather the brutal economic downturn of 2001–2003 that hit the travel industry. If airlines aren't flying, they aren't buying GE jet engines, spare parts, or maintenance. The projects go far beyond the divisions related to the engines that GE sells and supports to include any aspect of airline operations (from finance to flight scheduling to the tire shop) that a GE black belt and Six Sigma effort might be able to help. After the 9/11 attacks, GE Aircraft Engines tripled the number of teams in the field. So far, the company estimates that it has helped kick off efforts that have saved airlines some $400 million.

Other divisions of GE have their own "At the Customer, For the Customer" efforts. For example, GE Capital performed over 500 such projects from 2001 to 2004. This included helping Home Depot to improve workflows across the 1,300-store chain. Other projects at other divisions have helped diverse customers improve locomotive reliability, waiting times for CT scanners in hospitals, and copier sales in Europe. Overall, GE did more than 6,000 of these small projects. GE's "At the Customer, For the Customer" is designed to help GE's customers by sharing GE knowledge and experience with them, strengthening the relationship, and building trust with customers.

5. COOPERATING DESIGN[4]

Does your company collaborate with customers to create mutually beneficial new products and services? In realizing that customers are intelligent and responsible, companies can go to them for information and even for design ideas. Some companies go even further and attempt to supply their customers with "tool kits" to aid them in creating solutions to their problems that may lead to successful product launches for the company.[5]

In contrast, except for employing the occasional focus group, push/pull-oriented companies seldom solicit customer's advice or incorporate customer suggestions into new products. Relationship-strategy companies do listen to customers, but they do not have a collaborative design process with customers. Companies pursuing an advocacy strategy partner with their customers, actively co-creating new solutions.

Firms can be engaged with customers individually or through communities. For example, a number of computer companies, including Dell, Apple, and HP, offer online discussion forums where customers can discuss the company's products. Given the complexity of many modern products and the myriad combinations of usage patterns, no company can be expected to have all of the answers ("I'm having a problem printing from application X to printer Y using computer model Z with operating system version N . . ."). An open community creates a venue for mutual support in which customers and the company can overcome the difficulties of using complex products with the wide range of peripherals and software packages that exist in the market. Such communities often provide solutions to problems and suggestions for future products.

[4] For more background information, see the following books: Hiebeler, Robert et al. *Best Practices: Building Your Business with Customer-Focused Solutions (Arthur Andersen)*. Touchstone, New York: 1998 and Prahalad, C. K. and Venkat Ramaswamy, *The Future of Competition: Co-Creating Unique Value with Customers*. Boston, MA: Harvard Business School Press, 2004, and Whiteley, Richard et al. *Customer Centered Growth*. Perseus Books Group, 1997.

[5] Thomke, Stefan and Von Hippel,Eric. "Customers As Innovators: A New Way to Create Value." *Harvard Business Review*. April 2002. For more background see Eric Von Hippel, *Democratizing Innovation* Cambridge, MA: MIT Press, 2005.

The advantages of creating such communities include the following: 1) the company fosters a relationship with and among its customers, 2) customer loyalty increases as customers receive better service and join the community, 3) the company sees lower costs for technical support, and 4) the company learns about new problems and opportunities.

ADVANCED MICRO DEVICES (AMD) EDGE PROGRAM

AMD is a company providing processors, flash memory, and connectivity solutions. AMD purports to uphold a "customer-centric" solution, whereby AMD products are developed with customers' needs always in mind and not for the sake of innovation alone. To that end, they have created a special customer-focused online information hub called AMDEdge. AMDEdge is a B2C marketing program that targets tech-savvy consumers who are able to build their own systems, or "do-it-yourselfers." It provides users who sign up with technical tips, news, and information geared to keeping consumers or those interested in the technology on the leading edge of PC performance and technology. Specifically, a user who logs in will receive information on AMD's products, general tips on how to better utilize and understand his or her computer, computing news, PC building component information, and online forums related to AMD technology and general technophile-related tidbits.

By providing consumers with a channel of information and additional resources on AMD products, the AMDEdge program provides consumers with information power and cohesion. AMD gets to learn of problems related to their products in the online forums. There is less of a need for tech support as communities of users of AMD products help each other resolve problems or confusion. In addition, AMD hopes that its Edge program will further sales through word of mouth. The theory is that besides being early adopters, these "do-it-yourselfers" influence others to purchase AMD-based computer systems.

How your firm rates on the cooperative design dimension depends both on what information you solicit from customers and how you use that information. If you do not listen to customers at all, then you will have a low rating. A moderate rating might come from segmenting customers into categories and tracking the preferences of different customer types. The companies that rate at the highest level actively seek free-form customer advice and actively incorporate customer suggestions into their new products.

6. ADVICE AND PRODUCT COMPARISON

Do you provide unbiased advice that helps customers choose your company and its products? In a world of high customer power, using push/pull marketing to sell inappropriate products to customers is more likely to create enemies than revenues. Although a company may have good products, only an arrogant marketer or salesperson would think that the company's products are the best possible products for every possible customer. Sometimes a competitor's particular product might be better suited to a particular customer. If a company wants to use an advocacy strategy, it must be willing to tell prospective customers when they should seek out competitors' products. Honesty is the best policy when there is a risk that dishonesty will be revealed—and rising customer power means that this risk is unavoidable. Because customers have a wide array of information available from other sources for assessment and comparison, an advocacy strategy is proactive in supplying the information that customers are likely to get anyway.

Push/pull strategy companies provide little opportunity for product comparison and may even attempt to obscure the properties of their products through copious fine print. For example, wireless companies do little or nothing to help customers make the best decision. In fact, they make comparison shopping difficult with their intricate conditions and arcane billing rules involving activation fees, roaming charges, schedules of "free" minutes, early-termination fees, and so on. In contrast, travel services (such as Expedia, Travelocity, and Orbitz) provide information on virtually all flights and fares, enabling customers to choose easily among different options. Such practices demonstrate to customers that these companies are on their side.

In finance, competitive comparisons are becoming more common. For example, Bankrate.com gives competitive rates across most loan types. As I mentioned earlier, insurance firms like Progressive, Geico, and Nationwide also give customers comparisons. Bellco.org, a credit union, has recently joined the ranks of advocacy and has added an advice center, complete with comparative rate information on loans, mortgages, and a financial advisor to help you plan your finances (see Figure 6-3 for more details).

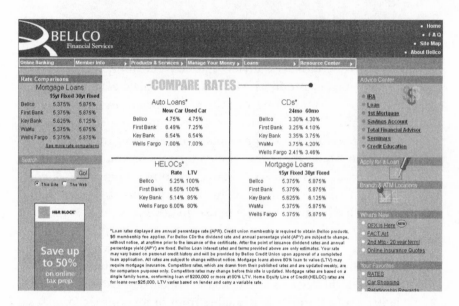

Figure 6-3   Bellco Advice Center and Competitive Rates

Another stellar example of nearly pure advocacy strategy is AutoChoiceAdvisor.com, a car selection web site sponsored by GM and J.D. Powers. (I talk more about this in Chapter 7, "Is Advocacy for You?") It is implemented as an independent site and is offered through third-party sites like Kelly's Blue Book and Car Talk as a "decision aid." The site provides honest and unbiased recommendations to consumers across all makes and models of cars. This kind of unbiased product comparison is still more the exception than the rule today. Strategies based on fair comparison would be rated like the advocacy profile in Figure 6-2: high on advice and product comparison. Travel services company strategies would rate high if they make comparisons and provide almost all rates and providers. Forthright dealing with potential customers also promotes the brand. If a customer is not going to buy from your company anyway, then why not leave them with at least a favorable opinion of your company?

Rating your company on the product comparison dimension means examining how your company helps its customers to select products. Companies that try to push/pull a single, high-profit product onto all customers will rate lowest on this dimension. Companies that listen to their customers and tailor their recommendations (i.e., companies using a relationship strategy) will rate higher. Companies that provide unbiased information and make recommendations that don't necessarily maximize profit (e.g., recommending a competitor's product if needed) will rate the highest on this dimension.

7. SUPPLY CHAIN[6]

Are your business partners trustworthy, too? A company is only as trustworthy as its least trustworthy business partner. If a company wants to become a true advocate of its customers, it must carry that advocacy to its business partners. The supply chain dimension rates the alignment of channel partners to the company's advocacy initiatives. Do your partners help or hurt your company's efforts to engender trust between you and your customers?

In many industries, a manufacturer relies on a network of channel partners, such as distributors, retailers, or value-added resellers to connect to the customer. Thus, these distributors and retailers play a major role in creating the brand image and customer relationship. Companies that implement an advocacy marketing strategy must work with their channel partners to create and reinforce trust. The actions of push/pull retail salespeople or shady distributors can damage a hard-won reputation for being trustworthy. Even suppliers can impact a company—for example, consider the

---

[6] For more background information, see the following books: Lewis, Jordan. *Trusted Partners: How Companies Build Mutual Trust and Win Together*. New York: Free Press, 2000, and Lewis, Jordan. *Partnerships for Profit: Structuring and Managing Strategic Alliances*. New York: Free Press, 2002.

impact of defective Firestone tires on Ford's sales of its Explorer SUV in the year 2000. Defective materials detract from the quality of a company's products. Although it may be the supplier's fault, the company gets the blame for selecting that supplier.

Travel services would be rated low on this dimension because their airline channel partners are not as trust-oriented as the travel sites are. Similarly, wireless phone service providers would be rated low because their channel sellers are very push/pull oriented. The channel is consistent with the company, but the strategy is push/pull, not advocacy, in these industries.

Many of these eight dimensions that underpin advocacy need to transcend the boundaries of the company. For example, incentive structures for retailers and distributors impact how customers will perceive a company's products. Even something as simple as volume-related incentives has an impact on trust. Volatile ordering patterns and erratic inventory levels lead to stock-outs and overstocks. Stock-outs frustrate would-be loyal customers by forcing them to buy other brands. Overstocks cause channel partners to push/pull the excess goods, creating mixed marketing messages. On the transparency dimension, the reluctance of suppliers or distributors to provide full disclosure detracts from a company's intentions for transparency.

Evaluating the strategies of business partners will determine your company's rating on this dimension. Of special importance are business partners with a direct connection to customers. Distributors, retailers, and service partners have the power to make or break a customer's trust. The quality and transparency of suppliers impacts a company's rating on this dimension, too.

8. PERVASIVE ADVOCACY

In the new paradigm of advocacy, the ideas must permeate all parts of the organization. Is advocacy and trust engendered at all levels and across all functions of your company?[7] The preceding

---

[7] For more background information, see the following: Harvard Business Review OnPoint Collection: *Building Trust in Your Company*. Harvard Business School Press, 2003.

discussions seem to imply that creating trust is, for the most part, the responsibility of the marketing, advertising, distribution, and sales functions of the firm. But in reality, implementing an advocacy strategy requires more pervasive changes that reach across the organization. For example, engineering, production, and R&D are critical to creating trustworthy products that meet customer needs. Pricing should reflect the premium value of the product and what trust is worth to the customer. Financial allocations need to reflect the long-run return horizon of an advocacy strategy.

Perhaps the biggest advocacy-related organizational changes are the cultural changes that inculcate respect for the customer. Human resources training and hiring must align with a company's trust-building view of customers so that all interfaces of the firm are coherent within an overall advocacy strategy. The culture of the firm must reflect the primacy of customer advocacy. This trust-generating culture extends beyond engendering trust from customers to include earning the trust of employees and stockholders. Although an accounting scandal does not impact customers directly (unless they are among the majority of Americans who invest in stocks), such scandals do damage the brand. High ethical standards and open, honest communication with all stakeholders are the corollary of a customer trust-based strategy. If employees do not trust the company, customers will not trust the company, either. The CEO must be active in this cultural revolution by leading the effort and by creating incentives and organizational structures that encourage long-term trust-building programs and reward executives who advocate for the customer. Therefore, the "comprehensive" dimension rates cross-functional participation and consistency in building trust.

Assessing the pervasiveness of advocacy in your company means asking the following question: Would you mind if customers could freely wander around your company, see how people are treated, read every memo, see how you make products, watch your design process, or listen to the CEO? The extent to which you are not embarrassed by any of the people or parts of your organization is the extent to which you rate highly on the pervasiveness of advocacy.

INDUSTRY TRUST ASSESSMENTS

Before you rate your company on the trust dimensions, let's look at specific industry ratings and examples of best practices to provide you with a deeper understanding of each component so that you can more accurately assess your position. Figure 6-4 shows examples of the overall trust scales for travel services, credit unions, autos, airlines, and wireless providers based on my judgment. In my example, trust varies from a high level for travel services (e.g., Orbitz, Travelocity, and Expedia) and credit unions to a low level for airlines (American, United, Northwest, etc.) and wireless providers (Verizon, Sprint, Nextel, etc.). Autos are in an intermediate position.

Distrust						High Trust
Skeptical Not Confident Disloyal	W	L	A	C	T	Belief Confident Loyal

W = Wireless/Telecom

L = Air Line

A = Autos

C = Credit Union

T = Travel Services

Figure 6-4 Overall Trust Ratings for Five Industries

In Figure 6-5, the typical firms are evaluated on eight strategy elements that contribute to an effective trust-based strategy. As I indicated in Chapter 5 in the section entitled "Caveat Emptor," wireless companies are the most vivid example of push/pull strategies in use, so they are rated low on almost all the scales.

Travel services are advocates for consumers and rate highly on the scales because they do the following:

- Provide full information
- Offer products to find the cheapest fares given customer requirements
- Offer incentives to find the best ticket and even reissue the ticket if the fares go down

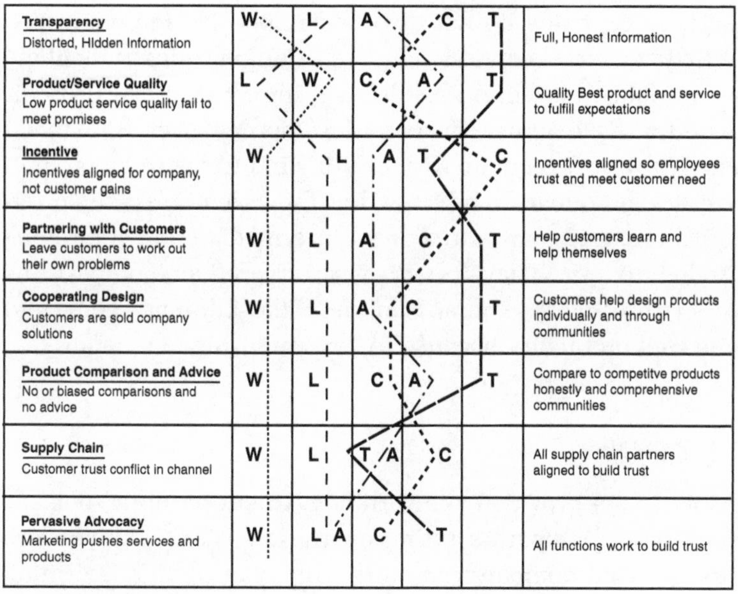

Transparency Distorted, Hidden Information	W	L	A	C	T	Full, Honest Information
Product/Service Quality Low product service quality fail to meet promises	L	W	C	A	T	Quality Best product and service to fulfill expectations
Incentive Incentives aligned for company, not customer gains	W	L	A	T	C	Incentives aligned so employees trust and meet customer need
Partnering with Customers Leave customers to work out their own problems	W	L	A	C	T	Help customers learn and help themselves
Cooperating Design Customers are sold company solutions	W	L	A	C	T	Customers help design products individually and through communities
Product Comparison and Advice No or biased comparisons and no advice	W	L	C	A	T	Compare to competitve products honestly and comprehensive communities
Supply Chain Customer trust conflict in channel	W	L	T/A	C		All supply chain partners aligned to build trust
Pervasive Advocacy Marketing pushes services and products	W	L A	C	T		All functions work to build trust

W = Wireless/Telecom

L = Air Line

A = Autos

C = Credit Union

T = Travel Services

Figure 6-5 Component Ratings for Five Industries

- Offer education to help customers (for example, explaining how consumers can save money with extra stops)
- Engage customers in product improvement
- Let consumers compare across almost all products
- Have company philosophies centered on helping the customer get the best ticket and vacation package

Airlines are not rated very well because of their inferior quality, the push/pull nature of their fare structures, and low levels of innovation. Specific airlines like Southwest and Jet Blue would rate higher than the industry average shown in Figure 6-5, though. They deliver what they promise and earn trust by consistently doing so. Credit unions are rated very well in Figure 6-5 because they stand up for customers and partner with them, but credit unions are ranked lower on transparency and product comparison because they generally do not display competitive interest rates, though Bellco is an exception. The credit union industry is likely to move in Bellco's direction resulting in improved ratings. Credit unions do not have active efforts to develop new overall financial products. They do a good job with existing industry products, such as mortgages, auto loans, and IRAs, but they are not usually product innovators. Autos are rated at an intermediate but improving level in Figure 6-5. They are highest on product comparisons because of third-party comparison sites like Edmunds.com, and they rate well on quality because of long-enduring TQM efforts.

RATING YOUR COMPANY

Figures 6-1 to 6-4 provided you with convenient profiling tools for visualizing your company's rating on these scales. Now you are ready to rate your company. As a first step, you should determine your company's overall trust position through market research or executive judgment (as discussed in Figure 6-1 and in the sidebar "Measuring Trust" in this chapter). As I cautioned earlier, be careful not to overrate yourself if you are using your own judgments.

The second step in determining your position on the trust dimension is to rate your company on the eight dimensions that underpin an advocacy strategy. You can evaluate your company on each of these dimensions by asking yourself the question that is paired with each dimension.

1. **Transparency:** How honest and open are you with your customers?

2. **Products/Services Quality:** Can you, in good conscience, recommend your products to your customers?

3. **Incentive:** Do your employees have incentives to be true customer advocates?

4. **Partnering with Customers:** Does your company create collaborative, mutually beneficial partnerships with customers?

5. **Cooperating Design:** Does your company collaborate with customers to create mutually beneficial new products and services after a fair comparison to competitors?

6. **Product Comparison and Advice:** Do you provide unbiased advice that helps customers choose your company and its products?

7. **Supply Chain:** Are your business partners trustworthy, too?

8. **Pervasive Advocacy:** Is advocacy and trust engendered at all levels and across all functions of your company?

Examining the profile of the component ratings allows you to determine why your overall trust ratings are high or low. After you evaluate your company on these dimensions, you should consider how you could change these ratings to improve your company's standing with your customers. It is also useful to rate your competitors on these same scales to determine whether you face a threat on the trust dimension or have an opportunity to gain on competition. You may also want to rate different customer groups to gain more insight. For example, if you were rating credit card endpoint customers, you would give low ratings on most scales, but ratings of the retailers who use the cards would yield a profile much more to the right on the scales.

BEST PRACTICE EXAMPLES ON EACH DIMENSION

The industry rating examples and ratings of your firm indicate where your firm is on each dimension. To illustrate the possible range on each dimension, I next describe some examples of best practices, in addition to those cited earlier in this chapter.

Transparency

This dimension rates the honesty and openness of company information. Great examples in the auto industry are Kelly Blue Book and Edmund's, which give accurate and complete information on new and used cars and provide customers with a range of ways to look at that data. KBB and Edmund's develop a trust-based relationship with customers by being transparent.

Product/Service Quality

Quality is a prerequisite for trust. Without good products and services, a company cannot recommend in good faith that customers buy its offerings. So, companies need to evaluate how good their products and services are. GE is a best-in-class example—their Six Sigma program has led to consistently superior quality. Another example is Toyota, which innovated many of the TQM procedures and continues over time to maintain top quality ratings.

Incentive

Customers are sensitive to what the incentives are for the seller, and they give full trust only when they are convinced that the firm is serious about creating a mutually rewarding long-term relationship. Salaried sales staffs tend to have higher consistency with advocacy strategies. eBay incentives are well aligned: Buyers and sellers benefit from honest ratings. Moreover, input from customers reveals any efforts to provide biased ratings. These incentives are reinforced by an arbitration procedure and the ability to eliminate identified buyers and sellers who are not trustworthy.

Partnering with Customers

Developing trust means showing the customer that a company is "on their side" or that the company and firm are on the same side. One good approach to this is to help customers help themselves. In addition to the GE and P&G examples cited previously, another example is the Trusted Advisor education program run by University Federal Credit Union in Austin, Texas. This site offers basic courses on buying a car called "Wheels 101," as well as "Home Economics 101" and "College Education 101." Wheels 101, which combines online information with an in-person seminar, is designed to make credit union members better auto shoppers. The course describes all the basics of good car buying and financing as well as dealer "secrets" that can exploit a consumer (see Figure 6-6). Although Wheels 101 may or may not lead to an auto loan for the credit union, it builds trust with the members based on useful information and learning. It is backed by the promise that University Federal Credit Union is "an oasis from pressure and deception" and will send consumers to another finance institution if that institution offers consumers a cheaper loan. University Federal Credit Union also sends low-key letters to members who have financed an auto loan through a dealer (they look at new registration data, merge them with their members' names, and determine if they have an auto loan with the credit union) offering to refinance the loan at the credit union rate. This often saves the customer money because the auto dealer may have charged the customer too high a price for financing. This is really representing the customer's interest, and it makes good business sense for the credit union—it results in new revenue and a new customer who now trusts the credit union more.

Figure 6-6   Trusted Advisor—Wheels 101

Cooperating Design

In realizing that customers are intelligent and responsible, companies can come to rely on their customers for information and even design input. A best-in-class example is 3M, whose use of lead user innovation methods has led to substantially improved new product success rates and larger market impacts. At 3M, lead user idea generation projects produced sales of $146 million—more than eight times the projects done by "traditional" methods.[8]

Product Comparison and Advice

In a world of high customer power, trying to push inappropriate products onto customers is more likely to create enemies than revenue. If a company wants to become trustworthy, it must be willing to tell prospective customers when they should seek out competitors' products. The consumer durables industry illustrates this best practice through sites like ePinions, Dealtime, and CNET. Retailers who fairly compare products represent the best practice, but those who sell their recommendation capability to the highest bidder are examples of the worst practice. Retailers who grant in-store preferences based on higher margins or online sites that display alternatives based on direct payment for the top position on the list of possible products can be trust-busters.

Supply Chain

A company is only as trustworthy as its business partners, so the supply chain dimension rates the alignment of channel partners to the company's trust initiatives. In many industries, the manufacturer relies on a network of channel partners, such as distributors or retailers. Dell is an example in this area, where the supply, production, and service chain is carefully populated with partners who maintain Dell's highest standards.

[8] Lilien, Gary L. et al. "Performance Assessment of the Lead User Idea-Generation Process for New Product Development." *Managment Science*, vol 48, No. 8 (August 2002): pp. 1042-1059.

Pervasive Advocacy

As described previously, trust is the responsibility of the marketing, advertising, distribution, and sales functions of the firm. But in reality, creating a trust-based strategy requires more pervasive changes that reach across the organization. Amazon and eBay are outstanding examples of implementing pervasive trust strategies and an effort to advocate for customers.

Another example is Legg Mason, who describes themselves as "global financial services company with only one product: *"Advice."* Legg Mason won the J.D. Power 2004 Investor Satisfaction award, competing against large firms like Merrill Lynch, Fidelity, and Smith Barney. Legg Mason's philosophy is "integrity, advice, performance, service, and an unfailing commitment to put our client's interest first."[9] That is a strong advocacy mission. Their product is advice, and the output is a valued relationship based on mutual success.

With the specific industry examples and best-in-class examples for each dimension, I hope you have the depth of understanding necessary to rate your company on the overall scale and component scales based on your judgment and substantiated by market research. The next step includes determining whether moving toward an advocacy position makes sense for your company and if so, learning how you can do it.

[9] www.leggmason.com/about

7

Is Advocacy for You?

In the previous chapter, I outlined a profiling tool that can help your company evaluate its position on the trust dimension. Next, you must choose a strategy and decide where to position your company on overall trust and the eight component dimensions. If you are now using a relationship strategy with a moderate level of trust, you may find it is not strong enough to meet the market challenges and therefore consider moving to full advocacy as a strategy. If you currently use a push/pull strategy (generally a very low level of trust), then you might consider moving to a relationship strategy with the long-term intent to shift to an advocacy strategy.

Various tactics can help your company become more trusted (i.e., to move farther to the right on the various trust dimensions shown previously in Figure 6-2). The first step is to examine the current profile of the company by using the ratings of each dimension. If, for example, your firm is low on transparency, it should build honest, open information systems for customers. If your company rates low on product quality, it can embrace one of many existing TQM programs.

Shifting from a relationship strategy to one of advocacy requires an even more extreme shift on the eight dimensions. Here you need more than just an improvement in transparency and quality. Your company could build advocacy through training, hiring better staff, and designing incentives so that employees are rewarded when customers succeed. It could partner with its customers through market research and communities to get suggestions for new product improvements. Your company could provide fair comparisons to competitor's products to build customer confidence that your company has the best products and can realign its supply chain to be as trustworthy as the company itself. Finally, your company can instill a culture of consumer advocacy across all areas of the firm.

Many firms could be cited for their success in moving toward advocacy by building trust among increasingly powerful customers. You may want to review the eBay sidebar in Chapter 1, "Now Is the Time to Advocate for Your Customers" and the examples (Amazon, Schwab, GE, P&G, Dell, and Bellco) and best practices (KBB, Mission Federal, 3M, ePinions, and Legg Mason) in Chapter 6, "Where Are You Positioned on the Trust Dimensions?" In this chapter, I examine specific trust-building programs implemented by General Motors, Intel, and credit unions, where systematic research has been done. After you see what these firms have done, you will understand what is now possible, and you can better decide if advocacy is the right strategy to follow.

DOES ADVOCACY FIT YOU?

Having evaluated your company with the scales in Figures 6-1 and 6-2, you should consider where you want to be. Are you comfortable with where you are, given the changes in customer power? Do you want to operate under Theory A and move more to the right side of the scale? Or is traditional push/pull marketing best in your industry and a better fit with your company, which makes staying to the left side of the scale the best strategy?

Developing high levels of trust through customer advocacy has the greatest benefits for companies in industries characterized by the following attributes:

1. Complex products
2. High customer involvement with products
3. High risk of loss if the customer selects the wrong product
4. Wide range of available products
5. Large volumes of available information

Many firms sell products that fit this attribute designation of advocacy and currently have relationship programs. Automobiles, health and financial services, high-tech industrial products, travel services, and consumer electronics are just a few examples of industries whose products have these attributes. Companies in these industries are likely to respond to the increasing levels of customer power with a shift from a relationship strategy to an advocacy strategy in order to increase their ratings on the trust dimensions. Relating to customers is good, but most of the time advocacy will be necessary to meet the demands of Theory A.

ADVOCACY IS NOT FOR EVERYONE

In contrast to the aspects described previously, some companies face competitive situations, company operating conditions, or customer characteristics that preclude the use of trust. Yet with each reason to not use trust, there are exceptions—reasons why conditions that preclude trust might change, or why trust might provide a competitive advantage to the companies.

Commodity Industries: Industries that are wracked by brutal price competition or that sell commodity products may not benefit from a trust-based strategy. Uni-dimensional price-based competition favors the most efficient producer rather than the most trustworthy one. For commodity products, the fact that competing products are interchangeable suggests that there is no benefit to developing a relationship with the customer. Yet trust-based marketing of commodity or price-sensitive products might be possible through differentiation (i.e., creating non-commodity product variants) or through service (e.g., superior delivery quality or a consultative relationship that helps the customer utilize the commodity). Service can be especially crucial if the commodity is a strategic material for the customer.

Monopolies: Companies that face no competition at all need not worry about trust. It would seem that customer power is low to nonexistent where there is no competition. Yet trust could improve financial performance even when customers have no choice but to buy from the sole source. At issue is the impact of push versus trust-based marketing on the quantity of buying. Trust could increase sales if push-based marketing breeds resentment for the monopolist—that is to say, customers might prefer not to purchase anything rather than purchase from an untrustworthy monopolist. A monopolist might also choose a trust-building strategy in order to forestall government regulation.

Uncontrollable Quality: Companies that face unavoidable disruptions to product or service quality may not be able to implement a trust-building strategy. If the company, such as an airline, cannot control service quality (e.g., weather and air traffic control congestion can cause unavoidable delays), then it is very hard to appear trustworthy. Although transparency helps customers realize that the company is doing all that it can to provide good service under trying circumstances, the reality is that unavoidably low quality of service can be a real trust-breaker.

Uncontrollable Quantity: Trust-based marketing is harder when a company can't forecast or respond to demand in a timely fashion (and thus has excess inventory or stock-outs on a regular basis). With excess inventory of some products and a shortage of other products, a company is more motivated to push the products it does have than to offer honest, trustworthy recommendations for the products that it doesn't have. Shortages of products also squander hard-won customer loyalty. Developing a better relationship with the customer can actually reduce this problem by providing a timely understanding of customer preferences that leads to more accurate forecasting.

Short-Term Financial Focus: Advocacy-based marketing is a "high-road" strategy that requires resources to create products and services that are worthy of being trusted. Moreover, it may take time for customers to change their opinions about a company's reputation. Companies with severe financial difficulties or short-term constraints may not have the luxury of becoming advocacy-based. However, maintaining a push/pull-based strategy to maintain short-term financial results may lead to long-term failure if customer power continues to grow or if competitors become trusted by customers.

Short-Term Customer Base: If customers do not engage in long-term or repeated purchasing of the company's offerings, then trust may be less relevant. The value of trust is dependent on the importance of reputation. The relationship strategy seems predicated on creating a long-term bond with each customer to create customer loyalty. If customers are making one-off purchases with little forethought, then trust is unlikely to improve the company's performance. The key exception to this exception is caused by customer power. If prospective customers have routine access to rating services or other experienced customers, then the need for trustworthy behavior may be high even if a given customer never makes a second purchase.

Low-Impact Products: The value of being a trusted company is strongly proportional to the impact of the product or service on the customer or the customer's involvement with the product or service. If a defective product has a negligible impact on the customer, then the customer will care less if the provider is trustworthy. For example, if the pattern printed on a paper towel has a defect, it may not have much impact on the customer's opinion of the supplier. In contrast, durable goods, mission-critical supplies, or health-related products need a higher level of trust because the impact of even minor defects is very large. Impact needs not be defined by monetary value alone—for example, a personally meaningful product like a bouquet of flowers can be a high-impact product.

In summary, industries are less amenable to a trust development strategy if

1. Customers don't care (commodity products, short-term customers, or low-impact products)
2. Customer can't care (sole-source or monopoly providers)
3. The company can't provide a trustworthy product (uncontrollable quality, uncontrollable quantities, or short-term financial needs)

Yet for each of the categories of exceptions, there remain reasons to consider a more trust-building strategy such as a relationship strategy or an advocacy strategy. Given the potential for further rises in customer power and the opportunity to encourage more sales, all companies should consider trust-building strategies.

IT IS UP TO YOU

Even firms with a push/pull positioning on trust should consider significant movement to the right. For example, when airlines faced short-run survival pressures for cash, many adopted tactics that emphasized short-term financial gain over long-term customer loyalty—cutting service, raising hidden fees, and adding more fine-print restrictions on passengers. This places these companies toward the left side of the scales in Figures 6-1 and 6-2.

Advocacy does not seem to be the best strategy for airlines, given price sensitivity of flyers, cutthroat price competition, and quality issues. It is not surprising that airlines have not pursued an advocacy strategy. Unfortunately, this has resulted in a cycle of lower quality, lower prices, lower trust, and lower demand, producing bankruptcy for some major airlines. However, as we have mentioned, Southwest Airlines and Jet Blue tried a different strategy. These airlines offer no-frills air travel, but they deliver exactly what they promise and emphasize loyalty. Customers trust them, and these airlines remained profitable during the prolonged post-9/11 travel slump. Southwest has consistently earned high customer satisfaction. This demonstrates that even though there are market- and consumer-related factors that deter trust strategies, a wise firm will consider advocacy even in these circumstances. For segments of the air travel market, trust is still important. In the market for international business travel, competition has developed to make the best business-class seat—one that allows fully reclined sleep, privacy, and Internet connections. In this segment, trust and premium service is valued and warrants higher prices. It is interesting that while international business has maintained or increased its level of service, domestic business class has experienced declines in comfort (smaller seats), quality (poor food), and service (stressed and overworked flight attendants), even though the prices have not dropped. It is the choice of the airlines to treat segments of the market differently, either by positioning premium services to them, or exploiting them with low value and high prices to subsidize overall operations.

Another example of unexpected trust building is in the telecommunications industry. Qwest (which acquired the Baby Bell

Company USWest) is a surprising candidate for a shift toward a trust-building marketing strategy. As a dominant provider of local phone service in the Rocky Mountain region and a telecommunications company, one might expect Qwest to be like other telecommunications companies. Many telecom companies practice old-style push/pull marketing based on the assumptions that customers are not smart enough to spot the tricks in pricing, and that customers want to buy only the lowest-price product. However, Qwest, a company that arguably started with the lowest levels of trust due to both fines for shoddy installation service and charges of fraud and accounting irregularities, is now pursuing a trust-building strategy. Under the leadership of its new CEO, Richard C. Notebaert, Qwest began a campaign called "generations of service" to rebuild employee trust and pride. The thinking behind the strategy is that a company cannot establish trust with its customers if it does not have the trust of its employees. The concept is to move toward what Qwest calls "blind trust," using a combination of relationship strategies and tactics that span all the functions of the company.

Although some market situations may seem to make the advocacy strategy an inappropriate choice, senior management must examine the space and see if advocacy is right for them. I predict that in most cases innovative managers will see that responding to the rise of customer power with advocacy-based strategies is the way to maximize long-run profits.

Some highly successful companies might argue that they already have some other source of competitive advantage—that leadership through some other means (innovation, efficiency, monopoly, etc.) precludes the need for explicit efforts to create advocacy. Such companies believe that they need not shift their profile on the dimensions of trust. Yet history suggests that any given type of competitive advantage can be transitory. New entrants, new technologies, new government regulations, and new customer needs all create hurdles to long-term competitive advantage. Thus, you can argue that a superior company should use its arguably transient superiority to maximize the trust of its customers while it has the advantage. Advocacy, with its attendant deep customer relationships, also helps the company adapt to many of the dynamic forces that might otherwise derail a one-time market leader.

Although some industries do not have all the prerequisites for advocacy-based strategies, such industries are relatively rare. Fundamentally, for most firms, it is a choice of three approaches. The first gives in to short-run pressures that drag a company into the pull/push game and often lead to anemic profits, stunted growth, and lackluster stock prices. The second is to stay with existing TQM and CRM methods but not respond innovatively to the growth in customer power, thereby missing opportunities for premium profits and growth. The third approach takes a long-run profit maximization view through respect for customers with explicit advocacy to represent customers' interests.

BUILDING AN ADVOCACY-BASED STRATEGY

MOVING TO THE RIGHT ON THE TRUST SCALE

Most firms will find themselves positioned on the scales similar to the auto industry's position shown in Figures 6-1 and 6-2. The decision they face is whether to increase trust, and if so, by how much. These firms typically have effective Total Quality Management and Customer Satisfaction programs. You may want to review the pyramid figure in Chapter 1 to see how CRM relates to advocacy. The firms also probably have basic customer relationship programs, although they are probably oriented to the promotion of selected segments to get short-term results.

Improving trust and moving toward advocacy is likely to be a good strategy a) if your company sells products that are complex and require customer education, b) if the products represent a risk to customers who make a wrong choice (for example, a high-priced item like a computer or a physical risk as in health care), and c) if your company's products/services are personally involving (e.g., choice of a vacation destination).

A program to increase trust could involve a range of components. Here are some examples:

1. Further improve product quality

2. Enhance customer service

3. Build a transparent web site that provides advice and education

4. Create employee incentives to reward representing the customers' needs

5. Develop long-range financial and customer measures to control the program (e.g., long-term sales and profits, improvement in trust measures and loyalty)

6. Jointly develop products with your customers

7. Develop tactics that allow customers to easily compare your product specs to others

8. Move your CRM from promotion-oriented communication to trust building, based on providing helpful information and education rather than mere price discounts

9. Build community involvement with your company and its products

Let's look at a few detailed examples of programs that build trust.

Intel: Intel is moving to build trust through a program at its customer support site (Intel.com), which gets over three million visits each month. Specifically, Intel decided it wanted to increase customer trust on the portion of the site where customers can download software from Intel. They wanted to increase the number of successful online downloads and save call center and channel costs to personally download software for the customer. The first implementation was on the PC camera download site. A personal advisor named "Rosa" was developed to help customers identify their PC camera, select the best download, and answer their questions. This advisor improved success rates for downloading by 19% and saved millions of dollars. Intel is now applying the personal advisor concept to the complete download site to help customers effectively identify their products. Such focused Internet strategies can aid in moving to the right on the trust scale (see Figure 7-1).

Figure 7-1 Intel Download Advisor Rosa

First Tech Credit Union: First Tech successfully services companies in the Northwest U.S. (including Microsoft and Intel) and wanted to enhance its already very good trust positions so that it could increase its share of financial business from their members. What started as an Internet advisor has expanded to a training tool for call center representatives, a "cross-the-desk" advisory tool for loan officers, and a comprehensive suite of tools to help customers across all wealth management areas. In this credit union, customer satisfaction has gone up, sales of mortgages, loans, and IRAs have increased, productivity of loan officers has increased, and coherence across all customer-facing channels has been achieved. Specifically, mortgage sales increased 60% (relative to the index of activity in the Northwest), and profit increased over $750,000 per year (see Figure 7-2 for the advisor provided by Experion Systems Inc.). Tom Sargent, CEO at First Tech, says, "We are simply ecstatic at having 900 mortgage advice sessions a month and that more than 54% of these customers actually applied."

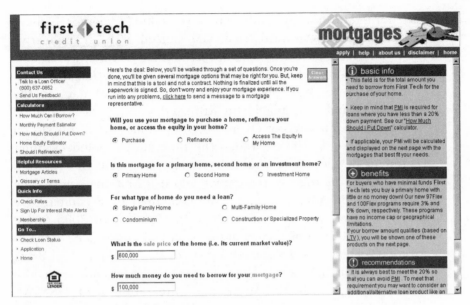

Advisor Questions and Answers

Advisor Recommendations

Figure 7-2 First Tech Credit Union Mortgage Advisor

General Motors: General Motors is making a comprehensive shift in strategy toward trust. GM started with an innovative advisor (see Figure 7-3) called Auto Choice Advisor, which fairly compares all vehicles. The site is sponsored by GM, JD Power, and AIC (the third-party supplier of auto specs data to the industry) and is available on KBB and CarTalk as a certified honest and fair advisor. Over 700,000 people visited this site in 2003 and 2004. GM expanded the program to include explicit product development feedback by analyzing why GM cars did not end up as the top recommendation for all customers. The Auto Choice Advisor is now complemented by a comparative drive program called "Auto Show in Motion." In 2003, more than 200,000 people drove autos from GM and other manufacturers. This was leveraged by a dealer 24-hour test-drive program for GM cars. Other efforts include enhanced loyalty programs through MyGMlink and integration with ONSTAR mobile services. Finally, GM is involving customers in the design of its new hydrogen fuel cell vehicle through an active Internet community sponsored by GM. These programs move GM to the right on all trust dimensions in Figures 6-1 and 6-2. The programs have increased the rate at which GM autos are seriously considered for purchase, and they are expected to increase sales and the level of trust in the relationship.

Companies should examine their strengths and weaknesses and look at the opportunity/threat posed by the growth in customer power. In many cases, the growth of customer power will lead a firm to move to the right (i.e., to create higher levels of trust). This will be especially true if the company has competencies in product innovation—that is, if they can create differentiated products that can stand up to fair comparisons.

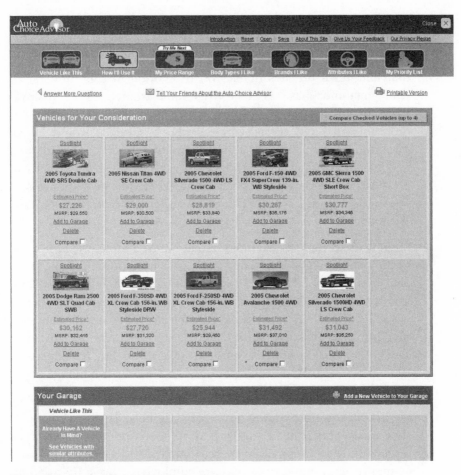

Figure 7-3 General Motors Auto Choice Advisor

STAY WHERE YOU ARE

You might decide that your current push/pull or intermediate strategy on trust is appropriate. Advocacy is not for everyone. If you are in the fashion industry, for example, leading customer tastes and aggressive advertising may be best. If your product involvement is rather low, such as in some frequently purchased consumer packaged goods, you may not want to be an advocate—you might prefer to stay with the kind of aggressive promotion that characterizes this industry. It is not uncommon to spend more than one-third of sales dollars on promotion in this industry. If your customer base is deal-prone and trained to be disloyal through ongoing promotions for switching, you may not find it profitable to build trust—wireless phone services would be an example. If your product is an image product, traditional marketing may be effective because you need to use aggressive advertising to establish a psychological positioning when physical differences are small. The use of celebrity endorsements for running shoes is one example.

But it is up to you. For example, Proctor and Gamble, a leading consumer packaged goods manufacturer, uses promotion heavily, but it has created an advisory site for mothers called Pampers.com, which provides education and services and does not directly sell products. P&G uses image-heavy advertising, but it also demands that its products have superior performance advantage. Reebok spends heavily on advertising with celebrities, but it allocates a large effort to build superior performance into its products.

Wireless companies may be stuck in a competitive war that makes movement toward building more trust unlikely. They practice old-style push marketing, along with all its assumptions. However, as we saw in the Qwest example previously, even a once distrusted company can rebuild trust with its employees. Qwest followed up the employee campaign with a "commitment to service" campaign aimed at building customer trust. This campaign was based on improved TQM procedures and better training of call center personnel. Next, Qwest simplified its rate plans by charging a flat five cents per minute and reduced its outbound marketing (uninvited calling). In 2003, Qwest called its best wireless customers and pre-emptively offered to move them to the newest lower cost plans. They gave up some short-term revenue, but they gained trust. Now, Qwest is enhancing MyQwest.com, which stresses "customer service that really serves customers." The concept is to move to the full trust level of Figures 6-1 and 6-2 by using trust strategies and tactics that span all the functions of the company.

Although some current market situations may seem to make trust an inappropriate choice, in the end it is up to the senior management to examine the space and see if trust is for them. I predict that, in most cases, innovative managers will see that responding to the rise of customer power with advocacy-based strategies is the way to maximize long-run profits in industries where one might not initially expect it.

MOVEMENT TO THE LEFT ON TRUST

Very few companies would like to move left and receive less trust from their customers, but competitive dynamics can result in companies sliding left. When large excess capacity exists and intense competition produces a price war, the firm may find itself on the slippery slope of cutting price, having to reduce service to stay in business, and then being forced to match further market price reductions. Airlines are a good example. We have all experienced decreased quality, frustration over price discrimination, and reduction in customer service. Probably most of us are less loyal and do not have high levels of trust in airlines. Airlines did not want this to happen. They would rather have high trust and loyalty and a stable price structure. Is there a way out of this dilemma? It is difficult, but one way is to cut expectations of service quality in exchange for lower price and then rigorously deliver what you promise (e.g., Southwest Airlines and Jet Blue). Another is to differentiate based on premium service at premium prices, as Midwest Express has done. They provide first-class-sized seats to all customers, have friendly personnel, and serve free chocolate chip cookies baked onboard the plane. All this is done at only a small premium over competition's rates, so it is no surprise that they have a growing corps of loyal customers.

Retailers can get caught in a slide to the left. Furniture retailing is a good example, where there always seems to be 50% off all the time, service quality is often low, and finance rates are high. An exception is Jordan's Furniture. It is the fastest growing furniture retailer in New England and has the greatest sales per square foot of any furniture retailer. They feature a huge selection (several mega stores), large inventories for fast delivery, entertainment (for example, live motion or Omnimax theaters), quality products spanning a wide price range, and low prices. However, they say their success is not due to these factors: "We can sum it up in one reason. It's trust."[1] They present the truth to their customers and treat them with respect. Rather than being pulled into a destructive price competition, Jordan's has differentiated and built a trust positioning.

EVOLUTIONARY STRATEGIES

In the end, it is up to management to decide where they want the company to be on the trust dimension. In general, customer power is forcing firms to the right, and innovative firms are preempting competition by moving to an advocacy position now in order to get a pioneering advantage and to maximize their long-run market positions. Although the Qwest strategy is revolutionary in that it is trying to move straight from push to advocacy (without an intermediate "relationship" phase), an evolutionary strategy is often appropriate because it may be difficult to determine the long-term payback of a shift to total advocacy. General Motors's strategy is emerging, and its transition to advocacy may take ten years. But, along the way, costs and benefits can be assessed, and evolutionary steps can be evaluated by market research.

Bellco credit union is adopting an evolutionary strategy toward advocacy. In order to move to the right of the scale, they first added trustworthy rate charts, then advisors, and finally competitive rate comparisons (refer to Figure 6-3). The result of adopting the strategy has been significant improvements in adoption of loans. According to Bellco's CEO Doug Ferraro, "We've seen a significant number of new loans generated through trusted advisors." As a result of adopting an advocacy strategy, they have seen loan growth rates nearly four times their peer group average for other credit unions, from 4.6% for the average credit union to an 18.8% change in dollar value of a loan portfolio for Bellco. Their consumer loan origination went up 26% in the 12 months after

[1] Radio ad on 98.5 FM in Boston, December 2004.

installing the web-based advisory center. The shift to the right has worked for Bellco and its members.

In the next ten years, we are likely to see considerable experimentation and learning by firms as they shift from Theory P to Theory A marketing. The paradigm is shifting, and new practices will emerge organically through experience and explicitly through research on tools for trust building. Many firms will find that push/pull does not work well and that even a good relationship is not enough—they will need to advocate for their customers. In the next chapter, you will be exposed to some state-of-the-art tools that can be used to establish an advocacy position.

8

Tools for Advocacy

In the last chapter, you considered whether advocacy was the right strategy for your firm. If it is, you need to have a range of tactics to build trust and move to an advocacy position on the eight profile dimensions. In this chapter, you will learn about the analytic techniques that underlie these tactics. You have seen examples of trusted advisors in the previous chapter (Intel, GM, and First Tech), but now you will explore the alternative methodologies you can use to build an advisor for your firm. This is an important building block in constructing the advocacy pyramid, but other blocks are available to establish a trusted relationship and reach the advocacy pinnacle. I will present a number of building block techniques and give you the managerial perspective to evaluate alternative methods of building an advocacy "tool kit" so that you can achieve the right level of trust and advocacy in your firm.

BUILDING THE FOUNDATION OF THE ADVOCACY PYRAMID

Figure 8-1 presents our basic advocacy pyramid. Before I review advanced techniques to establish the advocacy level of the pyramid, let me emphasize that the pyramid will collapse without the base of Total Quality Management (TQM) and Customer Satisfaction. There are many proven methods to establish TQM.[1] I will not review them here, but needless to say, although these methods are established and proven, they are not easy to implement consistently. For example, in the 1990s, Ford put high priority on quality and established a leadership position, but in the early 2000s, the quality levels slipped as the consistency of the program waned. Similarly, Customer Satisfaction programs are well known, but establishing and effectively executing them is no easy task.[2] After building a solid first level for the pyramid, you must build the next level by establishing trust with relationship marketing.

Figure 8-1   The Advocacy Pyramid

---

[1] See Goetsch, David L. and Stanley Davis. *Quality Management: Introduction to Total Quality Management for Production, Processing, and Services, 4th edition*, and John L. Hradesky, *Total Quality Management Handbook*. NY: McGraw-Hill, 1994.

[2] See Desatnick, Robert L. and Denis Detzel. *Managing to Keep Your Customer: How to Achieve and Maintain Superior Customer Service Throughout the Organization*. San Francisco: Jossey-Bass, 1993, and Keiningham, Timothy L. and Terry Vavra. *The Customer Delight Principle: Exceeding Customers' Expectiation for Bottom Line Success*. NY: McGraw-Hill, 2001.

THE DREAM VERSUS REALITY IN CRM

Customer Relationship Management is a valuable technique for building the relationship section of the pyramid. In the last decade, many firms pursued programs to build a newer, stronger relationship with customers, using information technology, better data, and improved business processes to increase brand loyalty and profitability. Many books have been written describing the methodology.[3] The dream was to understand customers and have a complete view of their interactions with the firm. With that understanding, the company could craft better products, communication programs, and promotions to build the relationship and earn premium profits. CRM is a potentially important tool for building trust with customers. The goal is to move up the pyramid and establish a trusting relationship that can be the basis of moving to an advocacy position.

The greatest success stories for CRM come from retailers. Firms like L.L. Bean, Land's End, and Orvis send specialized catalogs to customers based on their history of involvement with the firm and their recent purchases. The CRM program at these companies specifies policies of how many catalogs to send, which type, individual catalog customization, and special promotions. Some retailers have "opt-in" systems that allow them to collect more refined data on demographics (age, sex, income) and interests (product categories in which customers indicate that they want to see promotions and new product announcements). This enables further refinement in communication and promotion strategies across a mix of channels, from catalogs to stores to the Internet and call centers. These can often generate a healthy ROI. Las Vegas gambling casinos also have successfully used CRM. For example, Harrahs tracks individual gambling activity and allocates "comps" (e.g., free rooms) and perks according to the revenue potential of the customer.

---

[3] As recent examples, see: Brown, Stanley. *Customer Relationship Management: A Strategic Imperative in the World of E-Business*. New York: John Wiley and Sons, 2000; Swift, Ronald. *Accelerating Customer Relationships: Using CRM and Relationship Technologies*. Upper Saddle River, NJ: Prentice Hall, 2001; and Dyche, Jill. *The CRM Handbook*. Boston, MA: Addison-Wesley, 2002.

Unfortunately for most firms, the reality of CRM has not lived up to the dream. As I stated in Chapter 1, "Now Is the Time to Advocate for Your Customers," over 55% of CRM programs have not generated enough significant benefits to be termed a success, and firms are directing attention to their programs in order to determine what happened.[4] Typically, the CRM vision began in the marketing department with a goal of building a strong loyalty relationship, but soon the effort became concentrated in IT because the first step was defined as building a data warehouse.[5] Firms directed attention at "mining the data" and finding opportunities for profit. This profit emphasis was especially critical because the costs of building a complete database grew to millions of dollars at the same time that firms tried to reduce costs to survive the recessionary period of 2000–2003. The result was a focus on short-term profits and the use of promotion to gain these profits. In some auto companies, the thrust was toward identifying people who were ready to buy a car and giving them a special deal. For example, data mining might yield a list of people who owned a competitor's model car over four years old, had recently moved, and had income greater than $50,000. The dealer would then send these people a brochure of the new model, an invitation to a test drive, and a coupon worth $500 of free options. This may be effective, but it is a push tactic and does not build long-term trust.

In contrast, a trust-based CRM or "Dream CRM" would concentrate on helping the customer make an appropriate decision and supporting him or her throughout the lifecycle of ownership, from the purchase to the use, service, and re-purchase decision. Table 8-1 shows a number of techniques that can help convert a push-oriented CRM into a CRM that fulfills the promises of the original CRM dream scenario.

[4] See Freeland, John G. *The Ultimate CRM Handbook.* New York, NY: McGraw-Hill, 2003, p. 3.

[5] See Inmon, William. *Building the Data Warehouse.* New York, NY: John Wiley & Sons, 1996; Imhoff, Claudia, et al. *Building the Customer Centric Enterprise: Data Warehousing Techniques for Supporting Customer Relationship Management.* New York: John Wiley and Sons, 2001; and "Tera Data Center for Customer Relationship Management" at Duke University (www.teradataduke.org).

Table 8-1 Components of a Dream CRM

Component	Features
One-to-One Marketing	Individual treatment of customers
Branding	Brand as a trust mark
Loyalty Program	Reward continuing business relationship
Channel Partnerships	Trust-based channel
Permission Marketing	Opt-in system, custom communication, community
Full Information and Advice	Transparency, unbiased recommendations

One-to-one marketing builds relationships by treating each customer differently.[6] By understanding each customer's individual needs, the company can communicate to that customer exactly what he or she wants to know, and the company can use the channel that each customer prefers (Internet, email, phone call, direct mail, or media). One-to-one marketing also enables mass customization and fitting a product exactly to the customer's needs.

Branding is critical in a trust system. The brand becomes the trust mark and includes all of the customer's perceptions about the firm's quality, service, product positioning advantages, and the manner of its communication interaction.

Loyalty programs are important components in encouraging continuing patronage. Airline and hotel loyalty programs, which are backed by real customer benefits (e.g., free first-class upgrades, free reservation changes, and special services), can be a powerful incentive in building a special long-term relationship. Some premier travelers will change their travel plans just so they can fly on their favored airline.

Channel partnership programs are important in maintaining coherence throughout the customer experience. Partnerships ensure a common interest between the manufacturer, channel, and customer.

[6] See Peppers, Don, et al. *The One to One Fieldbook.* New York, NY: Currency Doubleday, 1999.

Permission marketing allows customers to opt-in to the company's system of individualized communication.[7] Achieving the voluntary opt-in from a customer is a strong signal of the customer's willingness to trust your company. Of course, you have to justify and build this trust, but if you have an opt-in, you can collect individual data that allows you to customize your communication, not only to observable data (e.g., ZIP Code and past data), but also to attitudes and needs (e.g., "My car is an important part of my identity," or "I am most concerned about safety"). This allows the firm to deliver needed and valued information and therefore earn the customer's thanks and trust.

Providing full and unbiased information is an important step toward the dream of CRM. One-sided and exaggerated claims are viewed with skepticism and lead customers to doubt that they should entrust their interests to you. An advanced form of this opt-in is a community sponsored by the company in which clients can exchange opinions, information, and usage experience with their peers. Advice through a phone center, channel salesperson, or virtual Internet advisor can be a big step toward a higher level of trust if the advice reflects the customer's interests and genuinely helps him or her make the best decision.

These Dream CRM components can help the customer as well as the firm (see the sidebar "General Motors and Tests of a Dream CRM" for an example from General Motors in which a Dream CRM program increased consideration of GM models, preference for them, and ultimately increased sales). This GM program builds upon the ideas underlying an unbiased advisor to help customers find the best car for them (refer to Figure 7-3). Moving CRM from a push/pull to a trust-based CRM is an important tool in building the advocacy pyramid. You should have a full tool kit available so that you can build the customer relationship program you need. This relationship building block helps establish the platform for customer advocacy.

---

[7] See Godin, Seth. *Permission Marketing.* New York, NY: Simon and Schuster, 1999.

GENERAL MOTORS AND TESTS OF A DREAM CRM

In 2004, General Motors conducted a field study to determine the benefits of moving from a traditional CRM to a Dream CRM. The new program consisted of four components:

1. An individualized mailing based on how consumers rated the importance of safety, style, performance, and economy—individual brochures were mailed on the most important topic.

2. An Internet advisor for unbiased decision support—refer to the Auto Choice Advisor in Figure 7-3.

3. Auto Show in Motion—a competitive test drive experience without any sales pressure (over 200 GM and competitor cars were available for test drives).

4. Community—500 customers in groups moderated and supported by product experts.

Approximately 1,700 prospective buyers (i.e., consumers who intend to buy in the next 12 months) were recruited in Los Angeles and assigned to the four components. An experimental design tested the individual and combination effects of the component treatments. Six attitude surveys were sent and collected monthly to measure consideration of GM, perceptions of the cars on attribute scales (e.g., quality, style, performance, safety), intent to visit dealers, preference, and intent to buy. The results showed that the competitive test drive had the greatest effect on consideration, preference, and buying, followed by individual mailings and the advisor. Community had a major effect on building trust (which is linked to consideration of GM cars). In each of the components, 90% or more of those who participated said they told one or more people about their experience. Statistical analysis suggests that if all customers could be exposed to all the treatments, GM share could increase multiple share points. Each share point in the national market is worth $5 billion, so the potential benefit is large. GM is now testing an integrated opt-in program in the market to build trust relationships and increase share and ROI.

CONTINUOUS LEARNING TO BUILD TRUST AND CROSS-CHANNEL COHERENCE

CRM should be supplemented by a continuous learning system that builds trust. Using market experimentation and market research to improve the trustworthiness of your marketing programs can yield significant and increasing benefits. This should be no surprise because continuous improvement has been proven to be a critical component of TQM. In the case of trust building, it means continued experimentation to improve the communication tools we use to build trust.

In Chapter 7, "Is Advocacy for You?", we showed Intel's virtual advisor, Rosa (refer to Figure 7-1). Figure 8-2 shows the continuous improvement of the Intel customer support site. In this case, it shows the improvement in the download success for PC cameras. Five experiments were done: 1) trust seals, 2) navigation decision assistance boxes, 3) a wizard with logical guidance, 4) a persona—Rosa, and 5) Rosa with a voice. The sequential experiments increased the online success rate of downloading from 63% to 85%. For cameras alone, this could save over $1 million per year, and if it were extended to all products at Intel with similar results, it could save over $40 million per year in costs to handle downloads on the phone or through the channel.

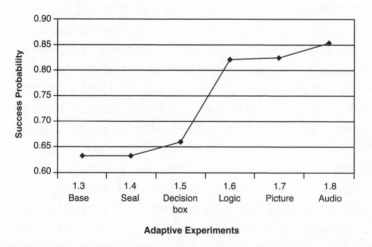

Figure 8-2   Sequential Market Experiments Improve Intel Support/Download Site

This progress is analogous to a total quality improvement program that conducts continuing experiments to improve quality on the factory floor, and over time, the result is that production quality and efficiency improve dramatically. Previously, production engineers thought they were doing well, but it was not until the Japanese showed them that they were far below their possible quality levels did they work to learn how to improve quality. The same is true of Internet site designs. Most sites were designed by IT engineers with little understanding of customer response. Norms for site design developed (e.g., tabs on top, menus on left, etc.). But these designs are far below their potential in terms of generating trust and building sales. This design effort is complex. Many site factors, as well as individual factors, affect trust building. Trust is an intermediate variable that drives action (such as download or purchase), and web site characteristics (e.g., format, information, recommendations, clear directions) and individual characteristics (e.g., level of computer expertise, education, and income) affect such actions directly as well. A statistical study across 25 Internet sites and over 6,800 consumers found (not surprisingly) that privacy, security, and no software errors were minimum requirements in building trust. But of equal or more importance were navigation ease, advice, information quality presentation (e.g., look, touch, and feel), and brand.[8] This analysis was the initial basis for the Intel experiments, but as the first experiments were conducted, they generated specific trust linkages that suggested high potential for the next experiment.

Although the Intel project was directed toward site design, the conclusions are relevant to a wide variety of channels. For example, in the retail outlet (e.g., dealership, bank office, or store), the minimum trust requirements are error-free pricing and secure, confidential transactions. These minimums are just as important in the physical world as they are in site design. If these minimums are not met, a "trust-buster" occurs, and people will walk out of the store just as they will leave a web site. In a store, the flow through the outlet (navigation), the quality of salespeople

[8] Bart, Yakov, et al. "Determinants and the Role of Trust on the Internet: A Large Scale Exploratory Empirical Study," MIT Sloan Working Paper (Cambridge, MA, MIT School of Management), 2004.

(advice), and the signage and labels (information) are critical to success. The outlet may vary from crowded and functional to warm and friendly (look, touch, and feel). Today, multi-channel marketing is typical (physical outlet, Internet, call center, direct mail, and catalogs). It is very important to have *coherence* across all elements of the channel, and trust cues must be consistent. For example, the advice and information provided by the site, call center, and salespeople should be the same—everyone should be on the same page. If the Internet site is devoted to trust, then the selling effort should be based on consultative selling principles (i.e., identify problems and needs, build a relationship, provide solutions to problems, communicate to all parts of the decision network, and get a consensus to move forward), not on product selling (make your pitch, overcome objections, and close the sale).[9] This is no easy task because most firms sell complex products, and changes are constantly occurring in the product offerings.

BUILDING TRUST WITH A VIRTUAL TRUSTED ADVISOR

As you approach and enter the pinnacle of the advocacy pyramid, a trusted advisor becomes a required tool. We have given several examples of such an advisor in this book (see the First Tech mortgage advisor and the GM auto advisor shown in Chapter 7, Figures 7-2 and 7-3). Now let's dig a little deeper and learn how to build a trusted advisor.

The best advisor is a well-trained person at the retail outlet or in a sales situation, but there are three problems with this option. First, good advisors are difficult to find; second, training and wages for good advisors are costly; and third, the turnover rate of customer contact personnel is high. In many segments, human advisors are prohibitively expensive. In typical retail outlets, wages are often low and cannot attract highly educated sales personnel. Training in basic skills is costly, and continual updating is often a substantial task. Training programs are typically multi-day intensive programs, and unfortunately, people forget many facts that

---

[9] See Maister, David H., et al. *The Trusted Advisor*. New York, N.Y: The Free Press, 2000, for a description of how the most effective sales people build trust.

are presented in such training efforts, resulting in a loss of effectiveness over time. Fortunately, Internet technology provides most of the benefits that a real person would provide. The most basic approach would be an email to a real person or a hyperlink to a telephone call center. Virtual advisors are a more substantial use of the Internet technology. These virtual advisors are low-cost, highly trained, and easy to update, and they work 24 hours with no breaks and have no turnover. Building an advisor that generates trust results in what we call a "trusted virtual advisor."

Analytically, there are several approaches to giving the advisor intelligence. The advisor needs to be able to generate good recommendations. The advisor also needs a set of trust cues so that customers will meaningfully relate with the virtual advisor. Figure 8-3 poses several approaches to the tradeoff between power (intelligence) and ease of use by consumers. For example, a very powerful approach is based on "conjoint analysis," but the ease-of-use of conjoint analysis is low because it requires that consumers fill out a 10–15 minute market research survey to generate the data needed for complex tradeoffs. I have found that few customers will undergo such questioning in an online advice context, even though they may get very high-quality recommendations. Active Decisions, Inc. originally used complex conjoint procedures, but after low levels of cooperation, they now offer a range of simpler methods. If you need detailed individual importance estimates, you can get this information by having consumers fill out questionnaires in a paid market research scenario based on new adaptive conjoint methods. On the other extreme of complexity, a very easy customer task would be to select the required product features and have the advisor identify all products that meet those specifications—we call this "attribute elimination." For example, the program could be instructed to find a red convertible sports car with over 300 horsepower and a price less than $50,000. A range of other advisor approaches lie between these two extremes. On the simple end are "product comparisons" based on selecting the products of interest from a list and looking at a matrix of technical specifications for each selected product. The secret is to develop an advisor that combines ease of use and power. One approach is to combine attribute elimination with advice on the pluses and minuses of each attribute selected (refer to the First Tech example in Chapter 7). Another approach is to ask customers for the "importance" of attributes and then calculate the value for each product by multiplying the importance by the attribute values and summing them up. MyProductAdvisor.com uses such an approach in its advisor for cameras. Nokia helps the user to select the best phone through six questions on topics like communication needs (business, creative/artistic, entertainment, socializing, basic) and preferences (spending preferences from basic to exclusive). More elaborate value calculations can be made based on "utility" models. The GM advisor is an extension of this approach because it asks about importance and how the consumer will use the product. This is a good balance between ease-of-use and recommendation quality. This utility approach can be achieved by simple or advanced utility calculators (e.g., Bayesian advisors are a good tool because they are analytically strong and consumers can use them easily[10]).

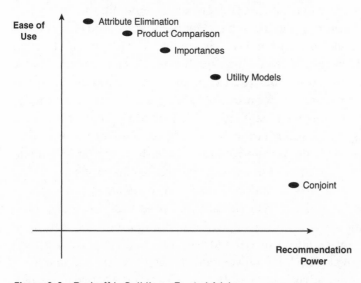

Figure 8-3 Tradeoff in Building a Trusted Advisor

[10] Urban, Glen and John Hauser, "Listening In to Find and Explore New Combinations of Customer Needs." *Journal of Marketing*, vol. 68 (April 2003), 72-87.

Features of the various methods are sometimes combined for maximum effect. XFI, Inc. has produced an auto advisor system where you select an advisor from a group of personas, and then you can go with the advisor's preferences or modify the preferences to reflect your tradeoffs. This combines filtering by choice of persona and attribute-importance ratings. Staples has created "defining quotes" to design seven personas for their segmentation strategies—this would be a natural input for advisor site design.[11] In some markets where repeated decisions are made, such as buying CDs or books, advanced methods called "collaborative filtering" can be a good way to give advice that has almost no burden for customers. Consumers' past purchases reveal preferences upon which new recommendations can be based. For example, if I bought *The Tipping Point*, Amazon.com might recommend *Don't Just Relate— Advocate* because other people who bought *The Tipping Point* also bought *Don't Just Relate—Advocate*. These correlations are the simplest form of collaborative filtering—advanced statistics can develop more elaborate algorithms to generate recommendations.

I recommend that you start with a simple approach. It is easy to implement attribute elimination and product comparisons. More advanced software is needed to build a utility-based advisor, and many trained modelers or consultants are available to build or supply such systems. The most powerful systems are usually supplied by outside firms, but you should be sure that your customers are comfortable with the input procedures before you use these methods. A range of techniques can also be used. For example, KBB has tips on buying, plus three basic decision aids: an attribute eliminator, a comparator, and a utility model (AutoChoiceAdvisor.com). Some people say, "Just give me the facts fast," while others say, "I want a personal advisor." You should have the customer decision support for both groups. Customers could select the approach they want, or you could ask them what their style of decision-making is ("I am an expert and want accurate information" or "I am just learning about these products and need basic help"). Finally, if you

[11] Manning, Harley, "Amazon, Staples Share Persona Secrets at Shop.org." *Forester*, January 29, 2004.

want to be clever, you could estimate their style from their click patterns and morph the site to move toward their preferred style of analysis.

In building a virtual advisor, the basic site design trust cues are important. The advisor must be easy to navigate, have a comfortable look, touch, and feel, and give good advice based on solid information. For those who want the facts, a crowded screen with lots of tables and links can work, but for those who want personal advice, use a persona, have lots of pictures, add audio, and leave lots of white space so that the site is warm and friendly—do not include one-sided ads.

John Deere (Deere.com) has built a set of advisory tools that are very attractive. For commercial utility tractors, they have a suite of product selector tools available to all web visitors. This suite includes a "tractor needs analyzer" to help pick the best size and type of tractor for your needs, a "tractor spec analyzer" that allows you to select the specifications that are most important to you and see which models meet those specs, and a "tractor build and price" tool to help you configure your tractor. (See Figure 8-4.) John Deere also allows you to compare their tractor models to multiple competitive brands and models. In addition they have many trust cues on their site. For example you can see videos of customers (e.g. contractors) explaining why they buy and trust John Deere. It is interesting that this kind of honest competitive comparison has resulted in some of John Deere's major competition (e.g, Kubota) also making competitive comparisons on their own web sites. The consumer gains from this information and the manufacturers earn the buyer's trust.

Advisors are not restricted to consumer markets. As we mentioned in Chapter 4, "Customer Power Is All Around You," G.E. Plastics uses an "engineering calculator" to help customer engineers select the best plastic material for their application. The advisor includes stiffness, fatigue, flow, costs, maximum strain, and heat management advice.

Figure 8-4 John Deere Advisory Tools

Designing an advisor requires that you understand how customers in your market make decisions and what segments exist in terms of decision style so that you can build an easy-to-use and powerful system. Concept-testing your advisor (see the sidebar earlier in this chapter) and continual experimentation can tune your advisory system so that it can build trust and provide advocate support to your customers. Building an advisor based only on your own products builds a trusting relationship, but the pinnacle of the pyramid demands that you honestly give customers advice about *all* products, not just your own products. John Deere and GM do this, but First Tech would have to add information on competing mortgages to its advisor before we would call it a customer advocacy advisor. Bellco credit union is farther up the pyramid with their competitive comparisons (refer to Figure 6-3), but they are not a full advocate because they do not actively give advice across all their competitors' products.

"LISTEN IN" TO LEARN CUSTOMER NEEDS

If you build a trusted advisor, you have the basis to learn about unmet customer needs, and you can set the stage for partnering with customers to design new products. By "listening in" to the dialog between an advisor and a customer, you can uncover opportunities for new products that meet customers' needs better than existing offerings.

Figure 8-5 shows a virtual engineer who is invoked in a trusted advisor system called "Trucktown," which was built at MIT in 1998 by my research team with GM support. In Trucktown, the customer chooses an advisor persona from three choices (a mechanic, a retired editor of *Consumer Reports*, and a contractor who lives next door). Based on importance/needs and preferences of the customer, a utility value is calculated after each question for each truck—and then the truck with the highest utility for that customer can be recommended.[12] When the advisor finds that she does not have the truck that fits all the customer's needs, she calls upon the virtual engineer to learn more about the customer's needs so that the company can build the right truck for the revealed needs. The magic in the system is knowing when to "trigger" the engineer. In this system, a need is revealed if the utility of the best truck among existing alternatives decreases after the advisor asks a question. For example, if a customer says he wants a small truck, that is fine—GM has them. If the customer wants a four-wheel drive—great, GM has that, too. But if the customer then tells the advisor he wants to tow his boat (6,500 pounds)—then there is a problem. GM has a large truck that can do that, but not a small one. So the advisor recommends the large truck, but the total utility is lower than it was before the customer said he wanted to tow a boat, and GM had a small truck that fit his needs. This implies the need to build a mid-sized truck or a small truck with more towing capacity. If this need is shared by enough customers, the company could consider starting a formal design and evaluation effort on this new opportunity.

[12] Urban, Glen and John Hauser, "Listening In to Find and Explore New Combinations of Customer Needs." *Journal of Marketing*, vol. 68 (April 2003), 72-87.

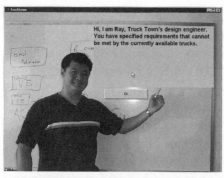

Introductory Screen

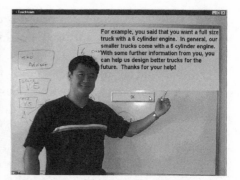

Example Dialogue

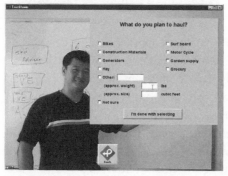

Specific Questions to Elaborate

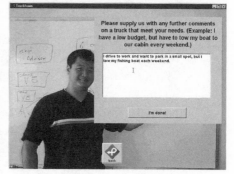

Open-Ended Questions

Figure 8-5 Virtual Engineer

In August 2001, I applied this "listening in" methodology based on over 1,000 advisory sessions. Three major needs were triggered. The first was for a small truck that could tow (this is the example mentioned previously). The second was a truck that was large but that maneuvered like a small truck—this can be done with four-wheel steering. Finally, some customers wanted a large truck with high fuel economy. Each of these segments is large enough to warrant investigation and initiation of the new product development process. In 2005, GM will offer a mid-sized truck called the Colorado that hauls and pulls more, a full-sized pickup with four-wheel steering for the maneuverability of a small truck, and a hybrid full-sized pickup truck.

This "listening in" method is one tool to uncover needs. But there are others. I identified "Lead User" analysis earlier in this book as another proven method.[13] In this method, an underlying trend in the market needs or technology is identified. Lead users are found from among the advanced users in the same or other industries who are working ahead on this dimension. The leading edge users participate in a workshop to help develop ideas for the base market using their solutions to problems in their industries. The success of the Lead User analysis method is demonstrated by companies such as 3M, which employed Lead User analysis and found that it is eight times more productive than 3M's traditional need identification methods.[14]

One way to enlist advanced customers in the design process is through a "design pallet." Figure 8-6 shows examples in which customers can create the pickup truck of their dreams. They can change the power (engine, transmission, hauling capacity, towing capacity, and four-wheel steering), size (height, width, number of doors, and cab size), style (modern, sporty, rugged, and retro) and options (stereo, GPS, air conditioning, etc). For each change, the car cost and miles per gallon are estimated. The figure shows a few of the screens used to create a truck for someone who commutes to work, parks in a low garage, and tows his or her boat on weekends. The final panel asks the consumer to compare this truck to the existing truck that best fits his or her needs. Inputs from a range of customers can identify clusters of customer design solutions that may represent new product opportunities.

The topic of partnering with customers to find new product opportunities is receiving a lot of attention these days. Recent books emphasize partnering between customers and companies to develop new products, renovate the selling process, and

---

[13] von Hippel, Eric. "Lead Users: A Source of Novel Product Concepts." *Management Science.* vol 32, no. 7, 1986, pp. 791-805 and "Shifting Innovation to Users via Toolkits." *Management Science.* vol 48, no. 7, July 2002, pp. 821-833.

[14] Lilien, Gary, et al. "Performance Assessment of the Lead User Idea-Generation Process for New Product Development." *Management Science,* vol 48, no. 8, August 2002, pp. 1042-1059.

improve service interaction—the total customer experience.[15] The result is "co-creation" between the firm and a customer, the firm and consumer communities, and even multiple firms with multiple communities. Partnering extends beyond individuals to the newly emerging communities forming on the Internet.

Partnering with customers, tapping lead users, and "listening in" are three tools you can use in building advocacy. They all should go in your tool kit for building the customer advocacy pyramid.

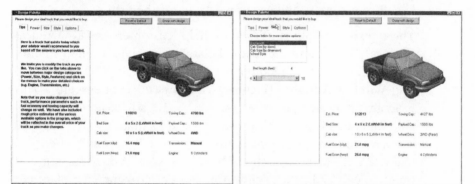

Introductory Screen   **Customer Selects Size**

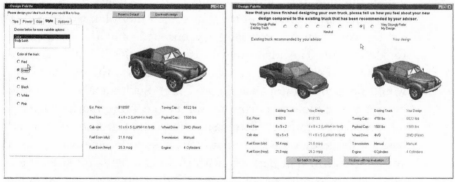

Customer Selects Color   **Customer Evaluates His or Her Design**

Figure 8-6   Design Palette

[15] Prahalad, C.K, and Ramaswamy, Venkat. *The Future of Competition—Co-creating Unique Value with Customers.* Cambridge, MA: Harvard Business School Press, 2004, and Vincent Barabba, *Surviving Transformation*, New York, NY: Oxford University Press, 2004.

BUILDING A VIRTUAL ADVOCATE

A trusted advisor that shows competitive products moves your company to the customer advocacy level of the pyramid. The use of tools to partner with customers for new product creation advances you toward the top of the pyramid. But the very top would be represented by an advocate that adds new customer benefit features to the trusted advisor. These new features would maximize the customer's interests while providing a framework for partnership that benefits customers and generates profit for the firm.

There exist simple advisors to help customers make wireless choices (WirelessAdvisor.com, Letstalk.com, and Inphonic.com). My team at MIT expanded upon these concepts in 2003 by creating "My Wireless Advisor" (Figure 8-7a shows concept screens). This program offers a choice of advisors, who give advice across all available suppliers. It provides advocacy features that describe how you can save money (e.g., make sure you are not roaming when you make a call out of your home area or extend your free minutes times to earlier in the night). You can design your own plan, put your plan out for bids, or take advantage of guarantees. These guarantees include retroactive pricing. For example, if the system determines after three months that some other plan would be better for you, you are retroactively enrolled, and the savings are rebated to you. The advocate will also automatically put you on any new plan (no matter who supplies it) that enters the market if that would save you money (see Figure 8-7b). Such an advocate would be a powerful tool for a firm that wants to capture market share or to enter a new market. Established firms that are not fully trust-based will find that the customer is the boss and that customers will switch to a firm that partners with them and fights for their interests. Perhaps some day companies will develop advocacy programs to help design systems for our total communication needs (wireless, land line, cable, Internet, and entertainment).

If a firm truly advocates for its customers, the customers will advocate for the firm by recommending the firm to other customers and by partnering to reveal needs that help the company design new products. This reciprocal benefit occurs at the pinnacle of the customer advocacy pyramid.

Figure 8-7a Advisor Choice

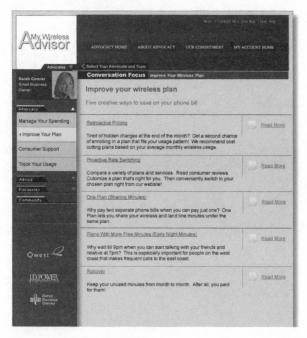

Figure 8-7b Advocacy Features

NEW TOOLS ARE EMERGING

The trend is toward trust-based relationships with customers. Innovative firms are using many of the tools cited in this chapter, and new ones will emerge as firms begin to compete for the customer's partnership. These tools will support tradeoffs between short-term and long-term ROI on assets employed in marketing and new product development, and they will lead to a pervasive attitude in businesses toward advocacy and a long-run trust building strategy. Firms will move from attempting to gouge customers toward a benevolence that presumes that as the firm works for the customer, the customer will reward the firm with purchases and will advocate for the firm because the firm so closely represents the customer's needs. But this revolutionary approach raises many questions, so I address them in the next chapter before emphasizing the need for top management leadership to make customer advocacy work.

Questions and Answers About Customer Advocacy

In this book, I have proposed some rather radical ideas: 1) Give your customers open and honest information and advice about your products and competitors' products, and 2) Passionately represent your customers' best interests. Customer power has grown due to the advent of the Internet, so these ideas are becoming required features of an effective strategy, not just nice-to-have additions. Firms are making these ideas work, as evidence has already demonstrated in the travel, automobile, and financial industries. The mindset is shifting from traditional marketing-driven strategy based on Theory P to partnering based on Theory A. Our basic assumptions about customers are changing from viewing the customer as someone who has to be coerced into buying to someone who is an active, intelligent, and creative decision maker. New tools are available to help you determine if advocacy is right for your firm and to help you implement advocacy strategies. But many questions are probably on your mind. Advocacy may sound attractive in concept, but will it really work for your firm and stockholders? Can you really trust your customers? What will happen to traditional advertising and promotion if trust-based marketing becomes the dominant practice? How widely will customer advocacy apply? Is advocacy a passing fad, or is it a paradigm shift?

I have presented much of the material in this book over the past few years to numerous executive classes. A number of questions have been raised. In this chapter, I answer each of these questions by highlighting quotes from those who have genuine doubts about advocacy and providing my own responses and counter-arguments. This question-and-answer format is a good way to review what I have proposed in this book and to enable you to form your own opinions about advocating for your customers.

WILL CUSTOMER ADVOCACY REALLY WORK?

Short-run costs will increase with customer advocacy, and I have to make my quarterly numbers—so does the advocacy strategy make sense for me?

It is true that short-run costs may increase as you provide customers with information about competitive products. You will probably lose some sales as you and your customers discover that your products may not be the best choice in all cases. Redesigning products and innovating in product strategy will take some time and resources, and if you suffer short-term sales losses, your profits may decline. In the long run, however, customer trust will pay off in more sales across your product line, greater customer loyalty, higher market share, larger margins, and reduced new customer acquisition costs. The long run will lead to increased returns for your stockholders, but there is a transition period.

Another transitional effect is the time that it takes to earn the customer's trust. In many markets, customers may be initially doubtful or baffled by a firm's unbiased information and advice. After all, they have seen companies use many unsavory methods to win their business in the past and may not view the firm's initial trust-building as genuine. Customers are skeptical, and they may view your openness as some kind of trick. But as some customers find out that you are really sincere, they will tell others because this kind of refreshing experience is worth sharing. In the long run, a consistent advocacy program will build trust, and advertising and promotion costs will decline. Your customers will advocate for you. Loyalty will mean more cross-selling opportunities for new products that fill a wider space of your customers' needs and more robust margins on existing products. However, implementation of a customer advocacy strategy does require some resources to fund the transition. Stockholders and financial markets will probably react negatively to earning reductions unless they are carefully communicated and positioned as enabling advocacy, which is the cornerstone of the firm's strategy to maximize long-run stock prices. So, in the long run, customer advocacy does "make sense" if the firm is willing to make the transition.

Only one firm can have the best products, and we cannot always be best, so we will lose customers by open and honest comparisons.

It is true that your firm will probably not have the best products *all* the time across the whole market, but you can consistently have outstanding products in your target market segments. These will be as good as, or better than, the competition after a transition to a line of products that stands up to unbiased comparisons. However, at times, a competitor may get the jump on you. They may find a new feature or an innovation in design and positioning. In these cases, you will have to make a fast response to match the competitor's advantage. If you have constantly been monitoring customer decisions and "listening in" to customer need statements, you should not get caught too often at a disadvantage.

If you have built a strong relationship with your customers, you should have a "trust reserve" you can draw on. If a competitor has a product advantage in one product, tell your customers, but indicate in your response when you will have a matching or hopefully superior product. Respond quickly, and your customers will show some patience. Their relationship with you is not based on one product and one quarter, but on buying a range of products from you over the years. You have earned their loyalty, and they will be likely to wait a reasonable amount of time to maintain the total trust relationship with your firm.

With that said, be sure you preempt competitive superiority and have a very aggressive innovation policy based on sensing and responding to customer needs and preferences. Customer advocacy depends on effective new product development, and innovation will be a core competence for firms using this strategy.

Customer advocacy is a nice 'hook'—I can use this positioning to improve my market share, but you are not really serious about trust, are you?

The "hook" is that "we want your trust." But saying "trust me" can be disingenuous. Saying you want trust but then not backing it up may trick a few customers for a short time. But it will not take long for customers to figure out your true intent and tell others about it on the Internet or by traditional word-of-mouth. There are no secrets in the world of customer power! Using trust as a hook will fail and will prevent a firm from becoming a believable advocate in the future. This is a "trust-buster," and customers will not easily forget it.

So, yes, I am serious about trust. It is not a short-run ploy—it is a long-run commitment to a new strategy of mutuality of interest with your customers. They get improved products, services, and decision support, while you get rewarded with increased sales and profits.

CAN YOU TRUST YOUR CUSTOMERS?

Customers want the lowest prices, so they will take our price and shop for a lower one.

Yes, customers like low prices, but they also want value. If you have their trust, they will believe your benefit proposition. With a customer advocacy strategy, you will have built products to fit customer needs, and you will have the features of merit. This will distinguish your products, and this differentiation will get you out of pure price competition.

It is possible for a customer to take your price and shop until he finds or negotiates a lower one. For example, in autos, a consumer may take your Internet price to another dealer and say, "Beat this price, and I will buy from you." Some buyers will invest considerable time and negotiating effort to save $100 on a car. This was true before the Internet, and it is still true with the Internet. You will have to be prepared to defend your price with these buyers, but with premium features and customer trust, you should be able to get the sale from all but such "deal-prone" buyers.

Deal-prone buyers come in two flavors. One group just wants low prices and is willing to forgo quality to get them. If your market is made up entirely of this kind of buyer, customer advocacy is probably not going to work for you. The second kind of deal-prone shoppers want a "deal" or bargain but are also concerned about quality. For this group, trust can work if you use honest prices and genuine promotions. First, you should not artificially raise prices so that you can continually discount them. Rather, set fair prices and do not discount them unless there are real reasons to do so—such as excess inventory or the need to rapidly phase out an older product. Deal-prone brand buyers will respond to such honest promotional price reductions and will trust that you make the best products at really fair prices.

I have some quality-oriented buyers and some price-sensitive buyers—with a trust strategy, can I reach both of them?

You cannot maintain trust if you discriminate between equal buyers of the same product. If you discriminate between buyers for the same service, they will find out and react negatively. How do you feel when the person next to you paid $200 for his or her flight ticket and you paid $1,000? This is not the basis of building a partnership and a trust-based relationship with an airline.

If you have two customer types, you should target the "quality" buyers and create premium products with good margins for them. You can honestly promote these products to "price only" buyers as they are being phased out. For example, stores like Marshalls and factory outlet stores fairly reduce prices for unsold or off-quality products. This can maintain the quality price segment while attracting deal-oriented buyers.

Another possibility is to have two brands—one representing high quality and the other representing lower quality and price. For example, Butler Steel Buildings has a "Widespan" premium line of steel beam pre-engineered structures and a "Landmark" lower-cost beam-based structure, so the company can meet two segments of price and quality tradeoffs. Both brands reflect fair price/quality tradeoffs. People pay different prices, but they get differing quality and service levels.

Trust is a good idea, but what if I get caught in a price war?

In this situation, products are equal, and buyers use price as the decision criteria. Excess capacity plus high fixed costs encourage companies to do whatever they have to do with price to get the business. In this situation, customer advocacy may not be effective. Airlines find it difficult to avoid price wars—excess capacity exists, costs are fixed, and the marginal cost of a seat is almost zero if a flight is going anyway. Lower prices lead to lower service levels and quality. Often, price discrimination between customers on the same flight exists. In these conditions, it is difficult to earn trust because customers react negatively to price discrimination and poor quality. Differentiated services are difficult to develop in the face of low margins and a negative cycle of lower price, lower quality, and reduced customer satisfaction. The only way to avoid this is to segment customers into groups who want a differentiated product and those who value more than low price. For example, custom charter airlines have taken the top-quality segment away from the airlines by fractional ownership or one-time charters.

Autos provide another good example of price competition. General Motors aggressively promotes cars (e.g., zero down and zero interest) because of intense competition and excess capacity. At the same time, however, GM is trying to get out of this situation through product innovation. Customer advocacy is very valuable in identifying opportunities for innovation. Prices do not need to be discounted for unique cars that precisely meet the requirements of a segment of customers' desires. It is easy to spot the cars that are not matched well to market requirements: They have the biggest discounts.

Price wars are not attractive unless a firm has a long-run cost advantage over competition. Customer advocacy is a valuable approach to avoiding a price war by focusing on product quality, innovation, and differentiation. If a firm also has a cost advantage, it probably will be most successful with a value proposition based both on trust and on low prices.

WHAT IS THE ROLE OF ADVERTISING IN A WORLD OF CUSTOMER POWER?

Will advertising always be the dominant marketing tool, even with the Internet's new information functions and higher cost per thousand viewers?

Advertising will continue to play an important role in marketing. Customers need to be made aware of improved products and need to be convinced of the differentiating features built into products to meet different needs. But the amount of money spent on advertising on traditional media is likely to fall in magnitude. The spending on TV and print advertising that was previously used to create minor perceptual differences will not be as effective when customers use comparative information to make decisions. Increased TV media costs and reduced audiences will also lead to decreased advertising as resources are allocated to other media.

Internet media may have new creative impact. For example, BMW developed a mini feature for the web that showed its cars in high speed and performance situations. It gained wide viewership at no media cost beyond the production and design costs. Honda spent $1 million to produce a three-minute web segment of a sculptural assemblage of an Accord that featured parts rolling and dropping artfully to create the car.[1] A buzz of word-of-mouth communication in the market resulted as the featurette was viewed on the Internet, and the URL was circulated through email networks. This kind of advertising may be more effective than traditional TV media spending. We can expect to see innovation in new media and messaging, but the overall advertising effectiveness per dollar is likely to decrease as consumers rely on rational information from advisors and customer word-of-mouth communication.

Advertising will continue to have a role in marketing, but the resources allocated to it will be reduced as allocations increase for product development, service, and Internet customer decision support.

---

[1] www.daboyz.org/honda/

Is more targeted spending on the Internet going to assure the role of advertising?

By targeting ads to potential buyers as they make decisions, companies will make media information more relevant. This is a strong factor in preventing the total fall of advertising spending. Ads in search engines like Google that are displayed in response to search queries are more likely to be effective, especially if they provide information that customers find useful as they make their decisions.

New "hot" animated media on the Internet can replace the static print ads now floated in windows on the screen. However, these hot ads are often intrusive, and many customers dislike them. Building trust is not likely to be effective if customers are annoyed by a manufacturer's ad. Similarly, linking ads to email content may have negative effects on consumer relationships unless the customer opts in to such practices that otherwise invade their privacy.

In the future, customers will be more in control of information acquisition. Firms will have to gain share-of-mind by providing valued and helpful information.

Sharing of opinions by customers will lead to inaccurate and biased rating, and in the end communities will be of little value.

Sharing information can enhance customer power, but this sharing has the potential to be biased. Amazon book reviews can be artificially improved when friends of the author write positive reviews. This is especially true when the total number of reviews is small. Of course, competitors can provide the opposite effect by entering negative information. Some firms say they can influence ratings and chat room conversations by hiring shills to make entries online and produce the client's desired objectives. This clearly biases the ratings.

Fortunately, customers will eventually discredit this false information. The best solution to the potential bias problem is a set of procedures like those used at eBay. Positive and negative ratings and specific comments can be reviewed. The seller can appeal or rebut false negative information. Such civil procedures are key in establishing reliable word-of-mouth information and effective functioning of communities. Reviewers are rated on some Internet sites.

ePinions has a "top reviewer" rating from consumers who consistently provide quality reviews. This practice helps eliminate biased and manipulative reviews. In the future, I believe more structured communities will be established, and rules of governance will prevail. Unregulated chat rooms will decrease in credibility for decision support.

HOW WIDELY CAN YOU APPLY CUSTOMER ADVOCACY?

This is interesting, but is it only useful in a few complex product categories?

It is true that trust-based marketing works best for complex products where loss can be large if the customer makes the wrong decision. In this case, open and honest information and advice are most useful. After all, "trust is not being afraid even if you're vulnerable." Thus the auto, computer, and home electronics industries are natural realms for customer advocacy. But the range of existing applications is large. In this book, we have cited applications in travel, health, finance, real estate, Internet retailers, telecommunication, autos, construction vehicles, and plastics.

We have not cited many industrial examples, but industrial product companies often compare their products to competition. For example, AMD compares their products to Intel processors, and AMD does not win all the comparisons. In its "Mobile Competitive Performance Guide," the 3.06GHz Intel Pentium 4 outranks the AMD Athlon 64 3200+ on AMD's Digital Media Benchmark.[2] Presumably, AMD is trying to be superior on all tests, but it reports even inferior results to build trust with potential clients. Buyers could get these test results from other sources, so AMD is simply making the comparisons easy. Also recall from the sidebar "Advanced Micro Devices (AMD) Edge Program" in Chapter 6, "Where Are You Positioned on the Trust Dimensions?" that AMD is actively pursuing lead users and is committed to finding products that will win fair comparisons. The rules of comparison have changed. Originally, companies only mentioned tests in which

---

[2] *Mobile Competitive Performance Guide* (AMD Corporation), p. 13 and www.amd.com/us-en/productInformation.

their product outperformed the competition. Now, some companies provide honest, comprehensive test results. Some industrial companies also practice trust-based marketing when they train their sales personnel to solve problems instead of just pushing products. Although it is tempting to go for every short-run sales opportunity, long-run relationships are built on trust, and often the salesperson will advocate for the customer by providing advice on solutions that may not include the salesperson's own product.

Even consumer package goods companies, where purchase costs are low, provide examples of trust building. Lever Brothers provides skin-care advice and information in an effort to strengthen its brands and substitute for some advertising expenditures. The range of applications is now broad and likely to be even more so in the future. It is difficult to find categories in which some elements of trust do not apply. Even for pure commodity goods such as sugar and salt, and unbranded food products like fruit and meats, freshness and quality are issues. Premium food stores like Bread and Circus and Nature's Heartland get premium prices for premium-quality fruits and meats. These retailers also provide dietary advice—they advocate for their customers' health.

Is trust only an American phenomenon, or can it work overseas, too?

It is important to point out that trust and advocacy are not restricted to the U.S.—this is a global phenomenon. Internet providers such as America Online and Microsoft are worldwide, and telecom companies are providing broadband Internet almost everywhere. Although Internet usage is highest in the U.S., Europe, Latin America, and Asia are catching up, so consumer power will likely spread in these countries as well. For example, in Europe, auto-buying sites abound from manufacturers, dealers, and buying services. Some make comparisons and give basic advice, and all supply valuable information. Travel services like Travelocity, Expedia, and Orbitz are global, but in Europe and Asia, dedicated travel services exist for those areas. Financial sites are global, and sites in Europe are often as innovative or more so in supplying information than U.S. sites. Asia leads the world in mobile Internet access. For example, DoCoMo provides extensive wireless shopping in Japan.

Blackberries, and now even mobile phones, can access the Internet worldwide. The Internet is becoming pervasive, and we can expect it to shift the balance of influence to consumers and the universal desire for trusting relationships.

Customers hate us and everyone in our industry. Is trust still a good idea?

Trust and advocacy have broad relevance, but of course the appropriate degree of trust varies across industries and countries. The scoring procedures I outlined in Chapter 6 can be used to see if customer advocacy applies to your product and company.

Nonetheless, a company in a deeply mistrusted industry might explore trust as part of a long-term strategic move to break out of the cycle of adversarial relations with customers. Understanding why customers hate companies in that industry could lead the company to breakthrough differentiation techniques that create better customer relations, high customer loyalty, and strong word-of-mouth marketing.

Some companies like Dell and Southwest Airlines are very successful without using customer advocacy—why are they not using it?

Dell is very successful with some traditional marketing practices. It advertises and promotes price discounting aggressively in conventional media, catalog mailings (over 50 million per year), and the Internet. It does not provide much advice and does not directly compare its products to competing products. Because its production model delivers the latest technologies in computers at very low prices, it wins over many customers who often search many sites for a computer. This is a successful strategy. It can be argued that Dell is trusted because its brand reflects its consistent delivery on its promises. But Dell could be even more successful with customer advocacy. Systems are getting complex, and Dell's original configuration system works well for very sophisticated buyers. As the market has matured and less technically trained buyers have entered it, many customers find the decision process bewildering. Probably many do not buy the right machine for their needs. Some may just delay purchase because they are not sure they are making a good decision. A trusted advisor that responds to customer needs would help Dell grow sales in the maturing market. Low price is important but not enough to give the new majority of users the confidence to upgrade their systems.

Dell's selling methods are product-specific, but customers are becoming more concerned about solutions to questions such as: How do I hook up to broadband? What about photos and printer integration? Can I use my PC for phone services? How can I integrate my entertainment systems (radio, TV, cable, stereo, and games)? These solution spaces are great opportunities for Dell's growth. Dell has achieved a good deal of brand trust in PCs, so it would be natural to leverage this into a wider relationship where customers would come to Dell for a range of products built around solutions. Dell now sells printers, but the company could move beyond product selling and take the responsibility to advocate for the customer by helping them design and implement the best system solution for the user. This could give Dell new paths for growth and profitability while giving the customer the solutions they want and need. So customer advocacy is a valid option for Dell. Should they move more to the right on the trust dimension? They can stay where they are and do pretty well, but they could do better by moving toward a customer advocacy strategy.

Southwest Airlines is also successful, and it does not even cooperate with travel reservation services by providing schedule information. Customers have to call Southwest to find the schedule and book tickets. This is part of the company's model of integration and efficiency. Southwest is far up the Customer Advocacy Pyramid with its quality of service—maybe not the very highest quality, but the service is consistent as promised, and at low prices. Customer satisfaction is high, and some customers are loyal in their relationship. As in the Dell case, moving to more trust and advocacy is a valid option for Southwest. If Southwest compared itself to other airlines through travel reservation services and on its web site, it could acquire more customers and then convert them into loyal fliers with its consistent quality and value. Especially as Southwest expands its routes, this trust building could help the company maintain growth and profitability and allow it to widen its service offerings as other airlines copy Southwest's model of delivery. Trust and advocacy could help Southwest capitalize on its pioneering advantage in air travel.

All firms should evaluate customer advocacy and decide where they want to be on the trust dimension.

Is customer advocacy restricted to use at corporations?

No. The ideas of customer advocacy can be used in non-profit organizations and government as well. For example, in public health services, client satisfaction can be increased with information and advice. Customer questions like, "How do I file cost reimbursement forms?", "How can I get timely patient information?", "Can I prevent diseases?", "What hospital should I use?", and "What do you recommend for me to improve my health?" can be answered with effective advice and information systems. Customers need the same open, unbiased information and powerful recommendation systems in non-profit and government sources as they need from private industry. Intel has implemented its Rosa advisor in human resources to answer these kinds of questions for its employees (for example, moving, selecting health plans, and choosing 401k investments), so government organizations could do the same.

There are differences between corporations and government, of course. First, in government, profit is not the dominant motive, but there is agreement in both that quality, customer satisfaction, and a positive relationship are important. Community development services find that a positive relationship with their clients is necessary for effective partnering and solutions. This also is true in education and even law enforcement, where mutual respect makes the job of providing a safe and secure environment much easier. Some government services even have advocates. The IRS has a free "Taxpayer Advocate Service," which is available to citizens "if you have an ongoing issue with the IRS that has not been resolved through normal processes, or you have suffered, or are about to suffer a significant hardship as the result of the administration of the tax laws."[3]

[3] www.irsl.gov/advocate/

An assigned advocate will listen to the citizen's point of view and will work to address his or her concerns.

The idea of building trust with our clients and developing a customer advocacy strategy has wide relevance to various products, industries, countries, companies, and non-corporate entities. In each case, the general principles need to be textured for the decision environment, but in all cases, advocacy deserves consideration. It may not be for everyone, and the degree of implementation intensity may vary, but I predict that more organizations in the future will find trust and advocacy as paths to success.

IS CUSTOMER ADVOCACY REALLY A PARADIGM SHIFT?

All this sounds familiar, and we do a lot of it now. What is really new here?

We have talked about quality, satisfaction, and customer relationships, and these are familiar concepts. But customer advocacy is the next step in this evolution toward customers dominating corporate strategy. The Internet has granted customers new power, and the old methods need to be refined to cope with it. For example, CRM has to be converted from a promotion tool to a trust-building methodology to achieve the dream of CRM potential. A firm reaches the top of the Customer Advocacy Pyramid when it is willing to compare its products to competitors in a transparent way, and when it truly adopts the proposition that it succeeds when it makes its customers succeed. New customer advocacy tools were outlined in Chapter 8, "Tools for Advocacy," and as you may recall, the tools include not only trusted advisors but also market experimentation for continuous learning, ways to "listen in" to customers in order to build better products, and virtual advocates. Customer advocacy is a new philosophy supported by new evidence on customer power. It is based on transparency, advice, and competitive comparisons and will often lead to reductions in spending on advertising and promotion.

Customer advocacy can be viewed as an evolutionary development building on quality, satisfaction, and relationship, but in many firms, it will be viewed as revolutionary. "Don't just relate—advocate" can sound radical in many firms.

New ideas come and go in marketing. Usually, it is the tried and true methods that prevail and persist over time. Will customer advocacy just be a fad?

If customer advocacy is revolutionary, then there is the danger that it will come and go. The history of business innovation suggests a cycle: New ideas come and promises are made. However, often benefits are over-promised, results are positive but less than expected, and the idea is eventually rejected because it failed to meet the inflated promises. Management is often looking for the silver bullet that will solve all problems and lead to success immediately. The famous Boston Consulting Group matrix is an example. This matrix showed that the fundamental tradeoff in strategy was market growth and market share. High share and high growth businesses were called "stars," low growth and low share were "dogs," high share and low growth were "cows," and low share and high growth were opportunities signified by a question mark. The concept was to milk the cows for cash, invest the cash in question marks to make them stars, kill the dogs, and nurture the stars. Almost all firms used the matrix in the 1980s, but it is rarely used now. The long-run benefit of managing cash flow across the product line proved to be difficult, and many firms dropped the construct when profits did not increase immediately. These same firms were off to the next wave of management excitement—core competence and focus—the opposite of the diversification implied by BCG. This cycle of innovation, over-promise, and rejection is not good for business. Rather, promised results should be achievable, and companies should realize that the results will not be easy or immediate. The fundamental concepts should be woven into a platform of solid knowledge that builds over time.

Customer advocacy has many benefits in terms of loyalty, cross-selling opportunities, long-run sales growth, reduced marketing costs, and increased profit. But achieving these benefits requires a carefully structured, measured, and controlled process of strategy planning and implementation. It takes time, resources, and an attitude of continuous improvement to be successful in customer advocacy. If expectations are correctly set, and long-run benefits are delivered, customer advocacy will become a paradigm shift.

Traditional marketing concepts are embedded in the minds of most managers. Modifying existing attitudes toward customers and changing the assumption that managers bring to the firm and to customer interaction is not easy. It will take time. Perhaps ten years will pass before advocacy becomes the dominant practice and traditional push marketing becomes rare. Pioneering firms will lead the way, and then traditional firms will find themselves at a disadvantage and will need to scramble to catch up. Some firms will just not get it—that customers are now in control—and will fail completely and go out of business.

If customer advocacy works, others will follow and compete on the trust dimension. Then the competitive advantage goes away, and we are back where we started.

It is true that if advocacy works, firms will begin competing on this dimension. There is no way out of competition, and there should not be. Profits go to the swift and innovative. Timing is critical, so it is important for your firm to be the first to use trust-based strategies and learn faster than others about how to effectively implement those strategies. One good thing about this competition is that pioneers have a very large reward potential. If they can earn customers' trust and consistently justify it, competitors will have a difficult time convincing the loyal customers to switch. The other advantage is that customer advocacy works to improve the customer welfare while the firm earns a fair profit for its efforts. In the end, innovation will be the key to profits, and with an advocacy strategy, the firm should be in a preferred position to combine technology with customer needs to develop successful new products. It will be a new world of trust, and you will have to compete in it. Advocacy is a potential advantage, but that does not mean you will not have to compete aggressively under the new ground rules of advocacy.

One of our competitors is gaining the customers' trust. What can we do?

A competitive trust gap can be hard to overcome. Once customers discover that one company can be trusted, they will tell their friends and will eschew that company's competitors. Less trustworthy competitors might eke out an existence in the cut-rate underbelly of the marketplace, offering second-rate goods for third-rate customers. Otherwise, companies have little choice but to pursue trust, too.

Catching up to a trust-leader is not impossible, and it may be the best strategy—it's better to become the second-most trusted company than to let another competitor garner that title. If more companies in an industry switch to advocacy and trust, they change the expectations of all customers, creating an industry where any remaining untrustworthy companies have no place. If many companies have advisors, you will have to compete in this new world of trust with better advocacy, more effective product development, and continuous innovation to maintain a trust advantage.

I want to build a customer advocacy strategy, but how do I get my firm to move to the new paradigm?

This question is from a CEO of a large firm. It is a good one and demands a long discussion to answer. So in the next chapter, I talk about how the CEO and all members of management need to change the corporate culture across all functions to be successful in customer advocacy. The CEO needs to be the number-one customer advocate in the firm, but everyone needs to be part of leading the change.

10

Moving to Advocacy

In this chapter, I respond to the question posed by a CEO at the end of the last chapter: "How do I get my firm to move to the new paradigm?" I discuss this question in terms of things you need to do as a leader in your organization. I assume you're a member of the management team that makes things happen at your firm. You do not necessarily need to be CEO; often the change agents in an organization are scattered throughout the organization chart. Viewing you as a change agent, I present here what you must do to make an advocacy strategy successful. First, you have to empathize with your customers and experience their decision process—feel their power. Then you need to change the culture of the company from viewing the customer as the person to influence to the person in power. If customers are in power and Theory A fits, you should advocate for them. Simple—right? Wrong! This is a really tough job! You have to change mental models built up from 50 years of Theory P and put in the right people, measures of success, incentives, and organization so that you will consistently represent the consumer across all functions of the firm and channels of distribution. This takes vision, courage, and passion. The CEO must become the number-one customer advocate in the firm, and a unified management team must be behind the CEO.

EMPATHIZE WITH YOUR CUSTOMERS

The first thing you need to do to implement an advocacy program is to empathize with your customers. Learn how they think. What issues and problems do they face? What is their buying process? How do customers collect information? You need to walk in their shoes and feel their thrills, disappointments, and frustrations. You and the whole management team need to empathize with your customers.

EXPERIENCE THE CUSTOMER'S DECISION

Go out and make a purchase in your company's product market. Actually make the decision. It is amazing how many executives do not actually make a real purchase decision for their own products. In the auto industry, few executives really go out and buy a car because they get company purchase plan cars. Few executives walk into a dealership without the benefit of the corporate identification to buy a car, and even fewer shop and test-drive competitive brands. Many airline executives do not buy tickets competitively and experience the reservation process. They do not go through the frustrating call-in process, and they travel first class. Instead, you should fly economy class and try to get the lowest competitive rate. If you are a telecom executive, try to find out what is the best plan among the competitive plans and experience the retail sales environment. Try to get your questions answered. Pay your own monthly bills—feel the anger at those extra charges and surprises. If you are in the financial industry, sign up for an account and make trades. See how coherent the multiple channels of the Internet, telemarketing center, brokers, and physical location are. If you are in a packaged goods company, make the weekly shopping trip to the supermarket. Consider the value you place on friends and word-of-mouth communication. What is the role of community?

A good way to organize this process is to keep a diary of each activity and day. Then look back and ask, "How would I have liked this process to go? What information would I have liked? How would I want to be treated? How can I get to a better decision faster?" Have all the top managers in your organization do this and share what you learn in an all-day meeting during which you define what the system should look like to maximize your interests as a customer.

Keep your diary up-to-date as you use the product. Document your experiences and frustrations with getting service, using the automated telephone system, and getting product problems resolved. Experience the whole lifecycle of ownership.

UNDERSTAND HOW ALL MARKET SEGMENTS EXPERIENCE THEIR DECISIONS

It is insightful but dangerous to study your own decision process. It is important to do in order to understand the customer's pain and power, but you are not a typical customer. You need to understand how all segments of the market make their decisions and sense their empowerment.

You can be a good observer and learn a lot. In the auto industry, listen in at an auto dealer as the sales process goes along. For example, be a sales apprentice for a day at a dealer. In the travel industry, watch carefully at the airport. Listen to the ticket agent interacting with a traveling family. Ask people in line about their feelings towards your company and travel. In finance, follow a broker for a day, listen to call-ins, and study selected Internet sessions. Stand in the supermarket and watch how shoppers go through the store, what they pick up and put back, what coupons they use, and how they load their car. These simple skills of observing and listening can help build empathy with your customer.

Although informal methods are useful, more structured methods of market research are required to really get an accurate understanding of the buying process. Focus groups are a useful method for understanding qualitative issues and structuring more formal market research questionnaires. Conduct multiple focus groups (at least five) and spend hours behind the one-way mirror watching them. In the travel industry, you will feel the anger when one customer discovers that another has paid less. In the auto industry, customers will describe how they reward honest dealers. In finance, you will find some people who really trust their account team—learn how this trust was earned. But in most industries, you will be surprised by how little people trust your firm. Most are not loyal, and you need to find out why. Those customers that are loyal provide many lessons on how to implement your advocacy strategy.

USE FORMAL QUANTITATIVE MARKET RESEARCH

Formal quantitative market research can provide a large sample of knowledge and insight into how customers experience the buying process and what they would like to see changed to better represent their interests and needs. This quantitative research can be motivational and can provide in-depth, open-ended comments, or it can contain structured attitude scales. We discussed some scales for formal trust measurement in Chapter 6, "Where Are You Positioned on the Trust Dimensions?" You should have customers rate your firm compared to the competition on the overall trust and component scales. You will probably be surprised how low your trust scores are in absolute and relative terms. But formal survey work is not a substitute for experience. First, build empathy through your personal decisions and observations and then be sure to get a representative view of your market through qualitative and quantitative market research.

CHANGE THE CULTURE OF YOUR COMPANY

Fifty years of push/pull marketing may have built a deeply ingrained set of beliefs about customers in your firm and about what the company needs to do to succeed. This is a culture—it includes the written and unwritten rules that govern decisions. These shared beliefs are often tacit assumptions about customers and the market structure. They may not even be written down, but they drive the company's response to threats and opportunities. Culture is the sum of what organizations have learned by coping with the environment over time. Ed Schein calls this the "organizational DNA."[1] Culture is deeply embedded and controls how the organization grows and responds. Growth and success build a body of conventional wisdom that is difficult to change.

[1] Schein, Edgar H. "Three Cultures of Managment: The Key to Organizational Learning." *Sloan Management Review.* Fall 1996, pp. 9-20.

IT IS A DIFFICULT TRANSITION

We discussed the assumptions of Theory P versus Theory A in Chapter 5, "Theory A—The New Paradigm." But here, I want to emphasize that these are cultural beliefs. Changing from the mental model of Theory P to Theory A is a very difficult task, and it may take years.

Not only does the organization share a culture, but also subcultures develop with their own beliefs. Sometimes these conflict with each other, so the task of changing the culture involves revising mental models and making them consistent across the firm's subcultures. These subcultures contain deeply imbedded beliefs, and you should map your organization's cultural terrain to understand what needs to be modified.[2] Often these subcultures are called silos. They are independent domains that operate by tight norms but rarely coordinate with other silos. For example, the following are some typical subcultures in a firm's departments and their goals, activities, and beliefs:

- *Advertising*—Be creative; win awards; psychologically position and brand to make a point of difference; increase advertising spending; change attitudes; influence, convince, and motivate customers.

- *Sales*—Make the sales numbers; do what is necessary to close the sales and book the business; be persistent; fill the funnel of customers' decisions (calls, interest, proposals, budgets, commitment); keep the pressure up.

- *Brand Managers*—Develop an annual plan and achieve it; invent new promotions; get more budget for your brand; create line extensions; grow market share.

- *New Products Managers*—Do new things; innovate, extend lines, get products out there soon; designing really new products is risky and takes a long time; do not do too much market research—customers cannot judge new products before market launch.

[2] See Schein, Edgar H., *DEC Is Dead, Long Live DEC* (San Francisco: Berrett-Koehler Publishers, Inc., 2003) for an example of mapping and diagnosis.

- *Service*—Keep customers happy but keep service costs within budget and product returns low; prevent abusive customers from taking advantage of the system; make service a profit generator.

- *Production*—Meet orders; keep costs low; maximize quality; be safe; improve efficiency; do not stop the production line.

- *Engineering/R&D*—Design is the answer; "we can solve the problem"; create the best design; cost is not the primary objective; seek approval from peers in your profession; customers do not know what they need.

- *Human Resources*—Hire talent; train effectively; create efficient systems; promote and reward by this year's results; keep labor happy.

- *Finance*—Make correct financial predictions; manage Wall Street expectations; cut losses; develop accurate accounting; be sure to pass audits; stay financially sound.

- *Executive Managers*—Make the quarterly numbers; win competitive wars; avoid crisis; simplify, develop vision; we probably do not get honest information as executives; advertising and promotion is a marketing task.

In this list, you can see many different beliefs. The marketing functions are influencing customers with whatever is necessary to achieve goals. Production is minimizing cost. Finance is meeting the numbers for the short run. Human resources is organizing its functions efficiently. Top management is creating a vision and keeping the company on track. Many of these activities are on target, but many are not, and conflicting goal structures cause problems for the company.

What is important here is to ask, "Who believes in advocating for the customer?" The answer in this example is no one! This should make clear the magnitude of the task of changing the culture to advocacy. The mental models of these managers do not include the concept of advocacy, which is directly in conflict with other beliefs like "we must influence the customer," "we must do what is necessary to close the sale," "we must invent new promotions," "customers cannot judge new products before market launch," "we must keep service costs and returns low," "we must cut losses," "customers do not know what they need," "we must promote by this year's results," "we must cut costs," and "advertising and promotion is a marketing task." These beliefs reflect push/pull-marketing as the mental model, short-term cost minimization, and the shared desire to make the short-term numbers.

Each organization will be somewhat different in aspirations and beliefs, so it is important to map your subcultures. After diagnosing the situation, determine what is necessary to build Theory A into the culture.

CHANGING THE MENTAL MODEL

To establish Theory A, you need to change these beliefs. You need to add the following activities and attitudes as dominant influencers of the culture:

- *Advertising*—Be transparent, honest, and genuine; think of communication to support the total decision process, not just awareness and perception; build positive attitudes over the lifetime of product use.

- *Sales*—Sell solutions; build a long-term relationship; meet needs; find opportunities for new products.

- *Brand Managers*—Be a leader in advocating for the customer; make the customer a success; build company-wide systems to serve customer decision making; build plans for new and changing customer needs.

- *New Products Managers*—Collaborate with customers to identify needs and solutions; look for lead users; create really new products; build a wider line of products that complement the customer relationship.

- *Service*—Fulfill lifecycle promises; trade increased service costs for long-run loyalty; build enduring customer satisfaction.

- *Production*—Build the highest-quality products; make total quality real throughout the entire value chain.

- *Engineering/R&D*—Co-develop products with users; build products for customer needs; provide comprehensive solutions; trust lead users to portend the future.

- *Human Resources*—Train employees in advocacy; reward based on long-term loyalty and trust; build internal trust-based services; build relationships between employees; change the belief structure to trust.

- *Finance*—Look at long-term numbers; manage market expectations for the long run; invest in advocacy even if short-run costs increase; control activities on the basis of trust, loyalty, and strength of relationship.

- *Executive Managers*—Make advocacy the core of the company mission; focus the organization on continuing long-run sales and profit growth; create a vision of partnering with customers.

This set of beliefs is strikingly different from the earlier set. Rebuilding the firm's subcultures around these new beliefs is not easy, and breaking down the traditional functional silos takes a lot of energy. These are fundamental changes for many of the subcultures, and change will require tolerance and humility by everyone in the firm. The subcultures can be viewed like separate countries, and you may not easily understand the differences between the entities. Cross-cultural problem solving will be needed. Establishing these new attitudes can change the culture as these beliefs become the underlying assumptions that drive the company's response to competitive threats and growth opportunities.

You need to understand the differences and revise the subcultures, but more importantly, you need to develop a unified view of the world across the entire firm. The dominant assumptions and rules must be shared by everyone. The sidebar "Advocacy Belief Statements" lists a set of beliefs and assumptions that characterize the overall set of attitudes that should pervade the firm if it is to reach the top of the pyramid and truly advocate for its customers. Some of these may appear overstated, but to be successful, you really need to be passionate about customer advocacy!

How do you change the culture? It would be naive to think that putting sayings like those in the sidebar on the wall will change the organization. To be successful, change first requires leadership at the top. The CEO must support and exude the beliefs of advocacy. There must be a team of top managers who believe just as strongly in the new strategy, and a set of change agents throughout the hierarchy to cause the change to happen. This top management advocacy team should create new systems to encourage trust building and advocacy. During the cultural change period, this team should meet regularly to assess how the belief structure is changing, correct cases where old rules have been reinforced rather than the new views, and formulate new initiatives. Many short-term versus long-term trade-offs will occur, and this team and the CEO need to be wise in preserving the firm's health while facilitating a transition to the new value structure. In the end, all employees need to believe in the thought structure represented in the sidebar.

ADVOCACY BELIEF STATEMENTS

- We live in the kingdom of Consumer Power.
- We believe in Consumer Sovereignty.
- We are transparent.
- We are the guardians of our customers.
- Trust rules the future.
- Don't just relate—advocate.
- We will be loyal to our customers.
- Our customers are smarter than we think.
- Customers design products better than we do.
- There are no secrets from customers.
- Our customers trust us, so they want to buy more from us.
- Fight for our customers' rights.
- If our products cannot stand up to competitive comparisons, why are people buying them?
- If you do not have the best products, build them.
- Climb the Pyramid.
- We are all responsible for building trust.
- ADVOCATE for your customers, and they will ADVOCATE for you.
- Be *passionate* about customer advocacy!

PEOPLE, MEASURES, INCENTIVES, AND ORGANIZATION

It is essential to have an informal team drive the cultural change, but the traditional top management change levers of hiring the right people, creating measures that evaluate program progress, building incentives around the measures, and formally organizing the firm should be used to enable continuing progress toward the advocacy culture. All managers accept using these levers, but there are differences when using these levers to change the culture to advocacy.

PEOPLE

When hiring people, you need to screen candidates for empathy with customers. Do this not only for marketing and sales functions but for everyone you hire. Some people just cannot learn this empathy because the notion of the customer as the adversary and someone to be manipulated are too deeply ingrained. If your new hires have the basic empathy, then you can train them in the philosophy and methods of customer advocacy. This will require explicit programs and resources. A training program should include cataloging your own decision experience, observing focus groups, and reviewing formal market research, as we suggested at the beginning of this chapter. Then, training on the design of programs and utilization of tools for advocacy will be appropriate. Finally, teaching people how to manage others to build the advocacy culture will be necessary. Some people will "get it," and others will not. Moving to an advocacy strategy may call for firing many of the managers who just "do not get it"—otherwise, they will be part of the problem rather than part of the solution.

MEASURES

Current measures of meeting short-term sales and earnings goals need to be supplemented by measures of long-term relationships. The firm does need to make the short-term goals it sets, but these short-term goals need to build a capability to generate the trust that will ensure long-term growth and profitability. You need to set both short-term and longer-term goals. With a transition to advocacy, the short-term sales and profit goals should be reduced and then met, while the longer-term growth and relationship goals should be aggressive. The average growth rate in sales, profit, and return on assets as a moving three-year average is a good measure of longer-term success. More detailed relationship measures should include 1) the share of the individual requirements met by your firm (this is the share among your customers and not overall market share), 2) repeat purchase rate (the fraction of first-purchase customers who make another purchase, the fraction of second-purchase customers who make a third purchase, and so on), 3) average margin among customers who make repeat purchases, 4) cross-selling (the fraction of customers who buy one of your products and then buy another of your offerings), 5) the fraction of sales accounted for by new products, and 6) attitude measures of trust and satisfaction (see Chapter 6 sidebar). These measures can be used as control parameters to evaluate programs and individuals if you want to encourage advocacy.

INCENTIVES

After you have the measures, you can create incentives around them. Bonuses can be established for the six advocacy measures cited previously. Most compensation should be in the form of salary, but healthy upside bonuses should be available to encourage building long-term trust relationships. For example, while the sales force may continue to get a significant commission for initial sales, an equal incentive should be given for increasing the share of business the firm gets from existing customers and cross-selling. Other marketing personnel should be rewarded primarily on the relationship measures (refer to the six measures in the previous paragraph). The bonuses should relate to overall company, group, and individual accomplishments and should also be based on the measures. Set the goals on the six measures, measure accomplishment, and reward those who exceed their goals on share of customer requirements, repeat purchases, margin, cross-selling, new product success, and attitudes of trust and loyalty.

ORGANIZATION

I have talked about an informal top management team to lead the cultural revolution to advocacy, but I would also recommend some formal organizational changes to encourage the evolution to the advocacy point of view. Everyone must advocate, but a VP of Customer Advocacy would be a useful position to create. This Chief Advocacy Officer (CAO) should report to the CEO. The key marketing functions, as well as customer service functions, should report to this person. This will allow the CAO to coordinate advertising, sales, marketing, new product development, and brand management around the core customer advocacy strategy. The CAO should work closely and have a dotted-line relationship to engineering, R&D, and production.

Some firms already have a senior manager for trust and customer advocacy. As you would expect, eBay has a Director of Trust. After all, their success is based on a trusting marketplace (refer to the Chapter 1 sidebar). Here are four other examples:

AOL

AOL has a Chief Trust Officer with the title of Senior Vice President who is tasked with providing strategic leadership for the development and execution of processes and practices that ensure the integrity of AOL, Inc. businesses. The Chief Trust Officer oversees the integrity of the user experience, consumer protection, privacy, online safety, accessibility, community standards and policy, and is responsible for setting internal standards and practices for various AOL businesses in areas such as product development, online programming, e-commerce, advertising, and graphics review.[3]

Siemens

At Siemens Enterprise Networks, the "Siemens Customer Advocacy Group" is headed by the Director of Customer Advocacy & Quality and the Customer Advocacy Program Manager. It was established in early 2002 to provide a customer voice within Siemens and to help Siemens better understand the needs of its customers and respond to them more efficiently. The

---

[3] See www.corp.aol.com.

group created the Customer Concerns/Complaints database for tracking the "voice of the customer." The Director of Customer Advocacy makes sure these customer concerns are heard, acknowledged, directed to the right people, and resolved. The Director of Customer Advocacy encourages customers to provide Siemens with feedback, concerns, ideas, and suggestions.[4]

Cisco

At Cisco Systems, the Customer Advocacy Group is headed by the Senior Vice President of Customer Advocacy. Its Customer Advocacy Mission Statement is to accelerate customer success with Cisco through innovative services and world-class people, partners, processes, and tools. Cisco believes that customer satisfaction equals customer loyalty. By listening to customers, meeting customer needs, and improving customer experiences, Cisco's customer advocacy group builds loyalty in the new customer-centric economy. When customers have issues and problems, the Customer Advocacy Group makes sure that those issues are escalated in the right way.[5]

AMD

AMD's Consumer Advocacy Initiative was launched in October 2001 and is headed by the Vice President of Customer Advocacy, who reports to the CEO. This represents AMD's commitment to being in tune with home and business technology consumers and being ahead of their needs. AMD formed the Global Consumer Advisory Board to discuss technology issues with the purpose of improving the quality of the end-user technology experience. The company believes that technology end users need stronger advocates and that a much larger customer base should be better informed. AMD recognizes that a gap has formed between technology innovation and users' understanding and adoption of technology, and it believes that bringing together experts from around the world to discuss these issues will help provide possible solutions to this problem. Consumer Advocacy also includes a "True

[4] See www.siemens.com and personal communication from Ms. Patty Clare, Customer Advocacy and Quality Manager.

[5] See www.cisco.com.

Performance Initiative" to provide a voice for customers inside AMD and to ensure that AMD is looking out for users' computing needs.[6] You may recall from the sidebar in Chapter 6 and comments in Chapter 7 that AMD backs up its initiative with a leading-edge users program and competitive comparisons.

You can see several of the CAO functions in these four example companies. AOL is focused on standards to guarantee trustworthiness, while Siemens is focused on service and complaint resolution. Cisco concentrates on customer satisfaction and includes listening for needs. AMD stresses user needs and adoption, and advocates for users understanding and adopting technology. AMD and Cisco advocacy officers report to the CEO. These positions are good starts toward organizing for advocacy, but I think they need to be defined more comprehensively to be successful in building a broad-based advocacy strategy. They should include responsibility for the advertising, sales, marketing, and new product planning functions, as well as customer service. The CAO mission should include building trust relationships, partnering with customers, and maximizing customers' interests.

CONSISTENCY AND COORDINATION

Although people, measures, incentives, and formal organization are powerful tools, they often leave inconsistencies between marketing, finance, production, and other functions. Cross-functional coherence is needed if the consumer is to have a unified trust-building experience while interacting with the firm. The CAO should be responsible for rationalizing the inconsistencies of the customer experience and breaking down the functional silos.

The first coherence requirement is that the firm must speak with one voice. All the customer-facing functions should have the same information. For example, in a credit union, the telecenter staff, loan officers, and online systems should have the same information on rates, should answer customer loan questions in the same way, and should provide consistent advice. A good way to do this is with a central online data and advice system. The advisor

---

[6] See www.AMD.com and www.Amdgeab.org.

shown previously in Figure 7-2 serves First Tech Credit Union with a consistent set of responses to questions, current loan rates, and advice standards.

There are many innate conflicts in organizations. One major conflict is marketing and cost control. For example, under cost pressure, airlines have cut the number of seats available for frequent flyer points redemption. This devalues the very loyalty incentives that premier passengers appreciate. Even at the highest level of awards, it is often difficult to redeem points when you want to travel. The answer from some airlines has been to institute "anytime seats" by booking any flight but at twice the award points per seat. This deflates the points' value by half. The move saves the airlines money but breeds distrust and resentment among the very customers the airlines are trying to win. In this case, short-term cost savings are overruling long-run loyalty and relationship.

Service and satisfaction also are classic conflicts. If you accept returns liberally, your costs go up, but customers are happy. If you lower returns with strict return policies, costs go down, but so does the likelihood that the customer will buy again. I broke my fishing rod on a big striped bass and then a week later broke my reel when it got crushed in my suitcase. Cabela's Sporting goods promptly sent me both a new rod and reel—you can be sure I'll buy from them again!

Sometimes service is cut because of customer fraud in returns. This is a tradeoff, but it is better to budget for (and of course minimize) false returns. The weight of attention should go to being sure you do not break trust but rather stand behind your products.

Quality and satisfaction are also difficult tradeoffs. If the quality is great, satisfaction is high. But if quality slips, loyalty is destroyed. The best policy is to keep the quality at the level promised to customers. In autos, the implication is the very highest quality, and companies pay dearly for slips in quality. Among airlines like Southwest, Jet Blue, and Song, the promised quality is not the highest, but it is consistently maintained, and satisfaction is good. But if you promise premium service on first class, it is a real trust-buster when you get poor food and surly treatment from the staff at the desk and on the plane.

Another conflict is evident in the insurance industry between sales and underwriting/claims. The sales staff wants new customers and loyalty that will lead to coverage of all the households' risks with a range of policies. The second sidebar in this chapter describes my personal experience with my insurance company. Although the company's sales goals were achieved through the purchase of my policy, the underwriting department's desire to minimize exposure led to the termination of over 25 years of loyalty. I am sure the CEO did not want this to happen, but because of the lack of coordination between departments and inconsistent policies, they lost my business.

TWENTY-FIVE YEARS OF LOYALTY THROWN AWAY

For over 25 years, a small insurance company in Stevens Point, Wisconsin, has gotten all my home insurance business (home owners, umbrella, and autos). My father-in-law was an employee at the firm for 50 years and ended his career as Vice President and Controller, so we had a long family tradition. It was natural that I bought my first apartment contents insurance from this company when I was in school. After moving to Boston, I regularly insured my cars with the company, and as I built my house, I added that coverage. I never compared rates and had a personal contact with my local representative, Joe. All went smoothly with only a few claims, and I consistently added more coverage as I raised a family and enlarged my house. But in 2000, my company dropped its personal representatives to save money, and I had to deal with phone operators who did not really understand my needs and were less qualified than Joe. This made me cautious. In March 2004, I got a "form" letter (unsigned) saying that my plans to add a workshop to my barn meant that the company had to cancel my homeowner's policy, and I had four weeks to get coverage elsewhere. Obviously this was a trust-buster for me! A few phone calls revealed that the problem was that my policy total value deviated from their accepted underwriting guidelines. Telling the phone operator of my long history did no good, and they would not connect me to the CEO, so I moved to Fireman's Fund. Both they and Chubb were eager for my business. My original company was surprised when I said I was moving my umbrella policy—"We can continue to insure that," they said. They did not get it—to me the relationship is more important than the "product" being sold. I do not buy just products from a firm, but most importantly I buy a relationship with a company I can trust to represent me. The underwriting part of the company probably did not know my customer history, and I would guess the policy limit setters did not consider the sales effects of the customer relationship on other products. This was a real lack of coordination! I wish my father-in-law had been living—he probably could have gotten the attention at the top of the organization and resolved this by being my advocate.

Channels are often difficult to control, and actual channel behavior may not be consistent with the company's policies. The Internet can help build coherence. For example, Sony has an Internet site for information and advice about consumer electronics. They refer you to the nearest dealer if you would like to go there, but in Japan, you can buy direct from Sony. In this case, Sony pays the retailer in your area a commission to be sure that the customer receives the best level of service when they come in the store. This is a great example of the use of incentives to preserve consistency.

Consistency is a real challenge, and coordination requirements are high. The previous examples are only a few of the many that exist in organizations. Fundamentally, the conflicts must be found and resolved. The tradeoffs must be made between the long-run value of relationships and short-run savings. These decisions should be explicitly made at the CEO level, and then standards should be put in place for the desired levels of consistency. If there is a Vice President of Customer Advocacy, it should be that person's responsibility to maintain coherence across all functions and elements of the customer experience. The highest levels of the company need to consider the customer relationship and preserve trust.

TRUST FOR ALL STAKEHOLDERS

We have been talking throughout this book about the customer relationship and the necessity of building trust, but trust building should not be restricted to just customers. You need to build trust with all your stakeholders. You cannot change your culture unless you advocate for all your stakeholders.

Employees need to trust that the company will stay in business and will reward their efforts to build quality. Total quality programs rely on a partnering relationship with employees to identify quality improvements and be sure that they are made. Quality circles are examples of the participatory management that most organizations use. In Chapter 7, "Is Advocacy for You?" we described how Qwest had to first build employee trust with their "generations of service" campaign before they tried to improve customer trust. As I stated earlier and repeat here for emphasis, Intel's persona Rosa, which was used originally for providing advice on the download site, has been adopted by the internal employees services group to provide information and advice in over 30 employee need areas. The human resources department feels that Rosa builds trust and relationships in what is sometimes a cold and bureaucratic interaction between the company and its employees.

Stockholders need transparency and long-term assurance that they are being treated fairly. Of course there are legal requirements, but often the firm should go beyond these requirements to give the stockholders honest, open information and not texture the stockholder reporting to look good and influence stock prices.

Regulators and the government can be viewed as an adversary, but often a proactive relationship between industry and government can prevent heavy-handed laws and enforcement. Communication to give all branches of government (legislative, administrative, and judicial) an accurate understanding of the industry and company situation can help lead to positive regulation to balance national needs and corporate profit.

All company business partners must trust the firm. You need transparency and rules of engagement with partners that lead to mutual long-term rewards. For example, technical cooperation between a manufacturer and supplier for joint product development is based on trust that benefits will be equitably shared. Retailers have power, but partnering can give the firm its required distribution and customer-facing trust relationships. Industry consortiums are often useful and are based on open cooperation. For example, realtors have developed an association site to gain exposure and provide customers with better information (Realtor.com). Airlines have formed Orbitz.com to participate in the reservations business. The members of the National Association of Auto Dealers have banded together to provide a common auto information and advice site (NADA.com), which includes step-by-step buying advice and impartial test-drive information through links to NewCarTestDrive.com.

Trust is particularly important in international relationships, and in some situations, formal contracts are not written because the strength of trust between the partners is so high. In many Asian cultures, trust is the prerequisite before any business gets done. In Japan, long-run trust between Toyota and its suppliers is one of its secrets of success. Instead of squeezing suppliers for short-run cost concessions that may jeopardize quality, Toyota carefully shares its problems with suppliers and works to find an improved solution that preserves the interests of all parties.

VISION, COURAGE, AND PASSION

It's not easy to build coherence and consistency in an organization, and it may be even more difficult to change the culture of an organization to customer advocacy. It takes a long time to change culture and construct the accurate IT and marketing programs needed to build trust. Measures, incentives, and formal organizational structures can help, but in the end, it depends on leadership from the CEO and the key managers who implement changes.

The CEO needs to describe a *vision* for long-range success that the organization can buy into. This vision may be in the CEO's mind, but it needs to emerge from participatory strategic planning. It takes imagination from the whole team of change agents throughout the organization. The team needs to be willing to take risks to deliver the vision. Theory Y was a new vision of organization in the late 1960s, and Theory A is a revolution in strategy in the 2000s. With a vision of customer advocacy, the culture is easier to change.

It often takes *courage* from the CEO to champion customer advocacy. It is much more comfortable to stay with the current situation and make marginal improvement. Customer advocacy is often a revolution in thinking, organization structure, and program design. Many people will resist the changes, and the CEO must lead the battles against entrenched subcultures and convince their members to adopt the new perspectives. A core of change agents is needed to help the CEO fine-tune the vision and implement it.

It requires real leadership to take on customer advocacy as the stamp of a CEO's reign. After all, the changes may take up to ten years, and most CEOs do not stay on the job more than five years. It takes *passion* for the cause of customers and conviction that advocacy is the best path to long-run success for the firm. The CEO must be the number-one advocate for the customer and for the required changes within the organization.

BUILDING THE TOTAL PYRAMID

Advocate for your customers, but remember—do not ignore the foundation of the pyramid (review Figure 8-1). Do not make advocacy a fad that will fade away. Build advocacy on top of a trust relationship, customer satisfaction, and quality. Start from the bottom in the pyramid. Be sure you have the best quality even before you think about advocacy. Be certain that your customer satisfaction is high before you embark on building a trusting relationship. Then use the trust to enable customer advocacy.

This all sounds very daunting, and it may be tempting to delay building a customer advocacy pyramid in your firm. But be careful—delaying may be throwing away your potential pioneering advantage. An even more convincing argument is that the future may not just encourage but may *require* customer advocacy to maintain viability as customer power becomes dominant. I discuss this imperative next.

11

The Advocacy Imperative

You have made a long climb up the customer advocacy pyramid. You have learned how the Internet creates customer power, how to use new tools for trust building, and how to change your organization. But what is most important to remember, and what will the future bring in terms of customer advocacy? In this final chapter, I review the key lessons learned from this book, predict that customer power will grow, and argue that because pioneers will gain lasting advantages by innovating along the trust dimension, customer advocacy will become an *imperative* for late adopters if they want to remain competitive. We will be living in a new world of trust and advocacy.

WHAT IS MOST IMPORTANT TO REMEMBER?

CUSTOMERS ARE IN CONTROL!

Customer power has grown over the last five years. It has been almost invisible to many managers, but because of the Internet, customers now have more information, options for buying, and simplified transactions. This fundamentally changes the company/customer interaction. Customers dominate the interaction and decision-making process.

THE BALANCE IS MOVING FROM PUSH/PULL MARKETING TO TRUST-BASED MARKETING

With the increase in customer power, the balance has shifted from aggressive one-sided advertising and promotion to *trust-based marketing*. Trust-based marketing relies on open, honest communication and great products to build long-term belief, confidence, and relationships with customers. This is especially true for differentiated, complex, and important products when buyers are very informed.

CUSTOMER POWER IS PERVASIVE AND GROWING

It is clear that customer power is growing in complex purchases like autos, travel, and health services, but customer power is increasing in many other industries like financial securities (for example, stocks and mortgages), real estate, insurance, consumer durables, and industrial buying. It is also present in some unexpected industries, such as consumer packaged goods and human resource services. Although the U.S. is farthest along in customer empowerment, the whole world is demonstrating that customers are gaining influence. The growth in power is converging with other strategic business factors: increasing skepticism, pervasive regulation, decreasing media effectiveness and efficiency, overcapacity, commoditization, and saturation of markets.

In Chapter 5, "Theory A—The New Paradigm," we described an advertisement where a small girl touched the face of a rhino after it stopped just short of her after a full charge across the Serengeti Plane. The buy line was: "Trust is not being afraid even when you are vulnerable." We probably all envisioned the girl as the customer and the rhino as the company. But in the future world of customer power, it would be better to think of the rhino as the customer and the little girl as the company. This may more accurately portray the future customer-company relationship. Customers will be powerful and companies will be vulnerable.

THEORY A IS THE NEW PARADIGM FOR MARKETING

The convergence of customer power and other strategic business factors is changing the paradigm for marketing and corporate strategy. Just as in organization behavior, where we moved from Theory X with its reliance on authority and punishment to Theory Y with participative management, marketing is moving from Theory P, which relies on push/pull techniques, to Theory A, which is based on trust and advocacy in the customers' interests. The assumptions we make about customers have shifted; instead of viewing customers as people who must be coerced and who are not very intelligent, we see them as natural decision makers who want to control the process of buying, make informed decisions, and have imagination, ingenuity, and creativity.

KNOW WHERE YOU ARE POSITIONED ON THE TRUST DIMENSION AND WHERE YOU WANT TO BE

In order to respond to the demands of Theory A, you must know where you are now positioned on the overall trust dimension and the trust components of transparency, quality of products and services, product comparisons and advice, incentives, partnering, cooperative design, the supply chain, and pervasiveness. When you know where you stand, you can decide where you want to be on the trust dimensions. Most firms will find they want to move to build trusting relationships with their customers, but many will find this is just not enough and will develop full customer advocacy programs.

ADVOCACY IS NOT FOR EVERYONE

Not all firms will want to move all the way to the advocacy level on the trust dimensions. First you must determine if advocacy fits your firm. Most firms will find that trust and advocacy are the path to future success. But if you are in a commodity industry, have a monopoly, cannot control quality and quantity, maintain a short-term focus, have customers who are short-term (one-time buy or deal-prone), or have low-impact products, trust and advocacy may not be for your firm. But it is up to you. Even in some of these industry exceptions, trust may be a path for added long-term profits.

TOOLS FOR BUILDING TRUST AND ADVOCACY ARE AVAILABLE AND IMPROVING

Trusted advisors on the Internet and throughout the communication channel (telemarketing, direct mail, advertising, point of purchase) are available and are proven trust builders. They are important tools as you build on the customer pyramid base of total quality and customer satisfaction. Advisors are one component in building a dream Customer Relationship Management (CRM) system to establish a long-term positive relationship with customers, earn their loyalty, and widen patronage. Use advisors aligned with your one-to-one marketing, branding, loyalty, channel partnerships, permission marketing, and collaborative customer design programs. Completing the pyramid with a customer advocate requires that you be willing to make competitive comparisons and provide information and advice that honestly represents the customer's interests. If other products are better, then recommend them. But, of course, you must get going on your new product development so that you can recommend your product as being truly the best.

MOVING TO ADVOCACY IS A CULTURAL CHANGE IN YOUR ORGANIZATION

The culture in your organization is most likely in conflict with trust building and customer advocacy. Moving from Theory P to Theory A is difficult—many deeply held beliefs in marketing and other departments work against transparency, competitive comparisons, and co-designing products with customers. In order to modify these long-held views, you should recruit a team of managers who have empathy with your customers in order to set up explicit measures for trust, advocacy, and long-term success, provide incentives that are compatible with these measures and with the strategies they engender, organize for advocacy with a senior manager for advocacy (Chief Advocacy Officer), and be coherent across all functions including finance, production, engineering, and human resources.

THE FUTURE OF TRUST AND ADVOCACY

Changes are happening rapidly. Internet use is becoming pervasive, and its impact on purchasing is growing. More people are getting data and making more informed decisions. These trends enable increased customer power, and they will continue. The early customer guides, such as *Consumer Reports* and the Better Business Bureau, were initially enhanced with the availability of online information. Now formal advisors exist to help buyers handle the complexity of available information. Industries from autos to travel and healthcare have implemented formal advice to help customers make better decisions.

FIRMS ARE GAINING MAJOR ADVANTAGES IN MARKETS

eBay is perhaps the most striking example of success because trust is the core of their business success and phenomenal growth. Especially noteworthy is that they created a multi-billion dollar business in used car sales by teaching used car dealers to be honest and trustworthy. Travelocity, Expedia, and Orbitz have revolutionized travel reservations with trust and systems that advocate for consumers by finding the lowest rates for them. Now new firms are serving travelers by searching across multiple sites to find the best flight and fares. For example, Mobissimo.com searches 58 sites (the usual Expedia, Orbitz, and Travelocity plus the airline sites and others). Large firms like General Motors have tested trust programs and found that they work to build sales and improve relationships. Intel has found that personal advisors help improve customer support, and they have averted millions of dollars in the cost of customer service. Medical suppliers like the Mayo Clinic, Aventis, and Novartis are increasingly basing their strategies on information, advice, and trust. Small firms also are finding benefits. Credit unions (First Tech, San Antonio, Mission Federal, and University Federal) are implementing advisors and finding improved sales, profits, customer trust, and strategic coherence. Trust building is pervasive, and I have cited companies across a diverse set of industries, including John Deere, G.E., Progressive, Amazon, P&G, and AMD. Innovation is rampant, and customers and firms are gaining from it.

In the future, we will see even more trust building on the Internet. ePinions recently implemented a "trusted store" designation for sellers based on consistent positive feedback, accurate price and shipping information, and quickness of resolving customer complaints. This designation cannot be bought and is a step toward empowering customers by rewarding merchants who earn and deserve their trust. Angie's List, an objective service company, has been introduced to allow service companies (e.g., plumbers, handymen, movers, etc.) at the local level to be evaluated by customers. This community rates service providers on satisfaction and makes the feedback available to other members. Companies do not pay to be on Angie's List, and over 132,000 homeowners rate services (customers pay $49 per year to be part of the community) in 20 major markets.

The Internet is leading the way in empowerment, but a diverse set of firms is increasingly embracing trust and fairness. In several places in this book, I have criticized the telecommunication industry for bad practices in terms of honesty, transparency, and reflecting customer interests. But even in this industry, trust and advocacy are emerging. Sprint has launched a new service called "Fair & Flexible." It eliminates high-priced extra plan minutes by retroactively recalculating your charges based on time actually used assuming you were in the best Sprint plan and sells you the extra minutes at the same rate as the best plan. This is customer advocacy because it protects customers from errors in estimating their usage. Sprint TV ads use an analogy of kids playing at a playground who have to estimate how many minutes they will play before they begin. In Sprint's characterization of the telecommunication industry, the rules for the playground include the following:[1]

1. "You have to guess how many minutes you're going to use your ball—for the next two years. Don't guess too high or low, or you will be sorry.

2. Whoever is new on the playground is more special. It's just a fact. Therefore, new kids get the new things, and old ones don't.

3. There will almost never be anything cool and exciting to play on. If there is, it'll be really tricky to get it to work.

4. If you don't like the rules, try another playground. It'll be exactly the same."

Although the "Fair & Flexible plan" applies only to Sprint services, the initiative is likely to shift the competition from deceiving customers to being open and honest and fighting for their interests. It remains to be seen if this specific campaign is successful, but the trend is clear. Third-party cross-brand sites like LetsTalk.com and InPhonic.com are becoming more popular and are a step toward advocacy by providing direct comparisons of brands and plans for mobile services. In Chapter 8, "Tools for Advocacy," I provided a definition of a possible future site called "My Wireless Advisor" (refer to Figure 8-7). No one is offering such an advocacy service at this time, but the trend is toward trust and advocacy in telecommunication, so we may see it soon. If the transition can happen in the traditionally push-oriented telecommunications industry, it will be emerging across industry after industry. Trust and advocacy strategies are becoming real. Experimentation will lead to success and diffusion of these new marketing and corporate strategies.

[1] Sprint "Fair and Flexible" ad, 2004.

FORCES WORKING AGAINST TRUST AND ADVOCACY

New Internet ad formats may make one-sided advertising more viable. For example, Google ads linked to keywords in the search request are able to get ads to people when they are interested in a product. Buzz marketing methods that include placing products in shows (reminiscent of the movie *The Truman Show*), creating word-of-mouth by using agents in public places (e.g., two guys sitting in a bar with tire tread designs cut into their hair talking about new high-traction tires for cars), and seeding community discussion groups with biased product evaluations may offer alternatives that are better than traditional media advertising. As companies have shifted out of advertising, they have created new message vehicles. For example, Coke sponsors Cokemusic.com on the Internet, and AMX created a series of web episodes that are entertaining and build interest. These new methods may enable marketing spending to gain new leverage and encourage firms to stay with traditional push/pull philosophies. On the other hand, these same new methods can be used for trust building and advocacy if they are honest, unbiased, helpful, and useful in supporting customer decisions.

New CRM data mining techniques may preserve push/pull marketing in some firms. New microscopic segmentation may enable firms to use intrusive methods of promotion and communication. More targeted special price discounts and messaging may increase productivity. However, my feeling is that the overall effectiveness of these methods will not increase enough to make traditional push/pull methods profitable in the face of the growth of consumer independence of information and action. Again, as in new media, the new data mining methods can be used to improve the customer trust, if you choose to use them that way. Recall how University Federal Credit Union in Austin, Texas, developed "Wheels 101" (refer to Figure 6-6). They also used data mining to find members who got an auto loan from a dealer and paid more than they should have, given their credit rating. University Federal then offered to refinance the loan at a lower rate. This is data mining to help the customer, and it represents advocacy.

Perhaps the strongest force toward maintaining push/pull market-ing is the short-term focus on profit and making the numbers. This will make a translation to a long-run trust relationship difficult. Firms that in desperation are running up short-term financial results at the price of long-term position will have a difficult time embracing advocacy.

Thus, overall the inertia is toward advocacy, and the new media and CRM methods are likely to support this trend. It may take five to ten years to complete the translation from push/pull to advocacy, but the forces and directions are clear.

THE ADVOCACY IMPERATIVE—IF YOU DO NOT DO IT, YOUR COMPETITORS WILL!

If the future will feature pioneering firms moving toward building trust and embracing advocacy strategies, your choice will be whether to lead or follow. Pioneers will face more risk than doing nothing, but they will also have the opportunity for major gains in market position. In this case, the gains are likely to be enduring. Earning trust is difficult, and if it is maintained, the customer is very unlikely to switch to an unknown supplier. Trust is precious, and few customers will risk the loss of trust by switching to a com-petitor. The cost of switching will deter changing brands even in the face of price promotions. If the pioneers continually innovate in products and trust generation methods, their pioneering advan-tage will endure. It is especially important to be consistent and be sure that no trust-busters occur in the relationship so that the cus-tomer can fully rely on the firm.

The second choice is to follow the innovators. It appears less risky, but in fact it puts the firm in the position of facing a major loss in its base of customers and sacrificing its past gains as customers migrate to trusted product suppliers. Often, if one firm in an industry leads on the trust dimension and achieves success, oth-ers have to follow. They have little choice because otherwise they will lose share and face going out of business. This is the *Advocacy Imperative*. If you do not lead, you will have no choice but to be an imitator in a market dominated by customer advocacy.

Consider the case of eBay and used cars again. eBay innovated by supplying the framework for trustworthy purchases of used cars. The imperative for used car dealers who wanted to get business from eBay customers was to adopt the trust paradigm. It is interesting that the National Association of Auto Dealers (NADA) has adopted a trust-based set of guidelines for their members, which includes the following:[2]

1. "Treat each customer in a fair, open, and honest manner and fully comply with all laws that prohibit discrimination.

2. Represent our product clearly and factually, standing fully behind our warranties, direct and implied, and in all other ways justifying customer's respect and confidence.

3. Advertise our products in a positive, factual, and informative manner.

4. Resolve customer concerns promptly and courteously."

If all dealers implement these guidelines, the auto business will be well along on the path of trust. If dealers in NADA are fair and honest, other dealers will have to match these tactics if they want to succeed with customers. As manufacturers such as GM lead in advocacy, other manufacturers will face the trust and advocacy imperative and will have little choice but to follow in the face of the customer mandate.

Credit unions have always been a membership cooperative, so they have a natural mutuality with customers. But, as I have stated, they are innovating in advocacy and trust. We examined First Tech's advisor in Chapter 7, "Is Advocacy for You?" (refer to Figure 7-2). Now over 17 credit unions have embraced this advisory format and capability. In Figure 6-6, you saw the example of University Federal's advocacy for their customers through a course "Wheels 101" on how to be smart when buying a car. Bellco has pioneered in advice and competitive product comparisons (refer to Figure 6-3). Mission Federal Credit Union in San Diego recently defined its commitment to the advocacy strategy with the development of an Advocacy Value Proposition (see Figure 11-1). This

[2] www.nada.org/Content/Navigation menue/autoshopping/codeofethics, August 2004.

contains sound and powerful concepts, and I like the tag line, "Live smart. Bank smart." This is a leadership commitment that reflects a decision to pioneer in the world of customer advocacy. Mission has recently appointed a Chief Advocacy Officer. The credit union industry will make major gains against the large banks with this strategy, and large banks will then face the Advocacy Imperative. They will then have to try to regain the trust of their customers by providing high-quality products, faultless customer service, and trust-based relationships and by truly advocating for their customers. This will be a major and difficult strategic transformation for them, and many will be ineffective unless they start now before they have lost their customer base to a trusted set of credit unions and small banks.

Key Concepts	
Internal	**External**
•A commitment to Member Advocacy and the Trust Imperative •Developing an "organization worth promoting" •Building loyalty and lifetime value for every life stage and every lifestyle All on a foundation of outstanding member service	•Protecting your long-term financial future •Addressing your immediate financial needs (relationship focus) •Serving in the member's best interest •Fulfilling each member's unique needs All on the foundation of Financial Education

Value Proposition Statement
We take the time to **understand** your changing needs and goals and then **educate and advise** you personally so you *can* make **smart financial decisions for life.**

Tag Line
Live Smart. Bank Smart.

Supporting Thoughts
•We earn our members' trust by educating them, and make it easy to get all the information they need to make an intelligent choice whatever their life stage. •We provide expert advice to empower members to better understand their options, and then pick the best financial products and services to fill their unique needs. •We blend member satisfaction and financial soundness with passionate member advocacy to represent the best interests of our members. •Our underlying philosophy is ultimately about serving our members, and we use trusted advice to fulfill that personal commitment. •Our mission is to become the kind of financial institution that our members consider worth promoting.

Figure 11-1 Mission Federal Credit Union Advocacy Proposition

In new companies, as well as in both large and small established firms, managers will face the Advocacy Imperative. Trust-based marketing and customer advocacy are coming, and you must decide whether you want to pioneer or are willing to accept the position as a late adopter of the new Theory A paradigm.

COMPETING IN A WORLD OF TRUST

If competitors do meet the advocacy imperative, you will be operating in a world of trust, and the innovators should be trying to determine how to maintain a competitive advantage.

The best way to retain the trust advantage is through continuing innovation. Develop new products and design them jointly with customers to meet their needs. Customers will reward firms for innovation and will quickly adopt new ideas because they trust the firm and because the firm has a record of advocacy. Profits in the long run will be based on how faithfully and effectively the firm represents the customers' interests through product and service innovation.

Another way to retain a competitive advantage in trust is by faultless execution and coordination. You may recall that I cited John Deere as having a good trust-based web site. When I was buying a farm tractor last year, I used this site and was impressed by their customer endorsements and competitive comparisons with Kubota, who also makes competitive comparisons on their site. So I had the choice of two trusted suppliers. The competition for my business next switched to the channel partners. The John Deere metro dealer I visited was large and efficient, but it did not engender my confidence, and the dealer's price was over the suggested Kubota retail price. Visiting a large Kubota dealer in New Hampshire gave me similar uneasy feelings, and the price was only $1,000 less than Deere (even with no sales tax for me because I live in Massachusetts and am not subject to New Hampshire sales tax). My final solution was a small local Kubota dealer outside of Boston where I got personal attention and a price $2,000 lower than Deere (after Massachusetts sales tax). I bought the Kubota.

This little story demonstrates the need for good execution. Deere had the best site, but the Kubota site was good, their price was lower, and the local dealer was more genuine and convincing to me. Trust building is a multi-channel experience, and you should never forget the importance of the personal interface in the final sale. The market research firm Yankelovich has found that personal experiences are the most important trust cues.[3] The firms that maintain their trust advantages will have a well-trained and coherent sales and distribution network and prices that maximize the value for customers relative to competition across the Internet, physical locations, and people.

THE ADVOCACY CHECKLIST

If you want to build an advocacy strategy, I have developed a checklist of the critical activities you must accomplish. If you successfully check them off, you will be well on the way to being a pioneer in customer advocacy. The checklist is shown in Table 11-1. It is organized around climbing the Customer Advocacy Pyramid. Be sure that the base of your product quality and customer satisfaction is sound—hopefully you already have this in place. Next convert your CRM from a push system to a Dream CRM trust-based relationship builder. Then cap off the pyramid with true advocate programs.

Most of the items are self-explanatory and are discussed extensively in this book, but a few deserve additional emphasis at the advocacy level. Writing an explicit advocacy value proposition makes clear the strategic commitment of the firm and defines the advocacy mission (refer to Figure 11-1). This is an important activity, and it helps to change the culture.

An "opt-in" program is a big step toward a mutual trust relationship with your customers. Customers opt in and get help and advice in making a better purchase decision because the firm can direct

---

[3] J. Walker Smith, Ann Clurman, and Craig Wood. *Coming to Concurrence.* Evanston, IL: Racom Communications, 2005.

information individually to them with their permission. Your company gets valuable product design input and gains a wider level of consideration and preference. If the opt-in program works, you will advocate for your customers, and they will advocate for you by recommending you and your opt-in program to their friends. Simple systems already exist for many retailers, and leading systems like J. C. Penny have almost 10 million members. G.M. is developing an advanced opt-in advocacy program called "My Auto Advocate." Figure 11-2 shows the first page of an interactive ad that serves to convince people of the advantages of the system and describes the unique program features. It includes a customer community called a "drivers forum," a virtual auto show with an advisor, competitive brochures, and test drives that fairly compare major GM and competitive models. Figure 11-3 shows the site built around a metaphor of an auto show. The virtual auto show is an interesting site design because it allows 360-degree panning and uses hot buttons to cue customer conversation bubbles as well as the major comparative information sources. The site also contains research on cars via the National Transportation Health and Safety Administration and the Insurance Institute, which give customers information they couldn't easily get otherwise. One very unique aspect of the site is the reward structure. The customer is paid through Amazon Coupons worth up to $20 to visit the advisor, test drive, participate in the community, or read eBrochures. In this time of media saturation and decreasing effectiveness, this payment for considering information may be the wave of the future for marketing and advocacy. The My Auto Advocate system is in market testing, and we will learn how effective opt-in advocacy systems with rewards are. I believe Figure 11-3 may be a precursor of the future.

Customer communities, such as the one in the GM advocacy program, are powerful in building trust. They can empower customers and cement the trust relationship with the sponsoring firm if the firm is truly a moderator/supporter and does not try to manipulate the group. This is an area in which rapid learning will take place and experimentation will yield benefits to firms pursuing an advocacy strategy.

Figure 11-2 My Auto Advocate Opt In Interactive Ad

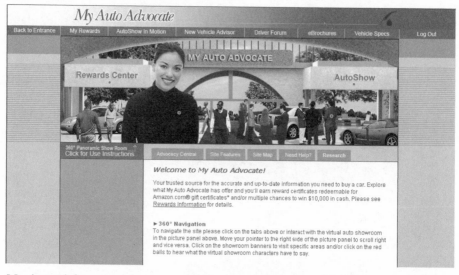

My Auto Advocate

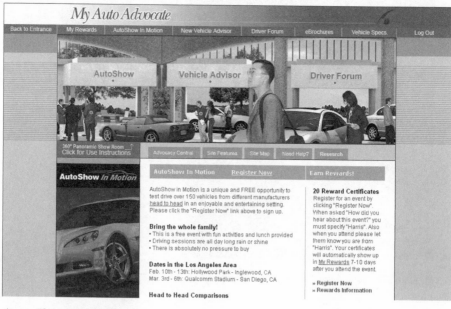

Auto Show in Motion

Figure 11-3 My Auto Advocate

Advocacy is not only a U.S. strategy—it is a worldwide program. Although trust cues will vary from country to country, trust is a universal value and is in fact valued more highly in many countries outside the U.S. Firms operating exclusively outside the U.S. can implement an advocacy strategy, although their reliance on the Internet may have to wait until the Internet capabilities equalize worldwide.

Every firm should develop its own checklist, but this one will provide a good start on the overall considerations. Detailed program management checklists should be built as the overall strategy is converted into detailed programs and tactics.

Table 11-1 Advocacy Checklist—What You Need to Do to Build an Advocacy Program

Build Quality

Have an effective Total Quality program

Be sure products consistently meet standards—zero defects

Design products customers want

Maintain quality throughout the value chain

Develop quality in all firm functions

Enhance Customer Service

Develop an effective customer service program

Stand behind your products

Be liberal in your settlements

Admit errors and correct them

Fulfill your promises

Create a Trusted Relationship

Be sure you do not have any trust-busters in your systems

Maintain the highest level of privacy and security

Take the push elements out of your CRM

Make your promotions genuine

Eliminate price discrimination

Mine data to help your customer

Have open and honest communication

Be transparent

Make the Internet the core of your trust building

Create IT and market research expertise

Reduce expenditures on mass media advertising

Spend more on product development

Increase budgets for Internet site enhancements

Provide unbiased advice to customers

Build a virtual advisor and persona

Advocate for Your Customers

Operate in the best interests of your customers

Write an advocacy value proposition

Make comparisons to competitive products

Collaborate with lead users and customers to build products

Create an *opt-in* Internet site for you and your customers

Build consumer communities

Provide incentives for channel members to align with your strategy

Build and implement advocacy tools

Be sure your customers are advocating for you

If prices drop, offer those lower prices to all existing customers

Be sure all functions are staffed for advocacy

Appoint a Chief Advocacy Officer (CAO)

Be consistent and coherent in your advocacy tactics in all channels

Create incentives for advocacy in your organization

Organize your firm around advocacy

Change the culture of your firm to advocacy

Build trust for all company stakeholders

Implement worldwide

Experiment, learn, innovate, and implement

THE CHALLENGE OF CUSTOMER ADVOCACY

You now know the steps you need to take to effectively advocate for your customers. It is clear that customers have gained power, and in the future they will gain more. The customer advocacy strategy components are already working for many innovative firms, and evidence is building to demonstrate that advocacy is a dramatic paradigm shift in corporate strategy. It can improve long-run sales, profits, and ROI. And equally satisfying, it is the right thing to do. Honesty, fairness, transparency, and helping customers is the ethical high ground—take it. Embrace trust and advocacy as core elements in your operations. Do not be a late adopter of advocacy because you will face the Advocacy Imperative and find yourself at a competitive disadvantage. Be a leader, not a follower, in working for your customers.

If you are a top manager in your firm, your challenge is to develop the vision, passion, and courage to lead your organization in the new world of advocacy. Most firms are not innovators, so you need to be the leader and head a team to move your firm forward in responding to the new consumer environment. Assure your firm's long-term growth and profitability.

If you are not in senior management yet, you can still function as a change agent in your firm. Bring in examples of advocacy and circulate them among your management team. Try small experiments and build a set of evolutionary steps to implement a test program in advocacy. Ferment change. Many innovations in firms start at the bottom and move up to the top as they achieve results. The best approach is to have a visionary CEO, an innovative top management team, and a set of change agents at all levels of the firm, but you can start the process by showing that trust works in your area of responsibility. It can help your firm and advance your career.

Innovate and advocate for your customers! This is a blueprint to profits in an era of customer power.

AUTHOR'S NOTE

BY GLEN URBAN, FEBRUARY 24, 2005

For my first 25 years at MIT, I did research and taught traditional push/pull marketing. I developed models to forecast new product sales and maximize profit by setting price advertising and distribution variables. After eight years in the dean's office (three years as deputy dean and five as dean) of the MIT Sloan School of Management, I began to appreciate the wider issues of marketing and management strategy. As I completed my term as dean, the Internet was blooming, and I was intrigued by the role of trust in this new medium.

In 1997, I began a project sponsored by General Motors directed at building a trusted advisor to help people make the right decision in buying a vehicle. This work at MIT was sponsored by a visionary GM executive named Vince Barabba. The result was a virtual advisor called "Trucktown," and our market research indicated that it did indeed build trust. As I mention in this book, GM took these ideas and developed AutoChoiceAdvisor.com. The parallel problem to giving honest advice was to find out why GM products did not come out on top of the list of recommendations. This resulted in a GM-sponsored project called "Listening In" aimed at finding opportunities to create new autos.

By 2000, I began to realize that markets and consumers were fundamentally changing. This was not business as usual, but rather a revolution in the making. I was working on specific pieces of trust work at GM, Intel, and McCann Erickson, but it took a while to realize that a new mosaic was emerging. The pattern of business practice was changing. As Bill Porter (founder of eTrade) said after my presentation on trust at the 2002 50th anniversary of the MIT Sloan School, "I knew there was something new in the atmosphere, but I did not know what it was—now I realize it is customer power."

The Internet was not just revising push/pull marketing—it was empowering customers. This new customer power has subsequently changed the ground rules for marketing. As I have discussed throughout this book, this power means firms need to fight harder in the old coercive methods of push/pull marketing or switch to a new paradigm of trust. I originally called this "trust-based marketing." CRM and relationship building helps, but it soon became evident that the future was beyond trust and would be reflected better in a strengthened concept—customer advocacy.

Momentum for customer advocacy has come from my work on customer advocacy, studies by other scholars, consulting companies' research (for example, Forrester Research in the finance area uses the term customer advocacy), and innovations by companies themselves. In 2000, I founded a firm called MyPersonalAdvocate.com to help implement my new ideas in practice. After the collapse of the Internet bubble, this firm was renamed Experion Systems and has implemented a focused suite of advocacy software products in over 20 credit unions to help customers make better decisions about mortgages, loans, credit cards, IRAs, and wealth management. Meanwhile, firms like John Deere developed advisors without any input from me. eBay staked its business on trust and fairness—and they have been phenomenally successful. Other companies like Expedia, Travelocity, Orbitz, AMD, Cisco, Mayo Clinic, and Progressive pioneered trust and advocacy techniques. All these examples are discussed in the text. Some of these experiments will fail and others will succeed—if you look back in a few years, you may find that some examples cited here were dropped, but other new ones will emerge. Evidence is building that customer advocacy really works to increase profits. Customer advocacy is growing, and new and improved strategies are being developed every day. This book has attempted to describe the existing body of work, provide a foundation for future innovation, and draw a blueprint for applying customer advocacy.

I hope you have enjoyed this book and will go on to create customer advocacy strategies and tactics of your own. Academics, managers, consultants, and regulators can move the paradigm forward. I invite you to come to a web site called DontJustRelate-Advocate.com (no apostrophe because it is an illegal symbol in a URL) and share your ideas. I will be posting new reports of my work (GM—My Auto Advocate, Suruga Bank—Trust/Advocacy Site Design, and British Telecom—My Wireless Advocate) and other researchers. If you have written a relevant paper, I will be glad to post it or create a link to it. In any case, please come to the "Community Members" section of the site to share your experiences and extend the threads of discussion on trust and advocacy. Report what works and what does not in your organization. Through a dialog, let's create the next generation of customer advocacy trust and advocacy innovations. Together we can improve the practice of management.

Customer advocacy and its tenants of open, honest communication and unbiased advice are ethically the right way to conduct business. In the long run, this is an easy ethical choice because doing the right thing corresponds to maximizing long-run profit. However, in the short run, it is a tough ethical decision because doing the right thing may result in lower short-run profits. It will take courage in many organizations to do this. Let's join together and collaborate to build a new and better marketing and management strategy around customer advocacy. It is the ethical way to do business, and it represents a blueprint for profit in an era of customer power.

Index

A

accessing alternatives, 3
accounting scandals, 72
Active Decisions, Inc., 149
ads, 8, 75
Advanced Micro Devices.
  See AMD
advertising, 20, 167
  cost of, 82
  Internet, 167-168
  push/pull marketing
    rules, 82
  slanted advertising, 88
advice, 19, 118
  trust components, 107-109
advisors, 21
  designing, 153
  listening to
    customer needs, 154,
    156-157
  virtual trusted advisors,
    building trust, 148,
    150-153
advocacy, 2, 10-11
  advertising, 20
  advice, 19

airlines, 126
applying, 169-170
benefits of, 15-16
building, 11-12, 202
building advocacy-based
  strategies, 128-129
  First Tech Credit
    Union, 130
  GM, 132
  Intel, 129
challenges of, 216-217
comparing self to
  competition, 19
competition, 163, 177
deciding if it's right for
  you, 22
determining if it fits your
  company, 122-123
foreign markets, 170, 215
future of, 175-176, 203-207
loyalty, 162
philosophy of, 18
versus push/pull
  marketing, 87
pyramid of advocacy, 11
shifting from relationship
  strategies, 121

short-run costs of, 162
supplier performance programs, 16
tools for, 20-21
transparency, 18
trust, 15
urgency of implementing, 207-210
when not to use, 123-125
who can use it, 173-174
who it is not for, 202
advocacy belief statements, 187
advocacy checklist, 211-212, 215
Advocacy Imperative, 207
advocacy pyramid, 140
  advisors. *See* advisors
  continuous learning, 146
  CRM, 141-144
  listening in, 154
  virtual advocate, 158
Advocacy Relationship Management
  (ARM), 12
advocacy-based businesses. *See also* trust
  advocacy, 94
advocacy-based management, 92
advocates, building virtual advocates, 158
advocating for customers, 88
airlines
  advocacy, 126
  price discrimination, 83
  push/pull versus trust/advocacy, 44-49
  trust scales, 113
  United Airlines, 75
  US Air, 75
alternatives, accessing, 3
Amazon.com, 68
  transparency, 99
AMD (Advanced Micro Devices), 106, 169
  Vice President of Customer
    Advocacy, 191
AMD Digital Media Benchmark, 169
AMDEdge, 106
AmericanSingles.com, 67
Ameritrade, 60
AMX, 206
Angie's List, 204

animated media, 168
antecedents, Theory A, 91-92
AOL, Chief Trust Officer, 190
Apple, 105
applying advocacy, 169-170
ARM (Advocacy Relationship
  Management), 12
Arthur Anderson, 6
assumptions about customers, 94
auctions, reverse auctions, 70
Auto Choice Advisor, 53, 132
auto insurance, comparison
  shopping, 64
Autobytel.com, 35
AutoChoiceAdvisor.com, 108
automobiles
  buying. *See* buying, automobiles
  Chrysler Crossfire, 83
  insurance, comparison
    shopping, 64
  NADA, 208
  shift in industry marketing, 52-55
AutoNation's Retail Network, 35
Aventis, 56

B

B2B online travel agents, 46
banking, checking accounts, 81
Bankrate.com, 62
banks, 113. *See also* credit unions
  CitiBank, 71
  trust, 91
Barclays Bank, 71
Bellco, 136, 153
Bellco.org, 108
benefits
  of advocacy, 15-16
  of trust-based strategies, 93-94
best practices
  advice and product
    comparison, 118
  cooperating design, 118
  incentives, 116

partnering with customers, 116
pervasive advocacy, 119
product/service quality, 115
supply chains, 118
transparency, 115
betraying trust, results of, 75-76
Better Business Bureau, 203
biased ratings, 168
bidders, eBay, 13
"blind trust," 127
BMW, 71, 167
Booth-Harris Trust Monitor
   survey, 72
Boston Consulting Group
   matrix, 175
brand building, 82
brand equity for packaged goods,
   online communities, 65
branding, CRM, 143
brands, quality, 165
broadband, usage, 27
brokerage firms, 60-62
Brown, Stephen, 85
Butler Steel Buildings, 165
Buyer Beware, 80, 82
buyers
   deal-prone buyers, 164
   discriminating between, 165
   industrial buyers, 70
buying
   automobiles, 81
      customer power, 32-36
      trust/advocacy models, 49
      vulnerable buyers, 50, 52
   stocks, 60-62
   treadmills, 68-69
buzz marketing methods, 206

C

California Association of Realtors
   (CAR), 62
CAO (Chief Advocacy Officer), 190
capacity, overcapacity, 74-75

CAR (California Associatioin of
   Realtors), 62
car buyers, 2
Car Talk, 108
Careerfish.com, 66
cars, 81
CarsDirect.com, 35
CarTalk, 132
casinos, CRM, 141
Caveat Emptor, 80, 82
cell phone services, 80
cell phones, 84
challenges of advocacy, 216-217
changing culture, mental models,
   185-187
channel partnership programs, 143
channels, 195
Charles Schwab, 61, 87
   incentives, 102
checking accounts, 81
checklists, advocacy checklists,
   211-212, 215
Chief Advocacy Officer (CAO), 190
Chrysler, Crossfire, 83
Circuit City, 69
Cisco Systems, Senior Vice President
   of Customer Advocacy, 191
CitiBank, 71
CNET, 118
co-creation, 157
co-payments, drugs, 56
Coke, 206
Cokemusic.com, 206
collaborative development of
   products, 17
commercials, 8
commoditization, 74
commodity industries, 123
communication between customers,
   customer power, 4-5
communities, 168
   brand equity for packaged
     goods, 65
comparing products, trust
     components, 107-109

comparison, 169
comparison information, 62
comparison shopping
  auto insurance, 64
  products, 68-69
competing in a world of trust,
  210-211
competition. *See also* price wars
  and advocacy, 163, 177
  benefits of advocacy, 16
  comparing to self, 19
competitive advantage, 127
components, trust components. *See*
  trust components
Cone Corporate Citizenship
  Study, 73
conflicts, 193
consistency, 192-195
consumer confidence, 90
Consumer Reports, 203
contacts, customer control over, 5
Continental, RewardOne
  program, 46
continuous learning, 146-147
cooperating design, 105-107
  best practices, 118
coordination, 192-195
corporations, 173
cost
  of advertising, 82
  of advocacy, 162
courage, changing to advocacy, 198
credit cards, interest rates, 81
credit unions, 208
  Bellco, 136
  First Tech Credit Union, 130
  trust scales, 113
CRM (Customer Relationship
  Management), 9-10, 12,
  141-144, 202
  branding, 143
  casinos, 141
  channel partnership
    programs, 143
  components of a Dream CRM, 143

continuous learning, 146-147
  Dream CRM, 21
  loyalty programs, 143
  permission marketing, 144
  profits, 142
cross-channel coherence, 147
Crossfire, 83
culture, 182
  changing mental models, 185-187
  consistency and coordination,
    192-195
  incentives, 189
  measures, 188
  organization, 190-192
  people, 188
  transitioning, 183-185
    to advocacy, 203
customer acquisitions costs, benefits
  of advocacy, 15
customer advocacy. *See* advocacy
Customer Advocacy Pyramid, 174
customer power, 1-2, 5, 7, 200
  buying automobiles. *See* buying,
    automobiles
  communication between
    customers, 4-5
  control over contacts, 5
  direct transactions, 4
  evidence of, 18
  growth of, 200-201
  healthcare, 36-37
  Internet, 25, 31-32
  lower rates, 45
  responding
    with customer advocacy, 10-11
    with push/pull marketing, 7, 9
    by strengthening customer
      relationships, 9-10
  trust, 6
Customer Relationship Management.
  See CRM
Customer Satisfaction, 140
customers
  advocating for, 88
  assumptions about, 94

buying automobiles, vulnerable
    buyers, 50, 52
deal-prone buyers, 164
empathizing with, 180-182
listening to customer needs, 154,
    156-157
loyalty to, 90
partnering with, 103
    best practices, 116
sharing opinions, 168
short-term customer base, 125
trusting, 164-165

D

Darves, Bonnie, 82
dating, Internet dating, 66, 68
deal-prone buyers, 164
Dealtime, 118
decreasing power of media, 74
Dell, 105, 171
Delta Airlines, 47
design, cooperating, 105-107
    best practices, 118
design pallet, 156
designing
    advisors, 153
    products, Theory A, 89
Despegar.com, 71
direct transactions, customer
    power, 4
discriminating between buyers, 165
DoCoMo, 170
doctor-patient relationships, 38
Dream CRM
    components of, 143
    General Motors, 145
drugs
    advertising for, 37
    co-payments, 56
    Medicare, 74

E

earning trust, 162
easyJet.com, 71
eBay, 13-14, 168, 203
    cars, 35
Edmonds, 33
EGG, 71
eHarmony.com, 67
empathizing with customers,
    180-182
enforcement of regulations, 73-74
Enron, 6, 73
ePinions, 118, 169, 204
eReality, 63
ERP (Enterprise Resource
    Management), 16
escrow services, 14
Escrow.com, 14
eTrade, 60-61, 71
eTrust, 67
evaluating transparency, 100
evidence of customer power, 18
expectations, 76
Expedia.com, 29

F

"Fair & Flexible," 204
feedback, eBay, 13
Ferraro, Doug, 136
Fidelity, 119
finances
    brokerage firms, 60-62
    financial rates, 62
    short-term financial focus, 124
financial rates, 62
FireFox, 76
Fireman's Fund, 195
Firestone, 110
First Tech Credit Union, building
    advocacy-based strategies, 130
flight, subsonic to supersonic, 17
focus groups, 96, 181

Fogdog.com, 68
forces, working against trust and
    advocacy, 206-207
Ford, 110
    Customer Satisfaction, 140
Ford Explorer SUV, 110
foreign markets, advocacy, 170, 215
fragmentation, 8
fraud protection programs, 14
FSI (Free Standing Inserts), 83
fulfillment, flawless fulfillment, 90
future of advocacy, 175-176, 203-207

G

GE (General Electric), 103-104
GE Plastics, 71
Geico, 108
General Motors (GM)
    Auto Choice Advisor, 53
    building advocacy-based
        strategies, 132
    Dream CRM, 21
    price wars, 166
    tests of Dream CRM, 145
    Trucktown, 154
GetThere.com, 46
Global Consumer Advisory Board,
    AMD, 191
global markets, advocacy, 170
globalization of U.S. sites, 71
GMAC Real Estate, 63
Google, ads, 168
government, 173, 196
growth
    benefits of advocacy, 16
    of customer power, 200-201

H

Harrahs, 141
Harvard Business Review, 85
Hauser, John H., 89
Health on the Net Foundation
    (HON.ch), 72

healthcare, 4
    customer power, 36-37
    doctor-patient relationships, 38
    HMOs, 57
    TQM, 58
    trust/advocacy model, 56-58
Herpes Outreach Center, 56
Hewlett Packard, 105
Hiding, transparency, 100
HMOs, 57
Honda, 167
honesty, 10

I

Iankelevich, David, 63, 71
IBS (Internet Buying Service), 35
incentives
    affects on culture, 189
    best practices, 116
    trust components, 102
Independent Financial Advisor, 62
industrial buyers, 70
industries
    airlines. *See* airlines
    automobiles. *See* automobiles
    commodity industries, 123
    insurance. *See* insurance
    telecommunications, 126
    travel. *See* travel
Inphonic.com, 158
insurance
    auto insurance, comparison
        shopping, 64
    Saint Paul Insurance, 88
Insurance Institute, 212
Intel, 21
    building advocacy-based
        strategies, 129
    quality, 146
    Rosa, 196
intelligence, advisors, 149
interest rates, credit cards, 81
intermediaries, 68

international relationships, trust, 197

Internet
advertising, 167-168
customer power, 31-32
travel, 28-30
usage, 26-28

Internet buyers, 63
Internet Buying Service (IBS), 35
Internet dating, 66, 68
investing in product superiority, 88
ISoldMyHouse.com, 63

J-K

J.C. Penney, 69, 212
J.D. Powers, 108
Jet Blue, 126
job searching, 66
Jobs.com, 66
John Deere, 152, 210
junk mail, 5
Jupiter Research, 67

Katz, Jeff, 29
Knowing position of company on trust dimensions, 201
Kubota, 210

L

L.L. Bean, 141
Land's End, 141
lastminute.com, 71
Lead User, 156
leadership, 127
changing to advocacy, 198
Legg Mason, 119
LendingTree.com, 62
Letstalk.com, 158
Lever Brothers, 66
licensing terms, 100
listening in method, 154, 156-157

loyalty, 44, 162
to customers, 90
example of lost loyalty, 194-195
loyalty programs, CRM, 143

M

mail-in service capabilities, 84
management
advocacy-based management, 92
participatory management, 86
managers, view of customers' trust, 96
market position, maximizing, 82
market research, empathizing with customers, 182
market share, measuring, 84
marketing
automobiles, shift in industry marketing, 52-55
buzz methods, 206
one-to-one marketing, 143
permission marketing, 144
push/pull marketing. See push/pull marketing
push/pull model, 7, 9
relationship marketing, 11
shifting paradigms, 22-23
strengthening customer relationships, 9-10
Theory A. See Theory A
trust-based marketing. See trust-based marketing
markets, saturation of, 74-75
Master Settlement agreement, 73
Match.com, 67
maximizing market position, 82
Mayo Clinic, 37
McGeehan, Patrick, 81
McGregor, Douglas, 86-87
measures, affects on culture, 188
measuring
market share, 84
sales, 84
trust, 97

media
animated media, 168
power of, 74
media fragmentation, 8
Medicare, 74
medicines. *See* drugs
Merck, 6
Merck Manual, 37
Merrill Lynch, 61, 119
"Miracle on 34th Street," 91
Mission Federal Credit Union, 208
MIT, Trucktown, 154
money-rates.com, 62
monopolies, 123
Monster.com, 66
Mullin, Leo, 47
My Auto Advocate, 212
"My Wireless Advisor," 205
MYOBTravel.com, 46
mySylvania.com, 70

N

NADA (National Association of Auto Dealers), 208
National Association of Realtors, 63
national broadcast networks, 8
National Transportation Health and Safety Administration, 212
Nationwide, 108
Netdoctor.com, 71
Nokia, 150
Notebaert, Richard C., 127
Novartis, Herpes Outreach Center, 56

O

observation, 181
Office Comptroller of Currency, 81
Omidayar, Pierre, 13
one-to-one connections, 9
one-to-one marketing, 143
online communities, brand equity for packaged goods, 65

online presence, automobile manufacturers and dealerships, 35
opinions, sharing, 168
opt-in system, 69
Orbitz.com, 29
organization, affects on culture, 190-192
organizational DNA, 182
Orvis, 141
OSRAM Sylvania, 70
overcapacity, 74-75

P

Pampers Parenting Institute, 65
Pampers.com, 134
paradigms, shift in marketing, 22-23
participatory management, 86
partnering with customers, 103
best practices, 116
partnerships, customer advocacy, 10
passion to change to advocacy, 198
PayPal, 14
people, affects on culture, 188
permission marketing, 144
pervasive advocacy
best practices, 119
trust components, 110-111
pharmaceutical products, selling, 82
pharmacies, 37
pharmacists, 91
philosophies, advocacy, 18
poor customer relations, trust, 171
pop-up ads, 5-6, 75
positions, determining where you are on trust continuum, 96
power
customer power. *See* customer power
of media, 74
price discrimination, 83, 166
"Price off," 83
price wars, 75, 166
prices, 164-165

pricing, push/pull marketing
    rules, 83
prime time TV, 8
Proctor & Gamble, 134
    Pampers Parenting Institute, 65
products
    collaborative development, 17
    comparing, 68-69
        best practices, 118
    designing Theory A, 89
    investing in superiority, 88
    low-impact products, 125
    quality
        best practices, 115
        push/pull marketing rules,
            83-84
        trust components, 101-102
profit margins, benefits of
    advocacy, 15
profits, CRM, 142
Progressive, 64, 108
promotions, 20
purchasing. *See* buying
push/pull marketing, 11, 85
    rules for, 80-84
    versus advocacy marketing, 87
push/pull models, 7, 9
    versus trust/advocacy models,
        42-44
    travel, 44-49
push/pull, 95. *See also* Theory P
pyramid of advocacy, 11

Q

quality, 147
    advocacy, 163
    best practices, 115
    brands, 165
    conflicts, 193
    employee relationships, 196
    push/pull marketing rules, 83-84
    trust components, 101-102
    uncontrollable quality, 124

Quality Service Certification, 63
quantity, uncontrollable
    quantity, 124
Qwest, 126, 134

R

RAacademy.com, 56
rates, customer power, 45
ratings, biased ratings, 168
real estate, 62-63
realtors, 63
regulation, 73-74
REI, 91
relationship building, 18
relationship marketing, 11
relationship strategies, 101
    shifting to advocacy, 121
relationships
    measuring long-run strength of
        customer relationships, 90
    strengthening customer
        relationships, 9-10
research, market research
    (empathizing with
    customers), 182
resume matching, 66
reverse auctions, 70
reviews, 168
RJ Reynolds, 73
rules
    of marketing based on Theory A,
        88-90
    for push/pull marketing, 80-84

S

Saint Paul Insurance, 88
sales, measuring, 84
sales results, push/pull marketing
    rules, 84
Sargent, Tom, 130
saturation of markets, 74-75
Schein, Ed, 182

SCM (Supply Chain Management), 16
searching for jobs, 66
segmentation strategies, 151
selling, 82
service, 115
  quality, push/pull marketing rules, 83-84
sharing opinions, 168
shifting
  paradigms, marketing, 22-23
  from relationship strategies to advocacy, 121
short-term customer base, 125
short-term financial focus, 124
Siemens Enterprise Networks, Director of Advocacy, 190
silos, 183
Site59.com Inc., 48
Six Sigma, 103-104
skepticism, 72
slanted advertising, 88
small business, reducing cost of building trust, 70-71
Smith Barney, 119
Sony, 195
Southwest Airlines, 47, 126, 172
spam, 5-6, 75
SPM (Supplier Performance Management), 16
Sprint, 204-205
Squaretrade.com, 14
stakeholders, trust for all stakeholders, 196-197
Staples, 151
Stewart, Martha, 72-73
stocks, buying, 60-62
strategies, segmentation strategies, 151
strengthening customer relationships, 9-10
subcultures, 183-184
subsonic flight, 17
successful companies not using advocacy, 171-173

superiority, investing in product superiority, 88
supersonic flight, 17
Supplier Performance Management (SPM), 16
supplier performance programs, 16
Supply Chain Management (SCM), 16
supply chains
  best practices, 118
  trust, 17
  trust components, 109-110

T

Takeda, 71
TD Waterhouse, 61
telecommunications, 126
  wireless companies, 134
telemarketing, 5
theories
  Theory A. See Theory A
  Theory P, 91
  Theory X, 86-87
  Theory Y, 86-87
Theory A, 77, 85, 201
  antecedents, 91-92
  rules of marketing, 88-90
  versus Theory P, 91
Theory P versus Theory A, 91
Theory X, 86-87
Theory Y, 86-87
The Tipping Point, 151
3M, 156
tobacco companies, 73
tool kits, 105
tools for advocacy, 20-21
Total Quality Movement, 83
Toyota, 197
TQM (Total Quality Management), 11, 140
  healthcare, 58
training programs, 188
transactions, customer power, 32

transitioning culture, 183-185
  to advocacy, 203
transparency, 18, 115
  hiding, 100
  trust components, 99-100
travel, 3
  and the Internet, 28-30
  push/pull models versus
      trust/advocacy models, 44-49
  trust scales, 112
travel agents, 30
  B2B, 46
Travelocity.com, 29, 48
treadmills, buying, 68-69
Trucktown, 154
The Trueman Show, 206
trust, 2, 5, 164, 23
  advocacy, 15
  banks, 91
  building, 202
    with virtual trusted advisors,
        148, 150-153
  for companies with poor customer
      relations, 171
  competition, 210-211
  continuous learning, 146-147
  customer power, 6, 25
  determining where you are on
      trust continuum, 96
  earning, 162
  eBay, 13
  measuring, 97
  moving to the left of the trust
      scale, 135-136
  moving to the right of the trust
      scale, 128
  rating your companies, 114-115
  results of betrayal, 75-76
  small businesses, 70-71
  for all stakeholders, 196-197
  supply chains, 17
"trust busters," 90

trust components, 98
  advice and product comparison,
      107-109
    best practices, 118
  cooperating design, 105-107
    best practices, 118
  incentives, 102, 116
  partnering with customers, 116
  pervasive advocacy, 110-111, 119
  product/service quality,
      101-102, 115
  supply chains, 109-110, 118
  transparency, 99-100, 115
trust dimensions, knowing where
    you are, 201
trust incentives, partnering with
    customers, 103
trust reserve, 163
trust scales, 112-113
trust-based marketing, 200
trust-based strategies, benefits of,
    93-94
trust/advocacy models
  automobile buying, 49
    vulnerable buyers, 50, 52
  healthcare, 56-58
  versus push/pull models, 42-44
  travel, 44-49
trusting customers, 164-165
trying your own products/services,
    180-181
TV
  ads, 8
  advertising, 167
  prime time TV, 8
Tyco, 73

U

United Airlines, 75
United States Census Bureau, 74
University Federal Credit Union, 116
Urban, Glen L., 89
US Air, 75

usage
    broadband, 27
    Internet, 26-28

V

value, Theory A, 89
Vauxhall, 71
Vioxx, 6
virtual advocates, building, 158
virtual trusted advisors, building
    trust, 148, 150-153
vision, changing to advocacy, 197
Von Hipple, Eric, 89

W-X-Y-Z

Wal-Mart, 69
web pharamcies, 37
Wellnesscommunity.org, 56
wireless companies, 134
wireless phone service, 80
WirelessAdvisor.com, 158
wizards, 71
World Economic Forum, 72

XFI Inc., 151

Yahoo!, travel services, 71
Yankelovich, 211
Yatra.net, 46

> "Great schools have... endeavored to do more than keep up to the respectable standard of a recent past; they have labored to supply the needs of an advancing and exacting world..."
>
> — **Joseph Wharton,** *Entrepreneur and Founder of the Wharton School*

The Wharton School is recognized around the world for its innovative leadership and broad academic strengths across every major discipline and at every level of business education. It is one of four undergraduate and 12 graduate and professional schools of the University of Pennsylvania. Founded in 1881 as the nation's first collegiate business school, Wharton is dedicated to creating the highest value and impact on the practice of business and management worldwide through intellectual leadership and innovation in teaching, research, publishing and service.

Wharton's tradition of innovation includes many firsts—the first business textbooks, the first research center, the MBA in health care management—and continues to innovate with new programs, new learning approaches, and new initiatives. Today Wharton is an interconnected community of students, faculty, and alumni who are shaping global business education, practice, and policy.

Wharton is located in the center of the University of Pennsylvania (Penn) in Philadelphia, the fifth-largest city in the United States. Students and faculty enjoy some of the world's most technologically advanced academic facilities. In the midst of Penn's tree-lined, 269-acre urban campus, Wharton students have access to the full resources of an Ivy League university, including libraries, museums, galleries, athletic facilities, and performance halls. In recent years, Wharton has expanded access to its management education with the addition of Wharton West, a San Francisco academic center, and The Alliance with INSEAD in France, creating a global network.